Managing information for research

Managing information for research

Practical help in researching, writing and designing dissertations

Elizabeth Orna and Graham Stevens

Second edition

McGraw Hill
Open University Press

Published by Open University Press
McGraw-Hill Education
McGraw-Hill House
Shoppenhangers Road
Maidenhead
Berkshire
England
SL6 2QL

email: enquiries@openup.co.uk
world wide web: www.openup.co.uk
and
Two Penn Plaza, New York, NY 1021-289, USA

First published 1995
Reprinted 2004

This edition published 2009

A catalogue record of this book is available from the British Library

ISBN 13: 978-0-33-522142-4 (pb) 978-0-33-522143-1 (hb)
ISBN 10: 0-33-522142-4 (pb) 0-33-522143-2 (hb)

Library of Congress Cataloging-in-Publication Data
CIP data applied for

Microsoft product screen shots reprinted with permission from Microsoft Corporation

Printed in the UK by Bell and Bain Ltd, Glasgow

Design, typesetting, page make-up and drawings by Graham Stevens. Typesetting and page make-up in Abobe InDesign and drawings in Illustrator version CS2; text typeface Fresco roman and Fresco sans designed by Fred Smeijers in 2003.

The McGraw·Hill Companies

Contents

From a review to a foreword

Invitation to self-reflection and visualization

'the visual image in science ... the style of scientific artefacts is no less integral to the communication of content and meaning than style in a work of art. ' Martin Kemp, *Visualizations: the Nature book of art and science.* Oxford, 2000, page vi.

Information management happens to be the subject that I teach and I try to follow the literature on it as closely as possible in these times when it seems that all kinds of publications breed by themselves with increasing rapidity. Elizabeth Orna's books stand out from the others as their author tries to follow her own recommendations on the presentation of information products. I happened to express appreciation of this particular feature of her books and, most probably, that was the reason why I earned a kind invitation to write a foreword for the second edition of *Managing information for research.*

I agreed immediately, as the topic seemed highly relevant for my work as a researcher and as a supervisor of master's and doctoral students, and so I hoped to be able to say something intelligent in relation to the book's contents.

All of us have certain routines that we apply in our daily chores and most of them concern looking for, storing, or using information in different formats. I am perfectly aware how inadequate are my own ways of treating information (the shoe maker usually goes bare-footed), but live in hope that I will improve them in the future. I always look for a good piece of advice, a tool, or a method but when I find one I immediately file it away, forget it, and proceed as always. So, my second reason was the commitment to read the book attentively, and even try some of the proposed methods in order to do the job properly, that I was undertaking in writing a foreword. Maybe this time some useful advice will stick with me ...

There was also a third reason—plain female curiosity. I knew that the book includes the experience of doctoral students and it is always interesting to learn how others solve (and, especially, fail to solve) the problems that one encounters every day. I also knew two of these respondents, having put them in contact with the authors of the book.

The second edition of any book is already an indicator of certain quality, or at least success. It is amazing how many first editions of books relevant to my interests I have missed, including the 1995 first edition of this one. I guess that there are two reasons for that: first, the invisible wall around the post-communist space endured much longer than the Berlin wall and blocked the flow of relatively expensive intellectual products or made it rather inconsistent; second, the number of publications is so great that inevitably most of them never draw the attention of all possible readers or users. However, I hope that this edition of *Managing information for research* will reach all who can benefit from it, as the book has fulfilled all my expectations and I can sincerely recommend it to both new and senior researchers. Now, I shall try to ground my recommendation by providing some arguments.

The subject that matters

This book approaches the research process from the inside, rather than the outside and deals with the problems that researchers can solve only for themselves, even if they are at the very top of the research hierarchy and can summon an army of assistants and doctoral students for help.

The issues of research methods are addressed in a variety of texts, both printed and electronic. Some provide a general introduction to the research process, others look deep into the sophisticated details of one research method. Some deal with quantitative, others with qualitative approaches. In the texts devoted to in-depth presentation of one or a group of related methods, a reader can find copious discussion of how to treat and process research data collected by different instruments. Some also provide fleeting advice on how to compose, store, index, or use research documents, like confidentiality agreements or field notes. Others give instructions and examples on how to write an article, a report, or a dissertation as a literary work, i.e. what is the appropriate style, terminology, language conventions for different genres, etc. Practically all universities provide students on all levels (including doctoral students) with courses on information seeking and searching and sometimes on more general issues of scholarly communication. Some of them also train researchers in writing skills. However, the main attention in these books and courses is concentrated upon the understanding, design, and execution of research methods as well as the exact presentation of research results.

This is also an important feature of this book and the presentation of research results is very much in focus. However, unlike other books that aim to instruct readers in how to do research, it deals with processes and objects that accompany research work from the very start to the end: information processes and documents. Research, conducted individually or in groups of different sizes, is an information-intensive activity. This usually means that it not only builds on and consumes information produced earlier, but also creates many different documents that are used in the process of research or become its end products.

All who have ever been involved in a larger and smaller research or development project know that in no time the space around becomes littered with scraps, slips, pages, sheets of paper, print-outs, copies and books holding vitally important elements for the final outcome. Nowadays, this is only the visible tip because the digital mass (sometimes the more accurate word is mess) stored in the computers is out of sight. The wood chips scattered around a carpenter‘s shop are the left-overs discarded because they are not necessary; but the white mountains in a researcher's office may hold golden nuggets of a new scientific discovery, or at least some shiny dust worthy of a doctoral degree.

I would also say that most researchers are aware of the significance of all this 'litter' and are quite good at managing their information resources on the intuitive level, regardless of which techniques they employ – filing or piling. I will never forget how my own supervisor, the late Prof. L Vladimirov (a notorious example of a piler), made me go through the papers collected over several years because he remembered that 'five years ago' he had put 'it (the document relevant to my research) right there'. You can bet, it was there and I found it!

I also admire my colleagues who manage to keep in order every bit of information that might be potentially useful for them or someone else and can trace it in the course of a few minutes. They are a tower of strength when one is in need or in a hurry. All of us, however, can benefit from some advice and training, or at least an opportunity to think about how to perform these activities better and help ourselves.

That is one of the positive features of this book: it invites reflection on how we act ourselves and how we acquire and treat the acquired information resources in relation to the whole process of research. The experiences of students who have just finished their dissertations or are in the final stage of the work related in the book is a very attractive element. They provide a glimpse into the real-life process and a variety of solutions for different information problems. Most probably, some of the respondents for this particular part of the book have regretted that the opportunity to think about their own practices has come after they have finished their project. But self-reflection never comes too late: they will certainly benefit from this exercise in the future and, moreover, many others will benefit from their experience.

The first two thirds of the book addresses information seeking and organization in parallel to the research processes. Time management issues earn a separate chapter in this part for a good reason. In relation to it, I would like to mention the informal and personal style of the text and advice throughout the book. I appreciated the advice about rewarding oneself for a job done well and in time; that should never be forgotten. The final part of the book deals with the idea that in addition to self-reflection and thinking of how to present their research results with precision and persuasion, researchers should also think of those who will be looking into and judging their final information product. The idea of considering the examiners who will evaluate the thesis and meeting their needs by providing a readable text with visual elements that aid comprehension is rather unusual in this context. This approach of relating the text to the reader is better known to those who deal with educational or leisure material. In scholarly writing, authors do think of the potential audience, but in a rather different way. We more often try to impress the audience by our knowledge and intelligence than to imagine the readers and think of their needs.

The authors' advice could, incidentally, be used by researchers from other countries whose traditions of scholarly writing differ from the Anglo-Saxon model. Their examiners might appreciate some other features of the text more than convenience of reading (e.g. refined style, abundance of special terminology, or usage of visual material of a certain type), and thinking about their specific demands would be most appropriate.

Consideration of the needs of the readers is indeed rarely thought of as part of scholarly writing or research work. And that leads me to the visual impact of the book.

Appreciation of the integrated design

The design of this particular book that you hold in your hands is an integral part of the content presented by the two authors. The book is a rare example of an author and a designer coming together to create the artefact not only as a source of knowledge, but also as an illustration of the methods advocated. The main subject and the architecture of the book, the content and the lay-out of pages, the text and the application of typographic principles go hand in hand and help the reader in more than one way.

Any book is an aesthetic whole that is produced by the harmony of the text, illustrations, design (format, cover, preliminaries, title page, lay-out, typesetting, paper type and quality, page structure and place of illustrations on it, binding) and the quality of printing. This harmony is usually visible in children's, art and, recently, popular science books. Unfortunately, research literature is often quite boring from this point of view and one can rarely speak of 'an aesthetic whole', especially, in relation to published dissertations. Partly, it can be explained by the lack of resources that does not allow one to hire professional book designers, but it also arises from the neglect of some basic and inexpensive principles of book design, resulting from ignorance. The inability to communicate with designers when they are available is in itself a result of this ignorance. The basics for this communication over 'professional boundaries' are provided here by the combined efforts of the two authors-designers. The figures in the book are not just illustrations, they visualize the thoughts of the authors. Their simplicity and elegance not only reveal the images hidden in the text, but also conceal the effort and time put into their design.

They also have provided a guide for researchers that introduces simple ways of making your own manuscript into a decent-looking and easy to use artefact. Chapters 9.1–9.3 are especially useful in this respect. The book itself serves as a model for a finalized dissertation text and just looking at it more attentively may help to improve structuring and presentation of one's own text. The content and the logic of the text is made visible and easy to follow by the elements of design present on each page. The illustrations are not only helpful for understanding the text, they are produced in a way that encourages others to try their own hand at them. At least I had an impression that I could achieve similar results by using familiar computer tools more imaginatively.

This quality of the book, stimulating thinking about the appearance and form of the research text, is an important achievement. Elizabeth Orna and Graham Stevens address their common creation primarily to first-time researchers on different levels. But I would also draw the attention of those who supervise and lead these researchers and students: senior researchers embarking on supervisory careers, seasoned professors, and even the managers of research institutions. They belong to the target group of the audience and the authors address them throughout the book. Reading the text in hand I have realized that as a supervisor for the doctoral students I often neglect to caution them on the perils of ill-managed data or documents. I readily assume that they should know them and, as students in library and information or communication science, will be able to take care of information seeking, organizing their documentation, and retrieving them from their own archives and shelves or libraries and databases. So far, my expectations of their professional skills have been justified. But it was not always true of the final production of the research texts, which require an additional competence or at least the sense of proportion.

Right here this particular sense of proportion suggests that the Foreword should not be longer than the text it introduces. So, I will leave readers to study and learn how to manage their own information for productive research work and for the benefit of the users of its results.

Elena Maceviciute
Vilnius, Lithuania-Borås, Sweden

Acknowledgements

In the course of our working lives, we have both spent a lot of time in actual conversation with the readership to whom this book is mainly addressed: students doing their first major research project. Writing it has been in some ways like a virtual, though perforce one-sided, continuation of those conversations. In another way, however, it embodies *real* conversations – even if mainly electronic ones – with several recent and current researchers, in a range of subjects and in various countries, who have been kind enough to answer our questions about how they managed the aspects of research which are the focus of this book.

Their very individual voices are an essential part of the text, the content of the book is enriched by them, and readers have them to thank for many of the 'Tips and time-savers' in the 'Dissertation Writer's Inquire Within' in Chapter 10. So our first thanks must go to them:

Paula Baker
Aragon Chen
Justin Chisenga
Hamid Jamali
Jane Jennings
Wouter Kritzinger
Mariana Cutino Moguel
Laima Nevinskaite
Karen Nowé
Kath Ward
Kerry Webb
Ismaril Wells

... and to the colleagues through whose kindness we were introduced to them:

Susie Andretta – Senior Lecturer in Information Management, London Metropolitan University.

Ben Hughes – Course Director MA Industrial Design, Central St Martins College of Art and Design, University of the Arts London.

Professor David Nicholas – Director of the School of Library, Archive and Information Studies, University College London.

Professor Pieter van Brakel – Head of Postgraduate Programmes e-Innovation Academy, Cape Peninsula University of Technology, Cape Town.

Professor Elena Maceviciute – Swedish School of Library and Information Studies and Vilnius University Faculty of Communication.

Our indebtedness to Professor Maceviciute does not stop there. She has also written a thoughtful foreword, which makes clear what this book seeks to offer its readers. Not many authors are so fortunate, and we cannot adequately express our appreciation.

We are also grateful to Dr Katy Deepwell, Head of Research Training in the University of the Arts London, for the opportunity to present the ideas underlying this book to current research students and supervisors; and to Professor Clive Holtham, Professor of Information Management, Cass Business School, City University, for information about his use of visual methods in the MSc in Management course, and the chance to meet students on the course.

The survey of recent dissertations would not have been possible without the help of Leo Geissler, Research Degrees Administrator University of the Arts London; Debbie Heatlie, Librarian, Joint Library of Moorfields Eye Hospital and the Institute of Opthalmology; Teri Harland, Learning Services Manager, Greenwich Campus, University of Greenwich; and Liz Harris, Head of Library Information, City University, London.

To our publishers we owe thanks not only for the excellent editorial and production support we have received from Kirsty Reade, Caroline Prodger, Catriona Watson, Melanie Havelock, Max Elvey and Beverley Shields during our work on the book, but also for their practice of commissioning detailed reviews in preparation for new editions. The thoughtful observations from academics who have used the first edition of *Managing information for research* in their teaching gave us the most helpful start on planning a new one that we could have wished for.

We are proportionately grateful to Deba Bardhan-Correia, MSc, Lecturer in Human Resource Management, Business School, University of Buckingham; Dr Mark Hepworth, Senior Lecturer, Department of Information Science, Loughborough University; and Dr Beverley French, Senior Research Fellow: Evidence Based Practice, Department of Nursing, University of Central Lancashire. We have no less than three reasons for gratitude to Beverley. She not only provided a review, but also put us in touch with Paula Baker and Kath Ward, *and* wrote the illuminating account of her own application of visual representation to interpret research data which appears in Chapter 8. Finally our thanks to Paul Leadbitter for his care and attention in checking the typographical detail and specification of Chapters 9.1, 9.2 and 9.3.

Liz Orna and Graham Stevens

First things first

C E M Joad, the resident philosopher on the BBC's wartime radio programme, The Brains Trust, used to demand that his fellow 'brains' should first define their terms. A reasonable request, and a good practice for authors to follow. So here are the definitions we use in this book for the terms that express the key concepts it deals with.

Information and knowledge

We take these two terms together, because we see them as distinct but mutually interdependent.

From the point of view of the user, *information* is what we seek and pay attention to in our outside world when we need to add to or enrich our *knowledge* in order to act upon it.

Knowledge is the organized results of experience, which we use to guide our actions and our interactions with the outside world. We all store our knowledge in our minds in a highly structured form, which is directly accessible only to us. When we want to *communicate* what we know to others who need to use it for their own purposes, we have to make it *visible or audible* to the outside world.

We do that by *transforming* our knowledge, and the result of the *transformation* is *information,* that is, knowledge which has been put into the outside world and made visible and accessible through a series of transformations.

One of the commonest ways of getting information is by using *information products* – which are so named because they contain information and have been produced, as a result of decisions by human beings, for specific users and use (this book is an information product).

Managing information and knowledge

In research, *managing information* means: defining the information we need to extend our knowledge; finding it; labelling, recording and storing the useful things we find, so that we can find them again whenever they are needed.

Knowledge management for researchers consists of making connections among ideas, integrating new information into what we already know, developing new ideas, and bringing knowledge from the depths towards the surface, where it's ready to be transformed into information. Most of us have to do all this in the light of nature because school education doesn't often give us any help with it, and the light of nature doesn't always shine too brightly! We can, however, learn a lot from the professionals who manage information and knowledge for organizations, and this book offers straightforward applications of some of their know-how for individual use.

Information design

When we come to putting the knowledge gained from research into information products to communicate it, we can benefit from the help of another professional specialism—*information design,* which can be broadly defined as everything we do to make visible our knowledge and ideas so that those who need them can enter into them and use what they learn from them for their own purposes. So the business of information design includes:

- The conceptual structure of information products
- Sequence of presentation
- Choice of medium and format
- Decisions about how the content is expressed (e.g. text, graphics, numbers, and combinations of all these)
- Management of the relevant technologies
- Writing
- Illustration
- Typography.

A brief definition from David Sless (2007) of the Communication Research Institute nicely sums up what information designers do:

> *'Information designers create and manage the relationship between people and information so that the information is accessible and usable by people and they provide evidence that the information is accessible and usable to an agreed high standard.'*

Typography

Typography is often described as 'visual language'. The typographer requires knowledge and skill in these areas:

1. The insight to analyse a document and recognize the writer's overall plan, and to identify each of the separate text elements that needs design attention. In particular, the typographer needs to be able to identify elements in the original document that could better be communicated in a different mode from the one its writer has used; for example: quantitative information conveyed in continuous prose that would be more readily understood if treated as a table.
2. Asking appropriate questions about the overall production requirements, starting (if it is to be presented in print) with the paper on which it will be reproduced, and its suitability for the nature of the product.
3. Finding appropriate typographical answers to the problems identified, designing individual pages that have due regard to the overall document plan, and producing a finished product that does not create undue eyestrain.
4. Choosing the most appropriate type (font) design, and making decisions on the size of the types to be used, and the spacing between lines and words, as well as on the software package that will be used.

Coda – a problem of naming

As you will see from Chapter 1 (page 21) we have written this book with the whole range of research projects in mind 'from the short undergraduate project through to doctoral studies, as well as research undertaken by working professionals who are extending their qualifications through part-time study or on study leave'.

That gave us a knotty problem – in this case, of naming rather than defining. What should we call the 'information product' that researchers at all these levels in all kinds of higher-education institution and in many different countries are required to produce?

The main candidates in English were 'thesis', 'dissertation', and 'research report'. The last was discarded because it is more usually applied to research which is done in the course of work after qualification, rather then in connection with gaining a degree at undergraduate or postgraduate level. Of the remaining two, both in common use in higher education, 'thesis' tends to be associated with postgraduate research at Master's or Doctoral level, while 'dissertation' can be applied at any level. A thesis, in the academic context, was in fact originally a proposition put forward by a scholar, which had to be 'defended' in spoken or written words; by the mid-seventeenth century in England (according to the Oxford English Dictionary) the sense was extended to cover the product containing the thesis and its defence – a 'dissertation to maintain and prove a thesis; especially one written or delivered by a candidate for a university degree'.

So we decided that 'dissertation' was a good portmanteau word for covering the whole range of written end products required of researchers on different courses, at different levels, and in various institutions and countries. When you encounter it in the book, please, if necessary, substitute the term your institution uses!

Reference

Website accessed on 18 March 2009

Sless, D (2007)
Defining information design.
http//www.communication.org.au/dsblog
30 03 2007

The territory

The chapters in this first part are by way of a welcome to readers, to help them envisage what we, as authors, offer them in the book, and what we hope they will contribute to the 'conversation' between us as they read.

Chapter 1 sets out the background and the basic ideas about research that underlie the book. Chapter 2 introduces one particular idea that runs throughout it: making the things we have to do in research visible – first to ourselves and then to others, initially as images inside the mind, and then as actual 'maps' and pictures in the outside world.

Doing that can help us at every stage in research to see more clearly what we have to do, plan our actions to accomplish it, and finally present an end product that does justice to the knowledge we have gained from the research – and that helps examiners to do the same!

Part 1

Dear Reader ...

Ch 1 Contents at a glance

1

In the light of experience ...

Answers from recent researchers to the question:

'If you had to start again, what would you do different?'

'I might try to communicate somewhat more regularly with my supervisors; this might involve writing in a rather more structured way. I would try to keep better track of my stored material and be just a little less untidy when it comes to information seeking.'

'I would make more effort to write an analysis of the present, throughout the project – a critical chronological journal.'

'Apply for ethics approval earlier.'

'Spend as much time considering how I was going to analyse the responses received as I did formulating the questions.'

'I would have asked my supervisor if I could use a professional design team. The finished product, despite all my efforts, would have looked so much better.'

'I think I would do most of the things differently. I would do a different research, I would be more organized, do things faster, do a more comprehensive and organized literature review. I would use my supervisor for my own benefit differently (more efficiently).'

In writing this book, we have paid heed to what they told us.

Introduction

The first edition of this book was addressed exclusively, or so we thought, to students undertaking research in English-speaking countries, and mainly to first-time postgraduate researchers, typically at Master's level. We were off the mark in both those assumptions. It is indeed used by that category of student researchers; but we have learned that lecturers use it in their work with research students, and that it is consulted in connection with all levels of research, from the short undergraduate project through to doctoral studies, as well as in research undertaken by working professionals who are extending their qualifications through part-time study or on study leave. We have also learned of a readership in many other countries; the first edition has been translated into Greek, Spanish, Portuguese and Chinese.

Our knowledge has benefited from detailed reviews of the first edition, commissioned by our publisher from academic users; their observations from experience have convinced us that the scope of this edition should extend to the readership whose existence we had not been aware of.

We have tried to keep this range of readers in mind in the writing and design of this edition. In particular we tailor the advice offered to various levels and circumstances of research, where it is helpful to do so, and we deal specifically with how both parties to the 'research contract' can help one another in their interactions.

Features of the original that have been updated include a wide selection of stories from the experience of recent researchers in various countries. Given the time that has elapsed since the first edition, there has been a complete update on the use of technology in managing information and in writing. There has also been a full revision of the typographical and layout advice in relation to the resources available to readers; and that has been complemented by a completely new approach to the visual presentation of the book itself (described on page 25).

One thing remains unchanged by the passage of time: the fundamental thinking about the research process, and what it requires in the way of handling information and designing and creating the end product. That has been confirmed and enriched in one respect by the doctoral research which one of the authors was just starting when the first edition was written, and the book to which it led (Orna, 2005, *Making Knowledge Visible,* published by Gower); they are the source of some new ideas about the 'information products' that are the end result of research.

The rest of this introductory chapter sets out the argument of the book, explains why the subjects it deals with merit a book, describes how it's organized, and says what it does *not* cover and why.

The argument of this book

Undertaking a research project for the first time (and even the second or third) is a demanding business; it requires most researchers to get to grips with some unfamiliar disciplines; and co-ordinating a variety of activities and bringing them to a successful conclusion to meet a deadline, and being 'project manager' in charge of the whole enterprise is a new and not necessarily welcome educational experience for many people.

This book is devoted to two sets of activities that all researchers at any level have to engage in:

1 Gathering and organizing material relevant to the focus of their research from the outside world *(information* for short), and *transforming* whatever in it is useful to them into *knowledge and ideas* inside their heads. We shall call those processes *information management* and *knowledge management.*
2 All the things that go into 'writing up' their research. That is, transforming the knowledge and ideas that they have developed back into *an information product* – report, dissertation, thesis, etc. – that makes them visible to other people in the outside world (see page 16 for why in this book we use the term dissertation to cover them all). There is more to this than just keyboarding a lot of words divided up into a set sequence of chapters in the shortest possible time. This is a critical product for success or failure; it's the only means by which others can see what researchers have been up to and enter into their thoughts, and the first people who encounter it are those who will judge the quality of the research and reward it accordingly. So creating it should be a work of thoughtful *information design,* in order to do justice to the work that it presents to the outside world. (For full definitions of all the terms in italics, see pages 14–15).

Why concentrate on these topics?

We devote a whole book to them because, so far as we can ascertain, the situation is still the same as when we wrote the first edition more than ten years ago. The support which institutions offer students on these critical aspects of research varies in amount and quality (see Chapter 2 for examples of some helpful programmes offered at the start of research); and few of the many guides to doing research which are available in print and on the internet offer realistic practical advice on them.

Guides which are otherwise comprehensive tend to glide speedily over information management and writing in a few pages. Sometimes the advice offered is sound, but does not descend from generalization to practical details of how to set about what it recommends, as in:

'It is a good idea to include tables, diagrams and other illustrations ...', or '[Notes on data sources] need to be stored in such a way as to offer some reasonable prospect of retrieval when required ... the easiest way to do this is on a PC.'

And sometimes it gives the irresistible impression that the authors know they need to say something on a topic but can't for the life of them think of anything useful, as in the list of things to do if a planned activity has to be delayed that includes 'surfing the web' and 'going to see someone'—desperate expedients indeed!

A 'design approach' to research

It is easy to think of information management and writing as separate stages of research, with little in common. Our argument, based on experience, is that they are linked by the transformations we have to make throughout the process — outside information into knowledge inside the head; inside knowledge into information product outside in the world (see Figure 1.1 on page 24). If we learn how to manage them rightly, each kind of transformation can help the other.

More than that, we would argue that there is an approach to the whole research process which can unify all the things we have to do in the course of it. It can fairly be called a *design approach* because it applies every side of our minds—rational, intuitive, reflective and analytical—to asking questions and using the answers in: forward planning, defining research territory, devising appropriate methods of investigation, setting up systems and procedures for getting things done, linking ideas, seeing patterns in data, creating mental and visible structures, and giving expression to them in verbal and visual language which allows others access to the fabric of our thought.[1]

How the book is organized

The four parts of this book reflect that thinking—each deals with a different application of a 'designing' approach to research, and draws on reflections from the experience of a number of recent researchers. The scope of the parts:

Part 1
Defining and mapping the scope of this book, and mapping the domain of research projects.

Part 2
Designing practical systems and procedures to support the researcher in dealing effectively with information, managing the research project, and staying friends with time.

1 In this, perhaps our 'design approach' is an instance of what Brenda Dervin (2006) calls the paradox of 'dialogic communicating', which 'is meant to invite us into the centre of the uncertainty that is our adventure and our struggle in the human condition. At the same time, it is meant to do this in a way that encourages and facilitates internal sense-making of ourselves and others; sense-making of the kind that allows us to go off enriched, confused perhaps but not empty and not alienated and thus better able to incorporate what we see as useful strengths in the work of others.'

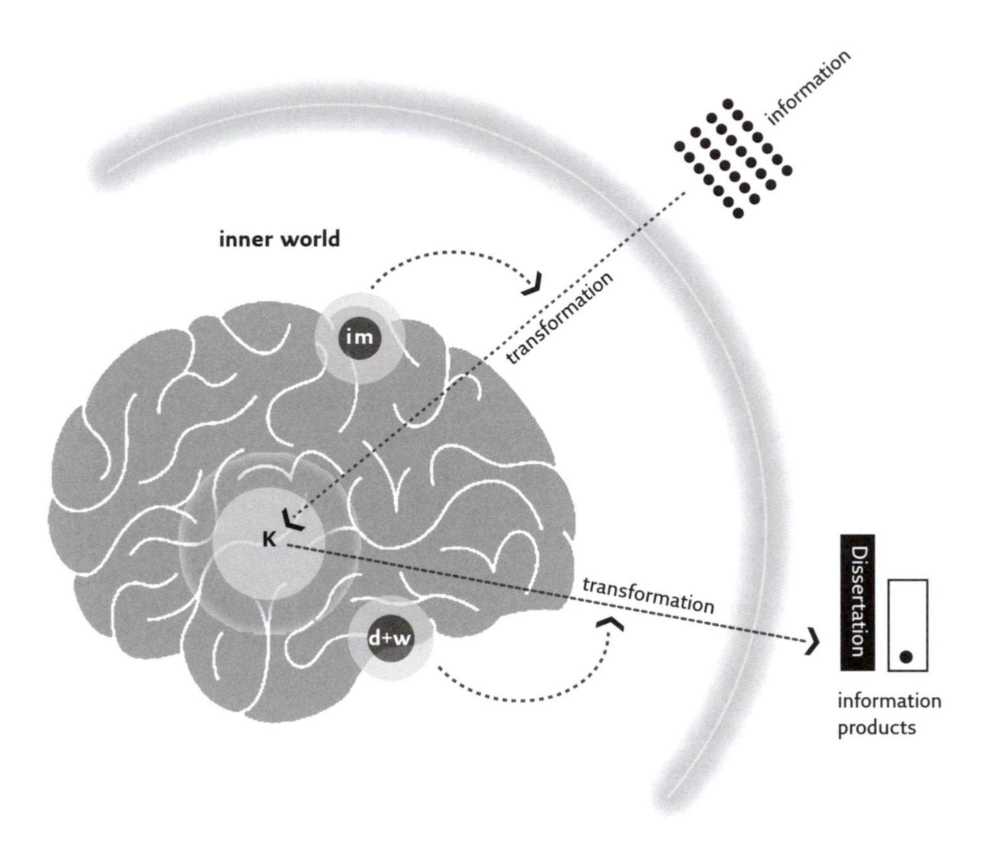

The transformations which our minds make in the course of research, as they move between our inner and outside worlds, link information management and writing.

We find information in the outside world, and transform it into inner knowledge; we manage it so that we can find and use it whenever we need it; and in designing and writing (as discussed in Part 4 of this book) we transform the knowledge we have created during research back into information, in the form of an information product – a dissertation – so that others can see and use it.

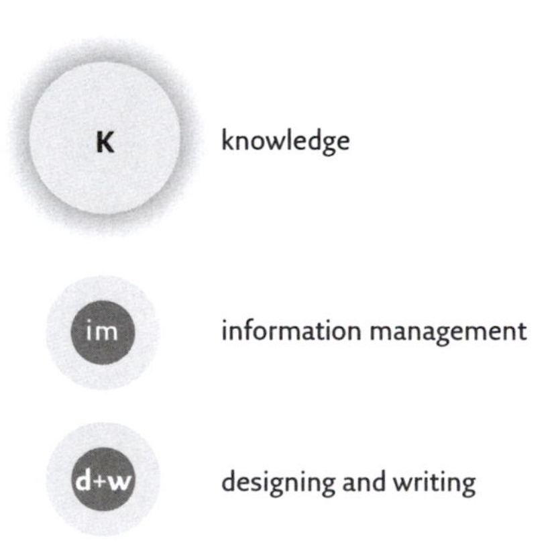

Figure 1.1 How information management and writing are linked through transformations

Part 3
Using the well-established design method of asking and answering questions in order to arrive at a 'brief' for the end product.

Part 4
The practicalities of information design as applied to transforming the knowledge and ideas generated during the research into the visible end product: first through the design of page structure and information elements, to make a visible framework for writing, and then through writing.

A book designed as a dissertation?

The designer-author of this book did some research in preparation for this new edition, by making a 'visual audit' of a number of dissertations (see pages 174–175), and talking with researchers about how they dealt with the visual design of their dissertations. They nearly all had a very hazy view of the process, knew nothing about how we read or how the typographic design of what we read can help or hinder us. The only advice they had received was to look at recent dissertations – which had been produced by researchers whose knowledge of these matters was no greater than their own.

From the point when the contract for this book was signed, we both followed our usual practice of discussing the design, because we always aim to make text and its visual embodiment on the page into a unity, with typographic design visually interpreting the writers' ideas, rather than being a formal surface addition. The exchanges about content in relation to design led to an early decision to give more focused and practical help on dissertation design than in the first edition, and you will find that in Chapters 9.1 to 9.3.

Other design decisions related to the size of the page that our publisher specified for the book: 240×170 mm, which is close to the ISO (international paper size) B5 commonly used for academic books. B5 is in direct proportion to the ISO size A4 – the standard UK and European format for research, institutional and business documents, and business stationery, as well as for laser and inkjet printers and photocopiers. The fact that the relation between width and height is the same throughout the whole range of ISO paper sizes provided the ultimate key to the final design solution, which was arrived at after a series of design experiments. Because the proportions of the B and A series of paper sizes are the same, it was possible to design a series of dissertation templates with margins and text areas that would directly correspond to the A4 document-size pages that researchers have to work with.

The complete set of templates is in Chapter 9.2 on pages 196–217, and the pages showing the underlying grid structures are on pages 192–195. All of the templates appear on right-hand pages and each of these pages can be enlarged to 159 per cent giving an exact A4 framed page on an A3 sheet of paper. There is also help for researchers wanting to use US Letter paper sizes. Guidance on designing and constructing the main features that make up a dissertation is also given, to help research students frame the questions before actually starting the design process.

Boundaries and limits

There are distinctions between what a book intended for the whole range of student researchers in any subject can reasonably offer, and what belongs to the proper province of their tutors and the library services of the institutions where they do their research.

The territory of the latter, which we are not qualified to deal with, covers the application of their professional knowledge to such matters as:

- Choice of research topics, and formulating research questions/hypotheses
- Guidance on sources of subject-based material
- Instruction in using software relevant to particular disciplines (e.g. SPSS for researchers in social sciences), web searching in specific subject fields, etc.

Ours is the application of our own kinds of professional knowledge, to complement what institutions and tutors provide for researchers with practical help in tackling the often neglected research activities that this book covers, and to provide pointers to useful resources, both traditional and digital, in these areas.

There are some overlaps between the territories, which we cover in the knowledge that they are likely also to be dealt with by tutors: keeping track of the progress of research and documenting it, time management, and the interactions between researchers and their supervisors/tutors.

That's the end of the beginning, now read on!

References

Websites referred to in this chapter accessed on 18 March 2009

DERVIN, B, REINHARD, C D & SHAN, F C (2006) Beyond communication: research as communicating. Making user and audience studies matter–paper 2, *Information Research* 12 (1). http://informationr.net/ir/12-1/paper287.html

ISO standard 216. www.cl.cam.ac.uk/~mgk25/iso-paper.html

Mapping the research domain

Ch 2 Contents at a glance

2

'the principle of subjectivity in maps, both personal and cultural subjectivity, needs to be emphasized ...

Subjectivity carries the implication of freedom, imagination, almost perhaps of play – elements whose role in mapmaking has not been sufficiently recognized ... The impulse to depict the world on paper has always been associated with the desire to make some statement about the world.'

Peter Whitfield (2002) *Outer Worlds and Inner Worlds: An Introduction to World Maps.* London: British Library (Introduction to the exhibition 'The Lie of the Land: The Secret Life of Maps')

'The crucial metaphor, as it is now understood ... is that of maps. The brain, and particularly the cortex, holds representations of the outside world, and plans of actions upon that world, in the form of multiple and complex patterns of neural activity in specific cells, in topologically defined relationships with their neighbours, which together provide models of the outside world – or at least models of how the brain and mind perceive the outside world, ...'

Steven Rose (2006) *The 21st-century brain. Explaining, mending and manipulating the mind.* London: Vintage Books, page 204

What are we doing when we do research?

Let us start this chapter by bringing together the various activities mentioned in Chapter 1 as things that researchers have to do:

- Seek and find relevant information in the outside world
- Store and manage it
- Transform it into knowledge inside their heads
- Act as 'project managers' for a project that is undertaken on their personal initiative. (Since research is undertaken in academic institutions, this task includes fulfilling their own side of a 'contract' with the institution – which requires them to know what their obligations are in the matter of quality, what they have to deliver and when.)
- Create a visible end product, by transforming the inner knowledge they have created back into an 'information product' in the outside world, where others can see, judge and use it.

We argued that in doing all these things researchers are engaging in what we called a design process, in which they need to apply every side of the mind – '... rational, intuitive, reflective and analytical to: forward planning, defining research territory, devising appropriate methods of investigation, setting up systems and procedures for getting things done, linking ideas, seeing patterns in data, creating mental and visible structures, and giving expression to them in verbal and visual language which allows others access to the fabric of our thought'.

Why a map of the domain?

That list makes clear that researchers have to manage a lot of activities, along many different dimensions, and bring them all together to a conclusion – usually at a fixed time. Just keeping them all in mind at the same time is hard enough, especially at the beginning of the process. When you are trying to plan your way forward at that stage it's fatally easy to get lost in a maze of words and partly formulated ideas.

I have found that starting with a metaphor and then making some kind of a picture of it keeps confusion at bay, because it gives a visible framework into which I can place ideas, and tasks that have to be accomplished; it gets them out of the mental space where they're jostling and shifting in and out of focus, and puts them outside into the world where I can see them. In the present case, on the basis of experience, here are two metaphors that express what 'doing research' encompasses:

1. Research as map-making: which entails exploring a territory – some of it familiar, some unknown. We start from a first rough map, with a lot of 'terra incognita'; we go to and fro between known and unknown areas, get lost and find the way again; we discover links between bits of the territory as we

revisit them, and in the process we clarify our map so that we can use it with more and more confidence to move freely about the 'research domain' and make sense of it.[1]

2 Research as a journey: but not the kind where we travel in a straight line between start and end points, through a defined series of activities, each of which is left behind for good once completed. The image I have in mind comes from a time when I lived not far from the Thames, and at sunset on winter days watched seagulls heading home to their roost on reservoirs upstream after a day's foraging at the estuary. Every so often their purposeful westward flight was broken by the irresistible attraction of a thermal, which drew them into a series of ascending spirals, from which they emerged to continue the homeward journey. That kind of progress is a good metaphor for another characteristic of research – going round a set of activities or ideas over again, but emerging at a higher level and with a better view. If we keep that picture in mind, we are less likely to be taken by surprise or despair by finding ourselves 'going round in circles'.

First questions to ask and answer

Map-making has to begin by asking and answering questions. If you answer questions like these for yourself, it should save you from being ambushed by nasty surprises.
What does the research seek to find out?
Questions it aims to answer/hypothesis it seeks to test?
Areas of knowledge, subjects, disciplines it will need to draw on?
New areas of knowledge and know-how you will need to get acquainted with?
Methodological options?
Limits to breadth and depth of inquiry?
Institutional requirements?

If your institution insists on you answering them and gives support and pointers to doing so, so much the better, but if it does not, researchers should ask and answer them for themselves.[2]

1
This is the kind of subjective and sometimes even playful, map-making referred to in the quotation on page 28.

2
The Quality Assurance Agency for Higher Education (2004) has published a code of practice for postgraduate research programmes, which offers a 'statement of good practice' that individual institutions should follow in such matters as telling students about their responsibilities as researchers, and how the institution works; provision of induction programmes; supervision arrangements; and training in 'research and generic skills'. But it leaves it to institutions themselves to decide how to do all this.

We asked our researcher-contributors whether they were required to ask and answer questions like these at the start of their research, and what support their institutions offered them in doing so. Their replies – some of which are outlined on the following pages – suggest some interesting differences among institutions and courses within the UK, and in countries further afield.

The help on offer

At Master's level, taught modules on relevant topics – for example, qualitative and quantitative analysis; statistical analysis; writing and presentation skills; project management; developing research proposals – with assignments to reinforce learning and prepare researchers for applying them, are offered in a number of the universities where our small sample of researchers studied. A different approach prevails at one institution: towards the end of their first year, students have a number of seminar/workshops with academic staff to help them develop their thinking about the major research project that occupies the second year of the course; and a visiting lecturer gives a seminar/workshop on managing information.

The replies of PhD researchers show variation in the range and level of support offered. In some institutions they are expected to answer the questions at various levels of detail at different stages, from their first application to undertake a PhD, to their research proposal/plan, and their thesis plan. The support offered ranges from an initial guidance document from the university and discussion with supervisors, to a selection of short courses on research skills (e.g. using library resources, 'personal and professional management skills', information literacy, use of bibliographic and word-processing software, thesis writing). The wide variation, and its consequences for researchers, are revealed in the Research Information Network report *Mind the Skills Gap* (2008).

Note

Because of the way that the material on researchers' answers is presented, this page falls short of the page depth. The next section starts on page 32.

How researchers answered the questions

Here are some of the replies we received from researchers to the questions on page 30. First, Paula's comprehensive response about her MSc course in Professional Practice Research and Development.

Paula *What does the research seek to find out?*

The purpose of my study was to measure the extent to which physiotherapists use specific research findings from the evidence base of the National Service Framework for Older People (Department of Health (DOH) 2001) and to find factors influencing their stage in the research utilization process ...

Relevant knowledge?

The study drew on both theoretical and empirical literature; the former covered:

- The conceptualization and classification of knowledge
- The determinants of research utilization
- Types of decision making and decision-making activities, types, levels and frequencies of research use (implementation)
- Outcomes of research use
- Models of research use.

Empirical studies regarding research use in physiotherapy were appraised. A deliberate decision was made to include nursing studies because of the paucity of physiotherapy studies with objectives similar to the proposed study.

New areas of knowledge and know-how?

The new knowledge I required related to:

Clear definition and conceptualization of research utilization.

1 Measurement of specific research findings.
2 Necessary to find study designs that are sensitive to the different ways research may be used.
3 Necessary to detect confounding variables to determine the reasons for utilization or non-use, concentrating on organizational and innovation characteristics.
4 Measurement of the impact of interventions designed to increase specific research use.

The know-how I needed to acquire?

- Questionnaire design—inclusion of quantitative and qualitative analysis
- Use of SPSS statistical package

Q&A

- Process of application of ethics, R&D approval, insurance, etc.
- Qualitative data analysis using 'Framework' (Ritchie and Spenser 1993)
- Transcription skills
- Use of equipment, how to get it.

Likely sources of information?

Medline, Cumulative Index of Nursing and Allied Health, Allied and Complementary Medicine, Embase, Cochrane and NHS Research Register ...

... My supervisor completed her PhD in a related topic: this was a really valuable source as she had asked a lot of the same questions during her work ...

Results of piloting the questionnaire and cognitive interviewing

My peer group: we had group supervision meetings.

Methodological options?

The majority of physiotherapy research and practices are biased towards a reductionist approach. This contrasts with a more constructionist approach found in a significant proportion of nursing studies. The focus of physiotherapy research utilization studies has been the measurement of knowledge assuming a prescriptive linear knowledge utilization process in the positivist tradition. This has influenced the methods chosen which in the main have been surveys using self-completion questionnaires.

It was considered that traditional research approaches may limit the usefulness and relevance of information gained and the final study took a post-positivist approach. This was to attempt to capture some of the complexities of working in the NHS where many variables influence practice. In planning the research several methodological options were considered using several criteria:

1 The amount of information sought
2 The complexity
3 Sources of bias
4 Level of possible non-response
5 Resources.

There were some very useful nursing studies which looked at measuring specific research use and so these formed the basis of the quantitative methods I used. I added a qualitative element to capture the contextual information. Finally a cross-sectional pilot survey using an interviewer-administered questionnaire was chosen to collate an accurate and contemporary descriptive profile of the stage of research utilization that physiotherapists have achieved ... and to explore factors influencing uptake. The most influential factor informing the choice of methodology was the ability of the survey to achieve both descriptive and exploratory purposes.

Limits to breadth and depth of inquiry?
Time was a limiting factor ...
Length of time I was able to borrow equipment e.g. transcription machine
Dissertation was limited to 15 000 words ...
The topic of Research use/knowledge management is vast—I had to be pragmatic and limit my discussions to physiotherapy and significant nursing studies.

Q&A

Next, here are Hamid's answers about his PhD research in the University of London on 'Scholarly communication and information-seeking behaviour of scientists':

Hamid *What does the research seek to find out?*
I am not testing any hypothesis. The research is qualitative and seeks to find any existing patterns and tries to generate a model based on the scientists' information-seeking and communication patterns.

Relevant knowledge?
I need to know about research literature of information behaviour and scholarly communication, which are two well-established study areas in our field.

New areas of knowledge and know-how?
I needed to learn interview techniques because the main data collection [instrument] I intended to use was interview, though I am also going to do a survey and have some statistics to analyse. So I learned how to design an online questionnaire and how to use SPSS.

Likely sources of information?
I talked to other colleagues (researchers) who have used this technique (interview) before and knew a lot about this. I also read some books on qualitative research.
For using SPSS I just read its help and went through its tutorial.
For online questionnaire I know HTML, but I started learning PHP [a general-purpose scripting language that is especially suited for Web development and can be embedded into HTML] and used web-based resources for learning how to write scripts and use other people's scripts. Also UCL has an IT support, so I made an appointment

Q&A

with a guy there and went and talked to him about the questionnaire and he guided me a bit and also gave me one of his own PHP scripts that I could modify and use.

Methodological options?
I could do a qualitative (interview) or quantitative (survey) research as my approach. I preferred to do mixed-method research by using both qualitative and quantitative approaches (triangulation is more popular these days and more defendable!). Though the main part is qualitative, I will do a follow-up survey and am also using critical-incident data collection technique. I will also analyse some electronic-journals-usage data. The research can be also considered as a kind of case study as it is limited to UCL department of physics.

Limits to breadth and depth of inquiry?
The study is limited to a case, which is UCL physics department. The limitation of sample makes it difficult to generalize the results. With regard to the depth, I don't go much deeper into the interaction of the scientists with particular information resources, and rather focus on their info-seeking behaviour as a whole.

Institutional requirements?
Q&A The research involves human subjects and I had to comply with ethical regulations of the UCL ethics committee (data are to be analysed confidentially and anonymously).

Laima, undertaking her doctoral research in Lithuania on 'The Development of the Public Sphere in Lithuania 1988–2000: the Case of Newspapers', describes the factors that influenced her mapping of the research area.

Laima *Relevant knowledge?*
The first 'mapping' task was to investigate the theory of the public sphere, the state of art in this field, but also what research has been done in my country. As I found that research, not only on the public sphere but also on the media in general was very scarce, my choice was to pursue research that would produce a more general picture of the development of the public sphere, instead of focusing on some narrow problem.

New areas of knowledge and know-how?
Q&A I had to map for myself the areas of knowledge and disciplines that my research will need to draw on. I knew from the very beginning, that I will not be able to stay in the narrowly understood theory of communication, but I will also need to go into rather new for me

fields of sociology and political science. As one way to cope with this I took a course on 'Social change in Lithuania' in the Department of Sociology.

Likely sources of information?
It was obvious from the very beginning that I will have to use statistical data on newspaper publishing. Other important information that I knew I would have to gather was on the history of press development in Lithuania in that period: the development of press laws, the change of media institutions, the change of the relationship between politics and press etc. The easiest available source of this information was the periodical press itself, since it documented the most important changes affecting it and discussed the current situation of media and journalism in the country.

Methodological options?
I combined the methodological approach of media and communication studies with a broader theoretical framework of sociology and political philosophy. I used the theoretical framework of Jürgen Habermas's normative conception of the public sphere ... [while] in the empirical part of the dissertation I measured the number of arenas of the public sphere (based on statistical newspaper-publishing data), level of audience involvement (based on circulation statistics and public opinion surveys), and number and scope of actors taking part in public debates (using content analysis).

Q&A

Using the answers to create a first map

Most researchers who answer the kind of questions we have been discussing—whether they are required to or do it on their own initiative—probably stop when they have produced a plan in words, with appropriate headings. That's very useful, and some of the researchers who have contributed to this book did it very thoroughly, but it could become much easier to use if they took one further step, and complemented it with a graphic version. Why? A text that runs to perhaps 10 typed pages, with several sections and subsections, is not easy to find one's way around; it's hard to locate points one wants to refer to, and difficult to keep the whole structure in mind. But if it's accompanied by a pictorial representation that can show on a single page the different parts and how they are related to one another, with just sufficient words to act as labels and pointers to the relevant parts of the text version, it gains in value and becomes much more accessible.

One of the researchers was fortunate in having a supervisor who was interested in conceptual maps—the general name for this kind of graphic—and she herself created one early in her research to illuminate her answers to the question about methodological options for her research, which as quoted above (see pages 32–34) were quite complex. In its first version (see Figure 2.1), it was a PowerPoint graphic that brought together on one plane the stages of research utilization, the factors affecting it in the physiotherapy profession, and references to key texts in the literature on the various stages.

The version as developed for reproduction in her dissertation is shown in Figure 2.2.

When I was writing the first edition of this book, I was just starting my own doctoral research (on 'The role of information products and presentation in organizations'). I made a simple map showing the key concepts, a view of their relationship, and the topics on which I proposed to gather information (see Figure 2.3).

I didn't at the time make a map for the research journey in line with the second of the metaphors described on pages 29–30, but this is something I now suggest to research students. Mine could have been on the lines shown in Figure 2.4, and I rather wish that I had done something like it at the start; it would have helped me to develop more detailed schedules for different bits of work as the research progressed.

Using the map

Maps made early in research – whether in words alone or supported by graphic versions – go on giving value through the whole course of the research.

- They can refresh researchers' memory of their own thought processes (which is often necessary!).
- They help to explain to others what your research is about.
- They can be updated and amended, to form a running visual record of developments in thinking and action in the course of the research.
- They help in planning actions, charting the sequence of activities over time, planning dissertation structure and sequence of writing.
- They make a good basis for illustrations.

Kerry's preliminary mapping was purely in text, but extremely thorough. Her outline 'Research strategy' could easily be developed into a first map of the research journey.

Kerry

- Determine organizational ... objectives for information literacy provision in UK academic libraries through a review of the relevant literature.
- Determine if the accredited courses on offer within [the institutions studied] fulfil these objectives, with particular focus on user education and information literacy skills, by comparison and review of data within course information acquired.

continued on page 42

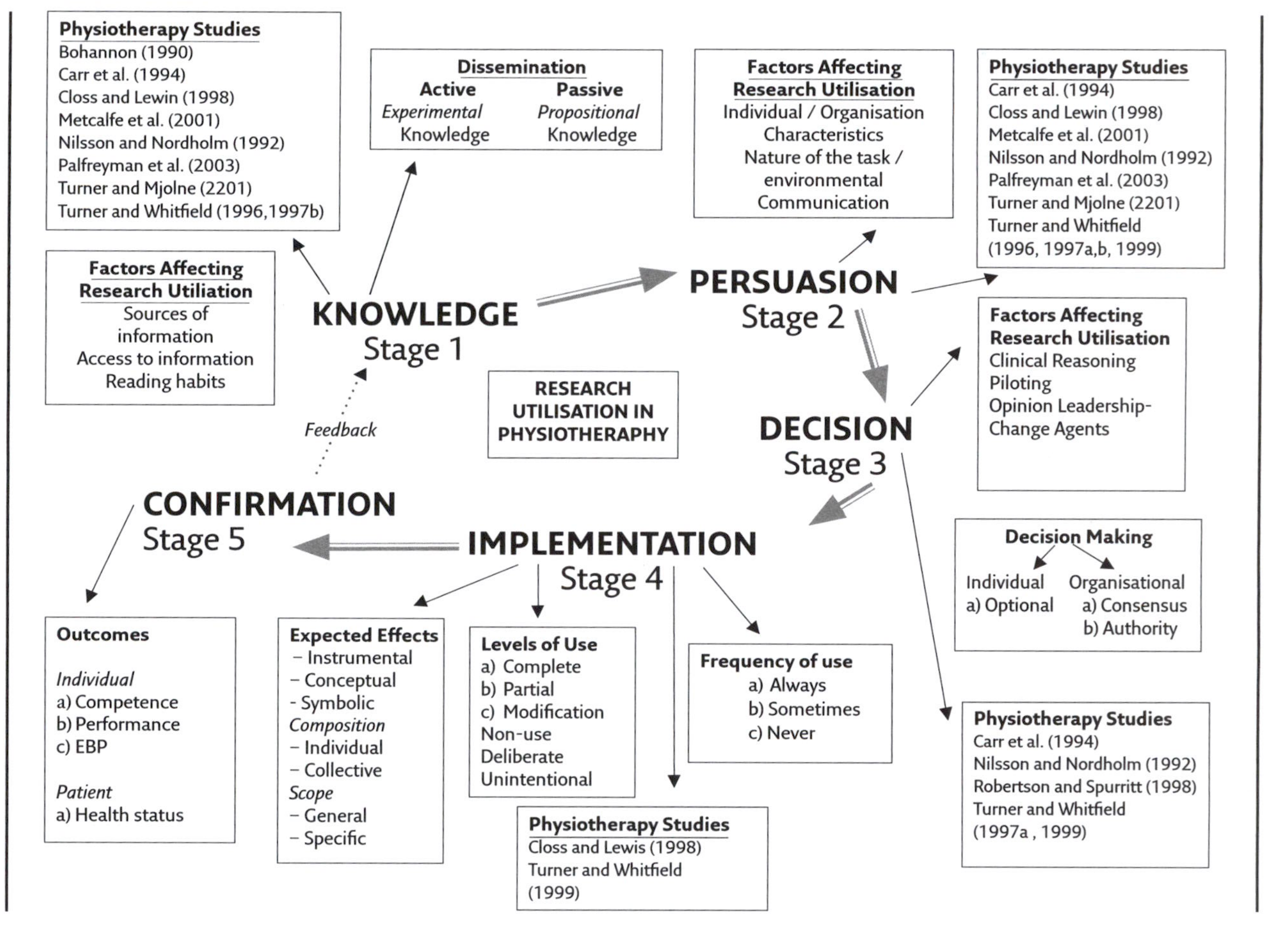

Figure 2.2 Paula's map – first version

A conceptual model of research utilisation.

KNOWLEDGE Stage 1	PERSUASION Stage 2	DECISIONS Stage 3	IMPLEMENTATION Stage 4	CONFIRMATION Stage 5
Factors Affecting Research Utilisation Source of information Access to information Reading habits	**Factors Affecting Research Utilisation** Individual / Organisation Characteristics Nature of the task / environmental Communication	**Factors Affecting Research Utilisation** Clinical Reasoning Piloting Opinion Leadership Change Agents	**Frequency of use** a) Always b) Sometimes c) Never	**Outcomes** *Individual* → a) Competence b) Performance c) Evidence / Research- based practice *Patient* → a) Health status
Dissemination **Active** → *Experimental Knowledge* **Passive** → *Propositional Knowledge*		**Decision Making** Individual → a) Optional Organisational → a) Consensus b) Authority	**Types of Research Use** *Expected Effects* – Instrumental – Conceptual – Symbolic *Composition* – Individual – Collective *Scope* – General – Specific	
Physiotherapy Studies Bohannon (1990) Carr et al. (1994) Closs and Lewin (1998) Metcalfe et al. (2001) Nilsson and Nordholm (1992) Palfreyman et al. (2003) Turner and Mjolne (2001) Turner and Whitfield (1996, 1997b)	**Physiotherapy Studies** Carr et al. (1994) Closs and Lewin (1998) Metcalfe et al. (2001) Nilsson and Nordholm (1992) Palfreyman et al. (2003) Turner and Whitfield (1996, 1997a,b, 1999)	**Physiotherapy Studies** Carr et al. (1994) Nilsson and Nordholm (1992) Robertson and Spurritt (1998) Turner and Whitfield (1997a, 1999) **FEEDBACK**	**Levels of Use** a) Complete b) Partial c) Modification Non-use a) Deliberate b) Unintentional **Physiotheraphy Studies** Closs and Lewin (1998) Turner and Whitfield (1990)	

Figure 2.2 Paula's map – final version

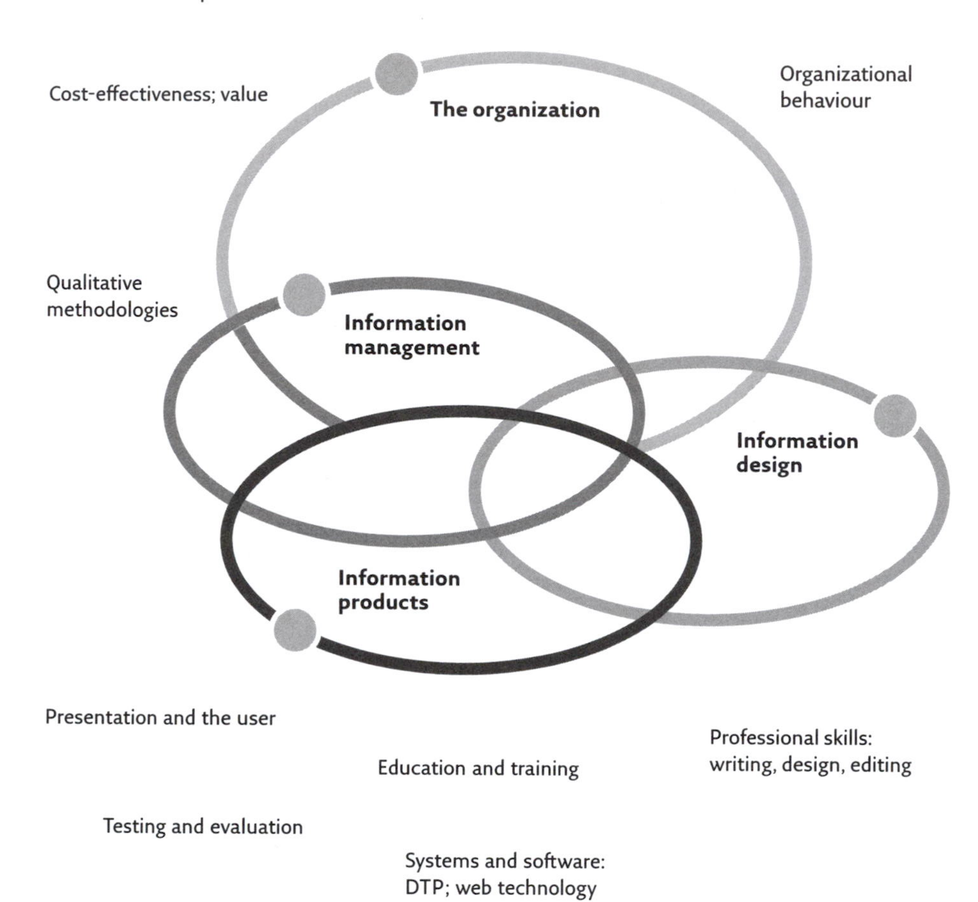

The interlocking rings in the middle represent the questions the research aimed to answer:
How do organizations manage the information products that they create for their inside and outside worlds?
What place do information products have in the organizational context?
Do information management and information design play any part in their creation and/or management?

The topics ranged round the diagram are the initial ideas about the subjects that I needed to know about in order to answer them – some I knew quite a lot about, of others I had some knowledge but needed to learn more, and I had yet to become acquainted with quite a number. So the topics represented a first set of search terms for reviewing the literature.

Figure 2.3 Liz's map of research territory

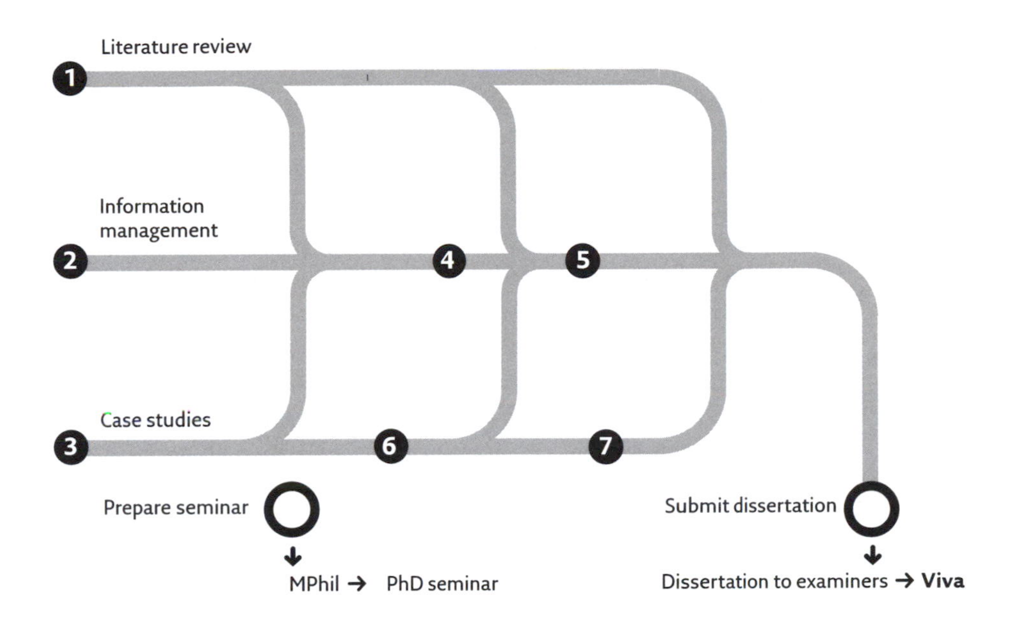

It would probably have helped me if I had also made a picture like this of the journey through time that I had to make during the research, to show how the things that had to be done should be organized to help one another forward, and reach completion at the right time.

It looks rather like streams joining the flow of a river along its course – and that is indeed the visual metaphor that emerged in discussion between the authors about how to illustrate what researchers have to do in the way of project- and time-management.

1 Plan literature review
2 Set up database
3 Set up case studies in 10 organisations
4 Plan dissertation structure
5 Start writing dissertation
6 Repeat visits at intervals
7 Final case study reports to organisations

Figure 2.4 A route map for the research journey

Kerry continued from page 37

- Contact 18 institutions and see if they would agree to telephone interviews, or develop a questionnaire to determine how they deliver practical help for new professionals within this field.
- Initial email to Department Head/Senior Lecturer, followed up by telephone interview—or initial telephone approach, followed up by questionnaire. (Rationale: distance/timescale involved in visiting each institution as research is on a UK-wide scale, so either telephone interview or mail survey most appropriate for data-gathering.)
- Qualitative approach preferred—interview will be developed to have fixed set of questions but use of one to one interview will hopefully encourage a diverse range of opinions. (May need to mail out initial questions if time is a factor for some interviewees.)
- Determine whether new information professionals (i.e. recently graduated) feel that they have received 'adequate' training in LIS schools to cope with the practicalities of user education/information literacy issues within their workplace.

The answers of another of the researchers reveal quite a contrast in institutional requirements. Hamid replied to our questions at a point when the collection of material through a case study and its analysis was completed but the thesis was still to come. In answer to the questions about the stage at which he began planning the end product of the research, he replied: 'Will do this in writing up stage.'

He was, however, required to submit a sample chapter during the first 21 months of his doctoral studies, and to make a presentation to gain approval for upgrading the work from MPhil to PhD, and my own experience of that process suggests that he must have done a lot of planning and mapping in preparation for it!

Help from supervisors and tutors

The help from their tutors and supervisors that researchers need most at this stage goes further than just optional lectures! It covers:

- Alerting them to the various dimensions in which they'll have to work, and how they relate to one another and to the business of research
- Requiring action that gives them experience of things they have to master
- Insisting on seeing actual plans of structure; pieces of writing; explanations of how they propose to go about the project; timetables for the whole process.

The responses of recent researchers to our question about support from their supervisors show how much they value this kind of help (and, incidentally, make it clear that the full benefit comes only when the researcher puts in as much effort as the supervisor).

Kerry	the majority of our discussions were done via email because we were both busy and in different towns. But the level of support received from my supervisor was excellent. She would challenge me regularly and this made me think hard about what I was trying to achieve.
Paula	The level of support I have received has been fantastic. The ground rules were clear from the outset and the relationship developed from student/teacher to a more equal footing with the tutor facilitating thought and questioning.

As well as giving their students the invaluable chance to practise on a small scale and in safety at the start so that they gain confidence for the real thing, supervisors can help them avoid potential difficulties by:

- Making themselves aware of whether researchers they supervise are affected by such factors as dyslexia, working in their second language, visual or hearing handicap; and ensuring that they receive whatever assistance the institution provides
- Finding out whether they lack familiarity with any aspect of the available technology for handling information, and ensuring they take advantage of the training on offer.

Software help

There are many software tools that can be used for graphic mapping of both research territory and research 'itineraries'.

One well-known form of concept mapping is through the 'Mind Maps', popularized by Tony Buzan in a series of books (see, for example Buzan & Buzan, 2000) and TV programmes. These began as a hand-drawn technique for note-taking, presenting the overall structure of subjects, summarizing information, etc. Now a range of mind-mapping software products is available from a number of companies, see http://www.mind-map.com, http://visual-mind. com, http://www.mind-mapping.co.uk (MindManager) etc. CMAP, developed for educational use in the United States, is a set of tools, available for download at http://cmap.ihmc.us/conceptmap.html/, that 'empowers users to construct, navigate, share and criticize knowledge models represented as Concept maps'. For background see Novak and Cañas (2006).

Useful though they are, software tools *will not do the thinking!* To get value from them, you have to do some hard thinking about the ideas you want to display; when you have done that, and not before, they can help to make them visible, and allow you to develop and organize them further.

I have to confess that the only software tool I use for making graphics to represent ideas is the AppleWorks drawing package. The process seems to start with visual metaphors for what I've been thinking about (see pages 29–30 of this chapter), that leads to hand-drawn roughs (very rough), which I can then turn into drawings using the software; experience shows that it doesn't work if I go straight to the computer. (When they are destined for books, as in this book, the output I produce goes to my co-author and designer, who transforms them into real illustrations!)

Maps which begin and end as hand-drawn[3] can be extremely clear and accessible; I have a particular liking for those which Checkland and his colleagues originated when they were developing what is known as 'soft systems analysis'. They are well worth a look because they can be used for a great many purposes and require very little manual skill (see, for example, Checkland & Scholes, 1999; Checkland & Holwell, 1998).

It has to be acknowledged that not everyone feels the need for graphic representation, and some of us feel inhibited at the thought of it. We would still encourage readers to suspend their inhibitions and have a shot at it!

Summary

Researchers have to manage a lot of different activities and bring them all together to a conclusion at a fixed time. Achieving that successfully and getting a good result depends on careful planning at the start of the project.

Making both mental and actual maps, of the 'territory' that your research has to explore and of the stages of the 'research journey' that you have to make, will clear the mind, and help you to make a good start—whatever the scale of the project, whether it will take three months or three years.

The map-making has to begin by asking and answering questions; your answers will help you define:

- The aims of the research
- The knowledge it will need to draw on
- The new things you will need to learn in the process
- Where you are likely to find the information you need
- Appropriate methods for doing the research
- The limits to set for it
- What you must do to meet the requirements of the institution where you are doing the research.

3
An interesting sidelight comes from recent work by Professor Clive Holtham at the Cass Business School, City University, London in using visual methods with students on the MSc in management. He has a long-standing interest in using drawings to explore ideas, and has introduced a course module in which the students use real traditional sketchbooks, 'applying arts perspectives' to help them design their research.

Some institutions insist on researchers answering such questions before they can undertake research; if yours doesn't, get on and answer them anyway for yourself.

When you have answered the questions, even if you have never tried turning ideas into maps before, have a shot at it—you may be surprised at how much they can show and how they can help your thinking and planning.

References

Websites referred to in this chapter accessed on 18 March 2009

Buzan, T & Buzan, B (2000)
The Mind MapBook. London: BBC.

Checkland, P & Scholes, J (1999)
Soft Systems Methodology in Action.
Chichester: John Wiley & Sons.

Checkland, P & Holwell, S (1998)
Information, Systems and Information Systems: Making Sense of the Field.
Chichester: John Wiley & Sons.

Novak, J D & Cañas, A J (2006)
The Theory Underlying Concept Maps and How to Construct Them, Technical Report, IHMC CmapTools 2006–01. Florida Institute for Human and Machine Cognition.
http://www.stanford.edu/dept/SUSE/projects/ireport/articles/concept_maps/

Research Information Network (2008)
Mind the skills gap: Information-handling training for research.
http://www.rin.ac.uk

Useful website

Quality Assurance Agency for Higher Education (2004)
Code of practice for the assurance of academic quality and standards in higher education, Section 1: postgraduate research programmes, at: http://www.qaa.ac.uk/academicinfrastructure/codeOfPractice
The Agency's recommendations and 'precepts'. Topics include supervision, progress and review arrangements, development of research skills, assessment.

Managing two kinds of information

This part gives practical advice, based on the professional skills of information managers and project managers, on how to deal with two vital kinds of research information:

1 The information we collect and create on the *subject* of our research, see Chapter 3.
2 The information we need to keep *about* the research itself as a *project*, see Chapter 4.

Chapter 5 offers lessons from experience on how to fit all that managment into the time available in your research project.

Part 2

P

Information to support research–and how to manage it

Ch 3 Contents at a glance

3

'I wish you would let me sort your papers for you, uncle,' said Dorothea. 'I would letter them all, and then make a list of subjects under each letter.'

George Eliot, *Middlemarch*, 1871, Chapter 2.

'Freedom is, in all things, an essential condition of growth and power. The purposes of readers in search of a book are as manifold as the names and subjects, or headings under which the book may be traced. Entering the book only once is giving but one of its many references and suppressing the remainder.'

Antonio Crestadoro, *The art of making catalogues of libraries or, a method to obtain in a short time a most perfect, complete, and satisfactory printed catalogue of the British Museum Library* by A reader therein. London: The Literary, Scientific & Artistic Reference Office, 1856.

'as I have always had several quite distinct subjects in hand at the same time, I may mention that I keep from thirty to forty large portfolios, in cabinets with labelled shelves, into which I can at once put a detached reference or memorandum. I have bought many books and at their ends I make an index of all the facts that concern my work; or, if the book is not my own, write out a separate abstract, and of such abstracts I have a large drawer full. Before beginning on any subject I look to all the short indexes and make a general and classified index, and by taking the one or more proper portfolios I have all the information collected during my life ready for use.'

Charles Darwin, *Autobiography,* edited by Nora Barlow, Collins, 1958, pages 136–138.

Introduction

In reading this chapter, the important thing is to get a grasp on the underlying ideas (which are commonsense rather than esoteric), and then decide for yourself what ways of applying them best fit your project and your own temperament. As we shall see, effective ways of managing information aren't necessarily all computer-based! Information management isn't synonymous with IT, though good information managers make knowledgeable use of appropriate IT. Software tools that can be helpful in various tasks will be mentioned where relevant, as will points that this book can't cover, on which tutors and supervisors are the essential source of guidance.

Why manage research information?

The short answer is, in order to:

- Get maximum value from the effort you invest in research
- Support your memory
- Help the transformations of information into knowledge and knowledge into information which researchers have to make (see Figure 1.1, page 24)
- Use time to the best advantage, and save yourself a heap of trouble. Remember, pressure increases throughout the research process and is heaviest towards the delivery end; managing information sensibly from the start helps keep pressure at the end manageable.

What information management covers

If we are to do anything useful with any information we collect for any purpose, including research, we need to manage it, but, as Karen observes, there are many different definitions of information management:

Karen I spent a long time trying to get a grip on the area of information management studies and create my own definitions and boundaries, since I experienced it as particularly vague, and felt that all kinds of people, both professionals and researchers, used IM (and KM) as labels for activities that were very much varying in scope, aims, and depth.

For the purposes of this book, this is what 'information management' covers:

- Defining the information we need to feed our knowledge
- Finding it
- Labelling and recording what we find, so as to create 'keys' to the information store that allow us to get in and find what we need at any time
- Storing it.

As Figure 3.1 shows, this is a cyclical process, repeated many times, because as we collect more information and transform it into knowledge, we realize there are new questions to ask and new information to seek.

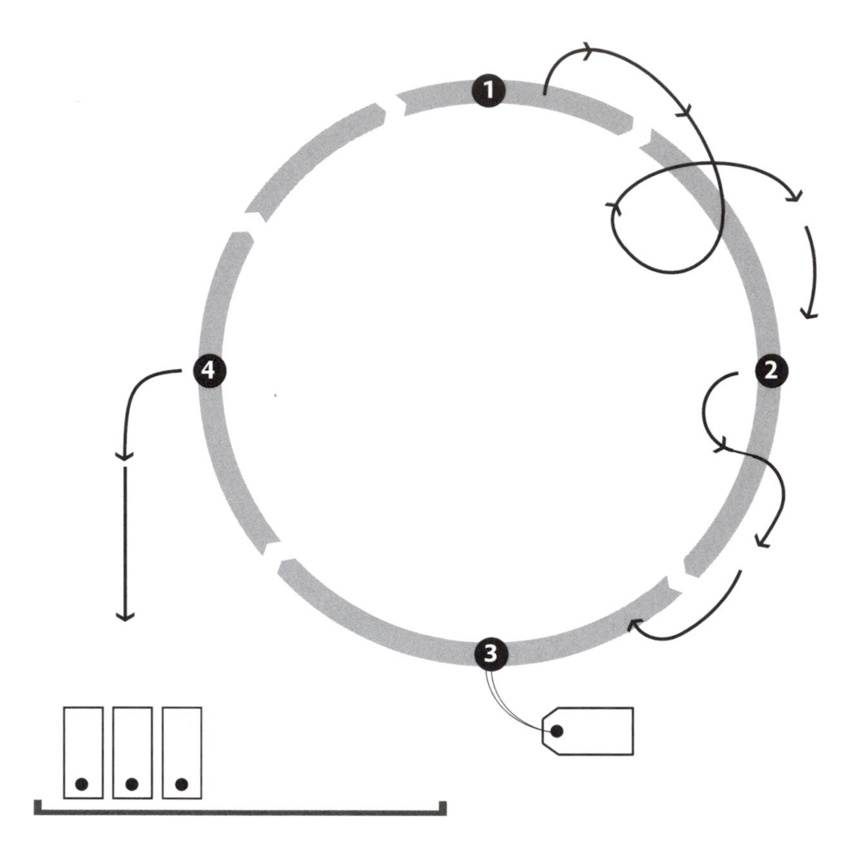

The four-stage process of information management shown here is a cyclical one, but it is not an enclosed system. The activities are repeated many times over in the course of research, but how we define our information needs and what we go looking for will change over time, as our understanding is progessively enriched by the information we take in and transform into knowledge. The information has to be labelled and stored so that we can find it whenever we want it, but its most important effects are through our interaction with it.

1. Define the information need
2. Find it
3. Label and record it
4. Store it

Figure 3.1 Information management for research

In research, as in most kinds of working life, we need to be able to:

- Locate sources of useful information
- Transform information that is useful to us into knowledge
- Store physical items that embody the useful information
- Get into our store of useful information, move around it easily, find what we need quickly, and get out with it as speedily as possible, ready to use it for our own purposes.

If we develop practical ways of doing this in the course of research, we gain something that will help us through the whole of our working life.

Lessons of experience

You *can* survive, and get whatever end qualification your research is intended to bring, without any of the support from information management advocated in this chapter.

I did it myself in my first research (for a Master's degree) because I knew no better, and there was no-one to tell me of alternatives. It wasn't a wholly enjoyable experience, and the end product didn't benefit to the full from the material I'd gathered, because I couldn't be certain of finding everything relevant to the arguments I was presenting.

When, many years later, I set out to do a PhD, I *did* know better, thanks to experience and education acquired in the course of work as information manager and information consultant, and I set about applying it from the start. It really did make a difference. The whole research process was more enjoyable and less fraught with anxiety, because from the start I knew I had the information I was gathering and creating under control, and when it came to writing I could find what I wanted, and incorporate it into the structure of my thesis at the points where it would do most good.

Reading the answers of recent researchers to our questions about managing information certainly makes it clear that individual temperament has a big effect on how they tackle it. If you're of a methodical disposition, managing information comes fairly naturally, as we'll see later from the responses of some very organized researchers (more organized than I've ever managed to become); if, like Karen, 'methodical' is perhaps not the word that comes to mind in describing yourself, then you have to find other approaches:

Karen — Another problem has to do with my rather untidy personality, when I can't find copies that I know I should have (that's relatively simple as long as there are electronic versions, worse with paper-based versions), and – more problematic – when I forget about texts that I have found altogether. The last problem 'solves itself' of course; I will be using less sources than I otherwise could do, but not be aware of the fact ...

> [However] ... as my research problem and cross-disciplinary, eclectic approach is rather original there are few texts that can be called truly essential to refer to.

And though she doesn't always refer to the 'scraps of paper' on which she writes notes in meetings or while reading, she finds that

> the act of jotting down my ideas and inspirations etc. seems to help enough in my thought process so that I usually 'come up with' the same ideas again when writing at the computer.'

Another researcher with a similar approach also observes the compensations that it can bring:

Laima — It might seem like a disorganized work, but when I look back now I am not totally unhappy with it. Of course, sometimes I had troubles to find again some particular article, but in the process of going again through all articles I would notice something that I have missed or something that I didn't regard as significant before. In any case, it didn't create major problems for my work.

As we shall see later (see page 66) this more intuitive 'right brain' approach is actually a valuable complement to the analytical one.

We all have to be realistic about the degree of unfamiliar discipline we can cope with, but experience suggests that most of us can become a little more organized in the way we approach research, to the benefit of the outcome, and without doing too much violence to our characters. *And the less experience of research and the less knowledge of the research topic we have, the more we need to provide ourselves with aids to putting more order into the business.* While Karen and Laima admit to being a bit short in the organization department, they are both experienced researchers who have built up a body of knowledge which helps them absorb new material and order it in their minds. Even so, both of them remark that if they had to start again, they would 'try to keep better track of stored material', and 'put some more order in the materials collected'.

Where and how information management helps research

There are six key research activities where information management can help researchers. Some are linked to specific periods of the research process; others recur more or less throughout. Figure 3.2 shows them on the spiral path that we considered in Chapter 2 (see page 30) as a visual metaphor for research.

1 At the very start, when you have defined the research question or hypothesis, and the objectives of the research
2 When you start collecting information and have to decide what's useful and how to take away what you need

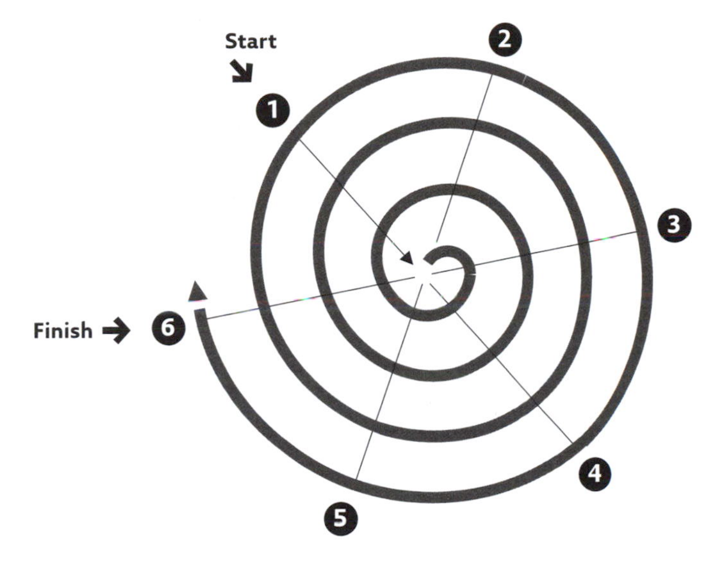

The spiral path is a visual metaphor for both the whole research process, and the repeated cycle of information management, which supports the key activities of research from start to end and beyond.

1. At the start, when you have defined research objectives
2. When you begin to collect information
3. When you have to store it so that you can find it again
4. Whenever you need to review progress
5. When you are writing the end product
6. When your research is completed and you want to make further use of it

Figure 3.2 Where and how managing information helps research

3 When you bring it back to base and have to store it so you can find it again whenever needed
4 When you want to review progress, decide where to go next, deal with new questions that arise
5 When you start writing and need to bring information together to support your arguments
6 When you want to use your research later as the basis for articles, presentations, books.

This chapter will look particularly at the first three, which are essential for the early stages of research; they make the foundation for the other uses, which are where you profit from the effort you invested. They will be considered in later chapters.

Making a good start

The thinking done in mapping your research territory and the answers to the questions set out in Chapter 2 (see page 30), make a useful start for managing research information.

Three basic questions

Your answers to these questions are specially relevant for planning what you need to do in that direction.

1 What subjects do I need to know about, what know-how do I need, what useful knowledge have I got to start with, and what do I need to add?
2 What kind of information resources will I need to use to add to my knowledge, and what do I need to take into account in using them?
3 What kinds of material will I collect? What are the implications for suitable storage?

They will give useful pointers for preparing to manage information, as the answers of recent researchers already quoted in Chapter 2 (see pages 32–36), and those described below, reveal.

Knowledge and know-how required

Assessing what relevant knowledge they already had, and the directions in which they needed to extend it, pointed them towards where to start and what to look for. (It is as well not to choose a research topic in which your knowledge – and interest – are minimal; on the other hand knowing too much can make researchers so confident that they already know the answers that they are unfitted to investigate their chosen subject, because they can't see what questions need to be asked!)

Kath (an occupational therapist on the same course as Paula, who has already been quoted) took the research aim of investigating how practising occupational therapists working in forensic mental health settings made use of professional theory in their day-to-day work. Her professional experience in that area, and her own existing knowledge of the work and its environment gave her a starting point for approaching the literature of the subject and identifying key themes for the information she needed to acquire. On the basis of her reading she went on to begin the main task of using people as the key source of the information necessary to extend her knowledge:

Kath I ... then conducted a focus group using the key themes as prompts for discussion. From the focus group discussion I designed a semi-structured interview schedule to carry out 10 individual interviews.

Another researcher with first-hand knowledge of her area of research (information management in voluntary peace organizations, and how board members' information behaviour influences and is influenced by patterns and values of the organization), Karen took a more informal and 'intuitive' approach.

Karen I simply started, looking first at the disciplines I was least familiar with, but also following other tracks, in other disciplines, at the same time.

I think the difference in approach may reflect a difference in research experience, as well as of temperament – Karen, a PhD student, had been there before, whereas Kath and Paula, as MSc students, were undertaking their first postgraduate research, separated by a period of professional work from their undergraduate studies. Experience does make it safer to take some short cuts, but you have to be sure that you feel comfortable with the level of risk-taking they involve.

Information sources

Once you have a fair idea of what relevant knowledge you have already, and where you need more, it becomes easier to locate sources where you're likely to find information that will help you extend and enrich your knowledge. It also makes you aware of where you need some guidance as to sources, and of the sources where special considerations apply.

The replies from the researchers who have contributed their experience point to two very different kinds of source: those based on the written word, and accessed through print or electronic media; and those which are embodied in people and are accessed through getting them to complete questionnaires or talk face to face in interviews. Nearly all research projects require at least some use of the first kind – for the 'literature review'; in some, texts are also the things investigated, the actual focus of the research. In other cases, the answer to the research question or the testing of a hypothesis depends on persuading a sufficient number of appropriate people to answer a questionnaire or talk to the researcher, and analysing their responses.

On text-based sources appropriate for your research subject, this book will say little or nothing, for the reasons outlined in Chapter 1 (see page 26); any guidance on them has to be the responsibility of your tutors. Some general guidance about making use of the relevant material you find in them, however, will be given shortly (see pages 66-68).

People as sources of information

If your research requires using people as your key source (as in some of the examples quoted above, and as in my own research, which depended on case studies in 10 organizations, spread over five years), you are in for an interesting time – and some problems that have to be tackled very early on. They include:

- Getting whatever ethical clearance the institution requires and observing its conditions
- Communicating with people who are potential and actual subjects for interviews, questionnaire surveys, focus groups, or workshops
- Drafting and testing questions
- Planning for analysis of qualitative and quantitative responses.

Even methodical and far-sighted researchers are liable to meet some surprises in this area, as Kerry did in the matter of questionnaire design – to which she also found a good solution:

Kerry — I was ... surprised at just how long it took to come up with two questionnaires that actually asked the questions I wanted to ask, in a format that wouldn't make my respondents lose the will to live before they'd finished it. I think from anyone's experience of filling out questionnaires, if you've got to really work at it you get fed up and the resulting responses are not therefore going to be as information rich as the researcher would like. Saying that, I didn't want just to be dealing with quantitative data as I felt this wouldn't really get to the crux of the matter.

What helped me get the final questions sorted was a little exercise I took upon myself to complete prior to a meeting I had set up with my supervisor for the following week. ... in order to try and get my rationale straight in my own mind before meeting with my supervisor I decided to actually write out the rationale behind each ... a really useful exercise although I didn't realize its full potential at the time of writing: not only in helping me come to terms with my ownership of the research (I actually started to believe that I really was designing a research strategy which I would then put into practice) and unwittingly developing my independent learning skills, but also because I was ultimately able to use some of this 'thinking out loud' material in my methodology chapter, so it was worth the time spent in the end.

That's not the end of the problem with questionnaires; once respondents have completed them, they have to be analysed – another can of worms, as Kerry found (fortunately she located an answer too):

Kerry I think if I'm honest I had not really considered the nuts and bolts of exactly how I was going to analyze my results – particularly the qualitative data, as I had never come across content analysis before, or at least not as a deliberate exercise. So it was only once my results were in that I started to really look at the methodology behind content analysis. The social research text books I referred to were helpful in this, as was an article I found ... in which the author states that the content analysis of LIS job ads conducted for their research had been along the lines of the content analysis described in x's article. This was a bit of a find as I could then use an established method of content analysis and justify my reasons for doing so by following a method already used within LIS research ...

If your research relies on getting people to answer questions, you need to plan your approach with a lot of care, as these contrasting stories show. Kath had to seek to persuade professional colleagues to be interviewed:

Kath The biggest problem was recruiting participants. I had not realized how threatened people would feel when they were asked to discuss their use of professional theory. I had to provide a lot of reassurance to people that my purpose was to discover barriers to using theory and not to judge their practice. I managed to recruit the number that I needed but only just.
... [If I were starting again, I would] provide a more detailed explanation of the purpose of the research in my invitation letters in an attempt to improve response rates from volunteers.

Hamid's research depended on getting fellow research students to answer a questionnaire:

Hamid The response rate was fine, more than I expected. But I have to say that this was partly because of the measures I took. I wrote all research students friendly emails addressing them with their forenames and tried to make the subject of the invitation emails and the topic of the research look interesting to them.

The explanation of the difference is probably that it is fairly easy to get fellow-students to help; there is not too much at stake there, and the main obstacle is likely to be natural human disinclination to mental exertion. On the other hand, it is often difficult to win the co-operation of individuals in work situations, where they may fear a threat to their job, or be sensitive to the possibility of criticism of their way of doing their work.

In my own doctoral research, I had to persuade a number of organizations in a range of fields from government to private, including commercial firms, cultural bodies, medical research organizations and academic institutions, to co-operate in long-term case studies, extending over five years. Setting up the case studies was the first major piece of work I did for the research. It took time and ingenuity to assemble 10 willing participants. Some industries and services are very cagey because they are anxious to avoid the risk of giving information to competitors; in other cases managers fear to overload already busy staff. Prior experience of winning over various kinds of businesses and organizations to participate in case studies for books came in useful – I was able to persuade some of them to help in the research; I also used professional contacts, and organizations for which I had undertaken consultancy assignments.

In 'practice-based research', of the kind undertaken by students of design, for example, where researchers often have to create artefacts of various kinds as part of their project, there is an extra dimension of getting potential consumers to test the products and of recording the results. Aragon and Ismaril, MA students of industrial design, provide observations on the problems involved.

Aragon had the interesting idea of using 'consumers' greed and laziness' in an attempt to get them to make sound environmental choices and avoid buying 'un-needed products', by creating a multifunctional product which would both achieve this virtuous end and satisfy the promptings of the two deadly sins.

Ismaril was investigating 'grooming practices' and the psychological background to them, with its related issues of self-image, and the products he made and tested were a 'height measure against which one compares one's height with that of celebrities' and 'Voice Mirror' a mirror with a built-in voice recorder to practice elocution.

His approach combined giving trial prototypes to subjects, questionnaires and follow-up interviews with them on their experiences in using the prototypes, and making video recordings of people approaching and using the prototypes when they were exhibited at a later stage. Like other researchers already quoted, he had problems with estimating the time required – 'I left trial prototypes with subjects for too long so got feedback at a late stage.'

He reflects in the light of experience that it would have been worth trying to 'configure prototypes so as to capture some element of their use (feedback)' perhaps by incorporating a small voice recorder in them.

Some general rules for survival if your research depends on inputs from people:

- Start early on deciding about the form of information-seeking, the number of participants, and where they need to come from.
- Plan the approach with care, anticipating the likely objections and reservations you may encounter. An introductory letter or email is probably the best way, as it gives the recipient time for reflection. A phone call is a useful first approach, however, if you need to find who is the appropriate person to contact in an organization.

- Provide clear, brief information about the project and what it will require of participants.
- Give assurances about confidentiality and getting drafts signed off by participants before any use is made of them.
- Never omit to thank people who respond to your requests – even if the response turns out to be not particularly useful for your purposes.
- Find out what the institution's ethical requirements are; remember that they take time to fulfil, and if you don't start early you may be delayed in getting on with an essential bit of your research. (*The Code of practice for the assurance of academic quality and standards in higher education* (2004) requires institutions to make researchers aware of ethical issues; if yours does not tell you about them, ask until they do!)
- Think hard about what you need to find out and how you need to use it, and ask the minimum number of questions for the purpose.
- Test the questions you plan to put in questionnaires or interviews on representatives of the people you need to participate (I have never stopped being surprised at how many wrong ends human beings can find to any stick they are presented with).
- Make sure the questions give analysable answers, and allow for how long the analysis will take.

Storing information – some practical ideas

Answering this question can give the business of research a reassuring touch of reality; in the early stages one can sometimes feel there's nothing really solid there, and it helps to have something tangible to do. Getting storage boxes, setting up folders and files, and having a visible place to put what you're about to start collecting helps you to believe it's all real. If your materials will include photographs or graphic materials or artefacts, think carefully about ways of storing them that will make it easy to put them away and extract.

If you expect to collect a lot of material from web searching, it is worth considering various free web-based tools that you can use to save, organize and search your collection. A useful article by Bates (2006) gives sound practical advice on using some of them, and Cameron (2006) describes similar facilities offered by the free CiteULike service he has run since 2004; it's described as being for academics, but is actually open to anyone – though links to copyrighted academic articles can be followed only by those who can access them from a university network.

Later (see page 74), we discuss how to make it possible to search the whole range of your information collection, regardless of physical form or storage medium.

Meantime, some examples from recent researchers, which show how they related the storage medium to the ways in which they wanted to use material in the course of their research. Kerry, who was researching the kind of information-skills training received by postgraduate Library and Information Science students, judged that, in using her information collection, it would best serve her purposes to be able to consult hard-copy material in the form of reports published in various countries.

Kerry — I used a very basic method of storing information, which involved a lot of sturdy A4 lever arch files! Main/key reports relating to information literacy were filed together as these were my 'primary' sources. These were then filed under the relevant countries of origin because I was comparing these to current practice in the UK.

It is interesting to see that researchers who found it met their needs in information searching to make extensive use of electronic sources, and who were fully at ease with using them, still found that traditional print on paper was a main part of the solution when it came to storing their collection.

Karen — I stored/store in folders, both folders on my computers, a folder called 'literature' in my mailbox, and paper folders for copied articles and the like.

Mariana (another Industrial Design student):

Mariana — Computer folders and files, with scanned or downloaded images from the web, or written information from such sources as electronic journals.
Folders and sketchbook.

Justin, on the other hand, used wholly electronic storage:

Justin — I first looked at the research questions and the proposed chapters that I had outlined in my research proposal and then examined the possible sources of information for each research question/chapter. Later I created a folder [Thesis] on my computer. Under the Thesis folder, I created sub-folders, each corresponding to the research questions or chapters that I had proposed for the thesis.

When consulting online resources, I recorded the information in Microsoft Word files and saved them in the appropriate folders. If I downloaded a PDF document or a webpage, this would also be saved in the appropriate folder.

In addition, whenever I used or cited information from an online resource, I would immediately add it to the Reference List which I was developing. This approach ensured that I captured all the details required for the Reference List at the time that I had access to the document/resource.

The commonsense criterion for all such choices really has to be what best suits the things you have to do with the information. This was the practice I followed (it's described later in the chapter – see pages 70, 73–75 – as part of the advice on how to make things in the information store findable).

Getting ready to go fishing

Once you have decided what information you need and likely sources for finding it, the next step is to prepare for 'fishing expeditions' to capture useful material. Here, researchers can benefit from applying some of the basic skills that information professionals use in organizing information and making it findable – skills that, according to recent research (Morgan & Bawden, 2006), are equally valued by academics and employers.

If you do nothing else, before you start make as much use as you can of whatever help is on offer from your institution and tutors in the way of training and advice on using relevant reference tools, abstracting services, electronic journals, and websites (subjects that are sometimes covered under the name of 'Information Literacy'). For useful material on the kind of help that Information Literacy teaching can give, see for example: Todd (2006) who describes interesting work in the USA; Verlander (2006) on an information literacy programme for users of the UK Information Services of the UK Health and Safety executive; Macoustra (2006) – for advice on formulating answerable questions when looking for information; and The Information Literacy Website – http//www.informationliteracy.org.uk (details of some other useful information literacy websites are given at the end of this chapter). Pay particular heed to guidance on searching the web and on evaluating sites – especially if you are doing your very first research project; people at this stage may be particularly liable to use the web as the first and only resort, and to treat everything they find as of equal validity.[1] And if you seldom darken the doors of your college library – you may think again about that if you read (on the web) Will Sherman's 33 Reasons Why Libraries and Librarians are Still Extremely Important' (Sherman, 2007).

As Macoustra (2006) remarks: 'A large number of students expect to find everything they need on the Internet and don't appreciate the free use of the proprietary databases that are available to them while they are studying.'

1

And maybe not just first-time researchers – studies at the Oxford University Internet Institute (quoted by Fry, 2006) suggest that 'In some disciplines they [search engines] are used as a way of bypassing' other electronic resources such as digital libraries or subject portals, without awareness of their 'limitations or even biases'.

'Fishing hooks for information'

Transforming useful information into usable knowledge can often be more difficult than actually locating it. It's easy to be overwhelmed by the sheer physical volume of information when we find a book or article or website that contains material relevant to something we need to know about. A useful way of preventing this is to identify before you start a handful of words or phrases which sum up the topics which are important for your research: they may be subjects, names of people or organizations, geographical areas, place names, materials, techniques, etc.

Jot them down quickly on paper. Then put each separate word or phrase on the top of a card and keep the cards by you as you start reading. You will find that the action of identifying important topics in your own words has brought those words to the front of your mind, so that they act as 'hooks' that catch relevant bits of text as you scan, as suggested in Figure 3.3.

It's important, for reasons that will be explained a little later (see page 70) to try to apply the same words and phrases to the same topics whenever you find them, and avoid alternative expressions.

The list of topics will be invaluable later too, when you want to find items on particular subjects in your collection. You can develop it as your knowledge of the field grows, adding more terms, and sub-dividing some of the larger topics, in the way that Kerry describes:

Kerry — I think the important thing was to come up with a list of general keywords, vaguely relevant to the topic area, but then narrow these down into more subject specific groups and then come up with more keywords/definitions based on these groups. What was very useful for doing this was the descriptor/keyword fields used by citation indexes. I tried to make a note of these and then use them to conduct my own searches—but it was important to try and keep track, which is why my trusty notebook was always to hand, because it was all too easy to get pulled further and further in to citation indexes/journal abstracts, find a fantastic article and then have no idea how you came across it [when you want] to try and find more of the same.

Paula too built up a set of terms to use consistently in her searches:

Paula — A structured and targeted on line search for primary research, literature reviews and theoretical articles was performed ... using terms including, information/knowledge/research and utilization/implementation/dissemination, evidence/research and practice/medicine/decision making, diffusion of innovation, health care evaluation and physiotherapy/nursing.

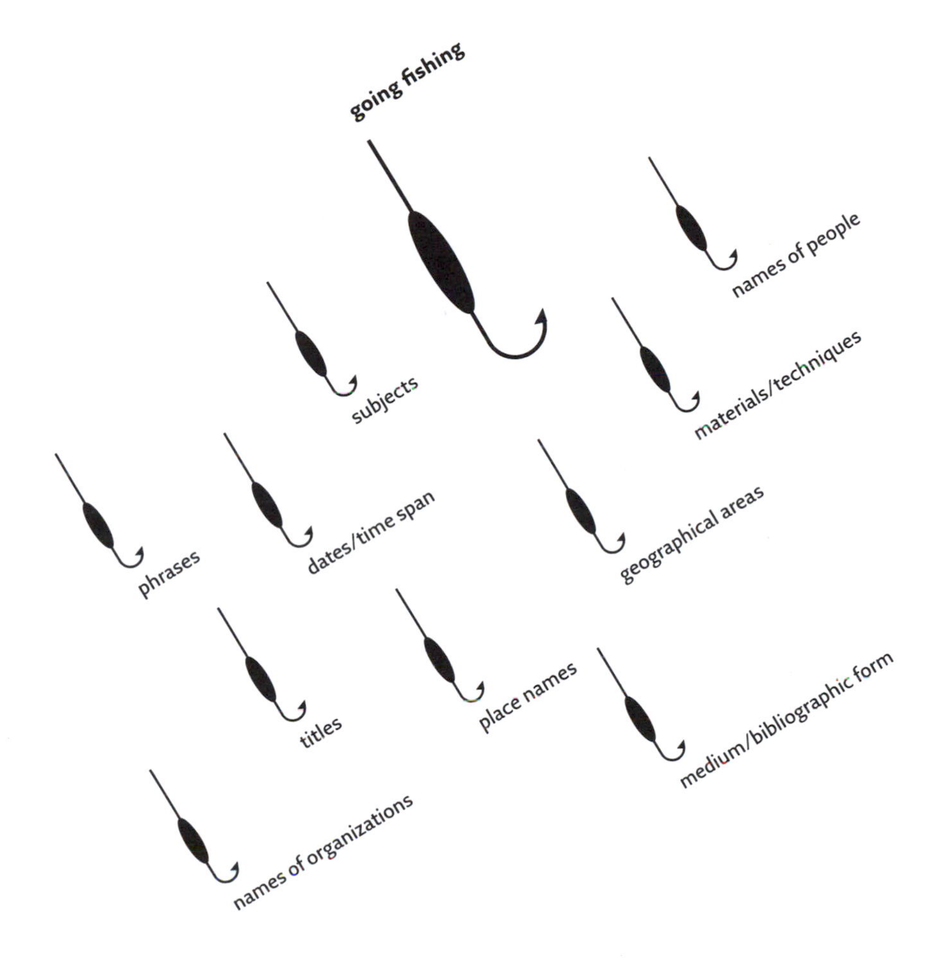

If you identify in your own words the important kinds of information you need for your research, in scanning for information your eye will be alert for references to them. They will act as 'hooks' to catch material that may be useful, which you can read with closer attention.

Figure 3.3 Fishing hooks for information

In my own research, I was able to derive a first set of key terms from the database of articles relevant to my work interests, which I have maintained for more than twenty years; others were added in the course of reading in fields that were comparatively new to me.

All these actions devised by researchers to help them find useful information are very conscious and analytical—and none the worse for that. It's nevertheless important to remind ourselves that much of what we do is driven by other parts of ourselves; as I suggested earlier on (see page 54) the 'more intuitive "right brain" approach is actually a valuable complement to the analytical one.' I owe the analogy with fishing in the heading of this section to a researcher in the field of art and design who observed in her dissertation that:

> Paul Klee's approach to everything he did was in conscious recognition of knowledge the unconscious already possessed. His forays, his journeying enquiries could be described as 'fishing expeditions'...
> (Chasseaud, 1993)

Wouter was in the fortunate position of doing his research while working as Research Assistant to his Supervisor.

Wouter   My supervisor pointed me in the right direction. He gave me a couple of names of researchers that are doing work in my field. Got hold of a couple of their research works and looked at their references. Also had to do a lot of reading. This helped me to pick up keywords and other prominent researchers in the field. All the research papers/articles I collected I stored as soft- and hardcopy. The softcopies I stored on my home computer as well as my work computer. So, if something happened to the one I always will have a back-up. The hardcopies I just sorted alphabetically by author in a file.

When you find something useful

Human memory is notoriously unreliable (we don't remember all we've read, or even all we've written, and if we don't remember it, or where we found it, we can't use it). IT on its own can't compensate for that; it can help a great deal, but we get full benefit from it only if we first think carefully about how we want it to help what we're trying to do. The thinking we put into compiling our own list of key terms for searching for information is an important contribution to getting benefit from IT.

When your search leads to useful items, decide whether you want a copy of the complete item for yourself—by downloading, printing out, or photocopying—or whether it will be sufficient to make a brief note of the parts of the content that are most important for you (see below, page 68, for more on note-taking).

Never forget to label your catches!

Whether you make a photocopy or print-out of a useful item, or just write notes, *never forget to do two things:*

1 Note the full 'bibliographic details' on the copy or notes you take:

Books	Author Title Publisher Date of publication Place of publication
Articles	Author Title Name of periodical, volume number, pages on which the article appears Date of publication
Websites	Owner of the site Site address Date on which you found it

(and if you copy a quotation in your notes, put the page on which it occurs at the end of it). Experience shows that it's also worth noting where you found it – e.g. which library, which book or article cited it as a reference, which website – so that you can go back to the source if necessary, and where your copy or note of it is actually stored at the moment.

2 The topics (from your cards) on which it has useful information; the section(s) or chapters of the end product where it will be helpful (e.g. methodology; literature review).

If the main source of answers to your research question is people, as respondents to questionnaires, interviewees, etc, rather than 'the literature' (or if the two are of equal importance); or if non-text materials are important parts of your information, these two bits of labelling are still relevant. Apply appropriate 'bibliographic details' to identify the origins and date of notes/transcripts from interviews, photographs, etc, and label them with the relevant terms to describe their content, and where they are stored. This will allow you to search right across your collection in one go, regardless of how and where different bits of it are stored.

There is one more action that is immensely helpful: before putting any information away, highlight the passages in it that are of particular importance, and that you may want to quote. For hard-copy material, use coloured highlighters; for electronic text, use the facilities of your word-processing package to flag key points.

Without going deeply into the important and confusing subject of plagiarism, here is a quotation from an excellent guide to remember and apply:

> *'This is the first thing you should learn about plagiarism—and how to avoid it. Always show that you are quoting somebody else's work by enclosing the extract in [single] quote marks.'*
> Mantex website (2005)

And the increasing use in institutions of higher education of plagiarism-detecting software such as Turnitin provides an extra incentive for learning about and avoiding involuntary plagiarism. Some universities now treat the subject in its wider context, and offer researchers classes on intellectual property rights (IPR) and copyright; see Ayris (2006).

Taking notes

In taking notes, avoid copying large chunks of text mechanically; time and effort are better spent on extracting for possible quotation just those sentences and phrases which say something important for your argument in a way that cannot be bettered (and when you do that, note the page number of the quoted bit so that readers of your dissertation can easily find it in its source).

You have to decide for yourself what medium to use for note-taking. The researchers who have contributed their experience on this tend to use what one of them calls 'Good old fashioned pen and paper'. The medium varies from notebooks to 'separate pieces of paper or post-it stickers', and one researcher confesses 'I started out with specific notebooks for notes and ideas, but I have "regressed" to writing down ideas on any scrap of paper that is handy'. One alternated between traditional and electronic note-taking: 'I used Endnote for a while but then I moved and I didn't have the software, so I used pen and paper or just wrote my notes in Doc files.' Another used a laptop for almost all his note-taking: 'I rarely used a pen and paper for taking notes. Whenever I consulted online information resources over the Internet, I would use my laptop to take notes, so that later I could cut and paste them into the chapters.'

I am mainly of the pen and pieces of paper persuasion, though I have occasionally taken a laptop to libraries. It cuts out the stage of inputting from hand-written notes, but unless you are working from books and periodicals whose binding allows them to open flat, there are problems in keeping them open at the right page! I always use separate sheets for each set of notes, rather than running them on in a notebook—because if you do that, you really need a subject index to the notebook (while notebooks aren't so good for this purpose, they are great for diary-type memos, reminders, recording things that you will later transfer to a more permanent form). If you keep them as separate sets, you can treat your own notes in just the same way as you treat photocopies of articles, etc.

Making it findable: 'keys' to the information store

Here, I shall tell you what I did in order to make the large amount of information I collected in the course of research findable, why I did it, and how. It's worth doing that, not because I think it's wonderful or the only way, but because it worked, and I can offer first-hand experience. Some readers may want to try it exactly; others may think of adopting it in part and making their own variations. Once again, by courtesy of the other researchers who were kind enough to answer our questions, I can give you their accounts of how they did it. Then I offer some alternatives – one that doesn't entail using database software and one that is essentially manual, and one real minimalist solution for very small collections. I hope all that will help readers to decide what will be most appropriate for them. Finally, at the end of the chapter there are brief details of software and web-based facilities of which I haven't got direct experience, but which are recommended by other writers I respect.

One container, multiple content – a problem

There is a fundamental problem in making information findable, which has exercised the minds of those who look after collections of books, articles and other containers of information for more than a century. This is the problem: any one 'container of information' is most likely to hold information on more than one subject; so the contents will be significant for different readers according to their individual interests and needs for information.

As Crestadoro (1856) observed about the British Museum Library catalogue in the pamphlet quoted at the beginning of this chapter:

> *'Entering the book only once is giving but one of its many references and suppressing the remainder; – it is serving the purpose of one reader and defeating that of others ... its light is extinguished and destroyed.'*

(He had a great idea for a solution, which he wanted the British Museum to apply to its collections, but rather underestimated the labour requirements, and readers had to wait more than a hundred years for the technology that was needed to apply it.)

More than that, different elements of the contents can be significant for the *same* reader at different times, according to what's of interest to h/h at different points. That is often the case with the material that researchers collect: any one article relevant to their research is more likely than not to cover a number of the topics that will be important at some stage in their work. See Figure 3.4, page 71.

If they follow the advice given earlier in this chapter (see page 67) to note, on every useful item of information they collect, all the topics to which it's relevant, *which of them do they store it under?* How can they be sure of finding it whenever they need information on any of the significant topics it covers?

The answer which I used takes some extra effort, but I can vouch for it as a good investment. This is where the list of words and phrases summarizing the topics of interest really comes into its own. It can become a tool that directs us to all the items in our collection where we will find information about a given subject, person, etc. And the more consistent we are in sticking to the same version of the terms to label everything we collect and create, the more likely we are to find everything we have that is relevant. If we use different words or phrases at different times for the same thing, we shan't find all the relevant information on it unless we are lucky enough to remember all the possible ways of describing it. (Some professionals have devoted most of their working lives to the theory and practice of solving all the ramifications of this problem, through the development of thesauri. It's a fascinating subject, but for the purposes of most researchers, who have plenty of other things to think of, just doing your best to be consistent in the terms you use will suffice.)

For an example of instructions to help non-specialists in the public sector of the UK in using a standard list of terms for labelling electronic information materials to make them findable, see Dextre Clarke (2006); and for details of Taxonomy Warehouse a free website directory of such tools, which go under the general heading of taxonomies, see the list of useful sites at the end of this chapter.

Ways of doing it

There is no one right, best way of setting up to find what you need in a collection of information, though there are certain things you have to provide for however you decide to do it.

The starting point is the list of terms that are significant for your research, which you will apply to the information material that you collected in the form of various *items*. The only other thing you need now is *records* that stand for the items – a record for each item. See Figure 3.5 on page 72.

> *Item:* An object in any medium, that contains information, for example a book, an article, a set of notes, a photograph, a map, an audio recording.
>
> *Record:* Something that stands for an item, and that can be used to represent it; it can be a material object, such as a catalogue card in a library, or it may be held electronically in a computer database. The records are like forms that you fill in for each item, with standard headings.

Figure 3.6, on page 73, shows the record format that I used for the material I collected during my research.

I made it as simple as I could. I had kept articles of interest for many years, and had made records for them in a database, so that gave me the starter for a separate 'research database'. My first step was to use my list of significant terms to search for relevant items in the original database, and copy them to start the new research database.

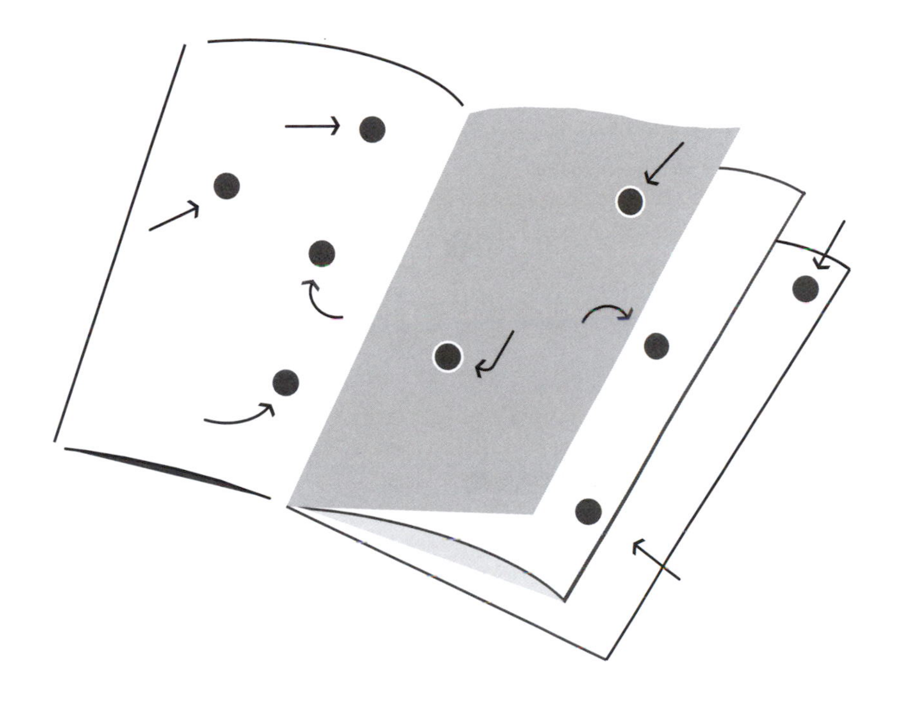

A fundamental problem in making information findable: a single container (e.g. an article) can give useful information on several different topics

 = useful content on a research topic

Each element of content can be significant for:

- A different user
- The same user at different times

Figure 3.4 One container, multiple content ...

Terms

1 Words or phrases for research topics

Items

2 Items containing information relevant to research
3 Descriptive terms + identifying details

Records

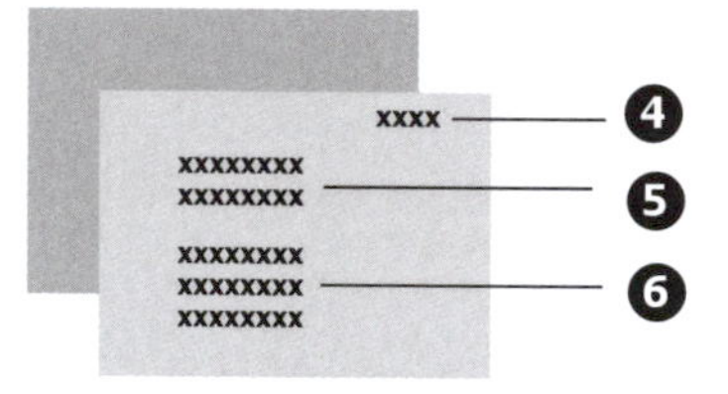

4 Item number
5 Identifying details
6 Descriptive terms

The *terms* are used in:

- Searching for information
- Labelling useful items when found
- Completing records.

Items; when found:

- Label with relevant terms and details that identify the item, including a unique number
- Make a record for each item, and enter terms and identifying details on it
- Store items.

Records enable us to find any item by any of the details entered on the record, e.g. subject, author name, title.

Figure 3.5 Making information findable: terms, items, records

Then as I collected new items, I labelled them with terms for the subjects on which they had useful information, as described above, and input details of them to the research database. All the records in it, and the items they stood for, were numbered in order of acquisition – because that was how I had set up the original database, and how I actually stored the hard-copy articles, in a series of pamphlet boxes (see page 74 for a discussion about decisions on how to arrange items).

Initially I used a new set of boxes to store the new research items I collected in the same way, but once I had a fair idea of the structure of my thesis, I first added a field to the records for the chapter(s) to which items were relevant, and then, as I started writing, physically took the actual articles, notes, etc. out of their original places, and put them in folders of material by chapter, amending the record to show this. All the way through the work, the research database was a reliable source for finding relevant material as new ideas occurred, verifying arguments, supporting memory, preparing for meetings with my supervisor, etc.

At the same time as searching in libraries, I was also gathering material from case studies. I stored this rather differently, filed by organization, with notes of all meetings with people in the organizations in chronological order, and examples of the publications they pressed upon me whenever I visited.

LIS No.	1942	RES No.	51	Date 1996
Author	Meyer, M H & Zack, M H			
Title	The design and development of information products			
Source	Sloan Management Rev, Spring, 43–49 (City U Business Lib)			
Keywords/ Notes	Information products Information design Information management Argues that research on development of product and process platforms for physical products has much to offer for information products. Case studies of companies 'that are creating competitive advantage by refining information through product and process technologies'. How companies can design information products in relation to 'customers' implied needs', take advantage of interactive technologies. Role of libraries and information management in this.			

Figure 3.6 Record format for material collected in research

I used a standard set of headings, linked with the main research topics, for asking questions, and for presenting the findings for all the case studies. I input my notes to word-processed files, printed them out, and highlighted them to show the major topics so as to make writing easier, and noted the links in them with arguments and theory presented in the main body of the dissertation. Printouts of the files, together with examples of the organization's information products, were stored in a set of boxes, one (or more!) per organization. By the end of five years there were a lot of boxes, and I was very glad when the day came that I could dismantle them and allow the files on the computer to act as the archive for the case studies. (In retrospect, I think it could have been useful to make records in the database for the sets of case study notes, so that I could search that material at the same time as the collection of articles.)

Not only do we have to decide what to put on records and how to store items, we also have to decide how to *arrange* the items in their containers. There are two choices: either grouping like with like, or just adding them as they come in—the most recent next to the last one you put in. In fact it's wise to provide for both as shown by my account above of how I stored my materials. It's also wise to have a heading (or 'field') on record forms in which you can enter exactly where you keep the items to which they refer. And, if you can face it, a list in numerical order of all items with their bibliographic data in a standard form (it's a valuable record of what you've got, and the basis for the bibliography). If I had to do it again, I think I would make the record form a bit more comprehensive, to allow for entering material other than articles and books, as shown in Figure 3.7. That would have allowed me to keep details of the case-study organizations, notes of meetings with them, and references to their publications in the same database and to search the whole range of material gathered at one go.

Now some accounts of what other researchers did.

Kerry's approach was similar to mine; she treated the reports that were her primary sources in the same way as I treated the material from case-study organizations, separately from the articles she collected. While she limited herself to filing the articles by subject keywords and didn't set up a database, she made a meticulous list of everything she had read, which minimized the time spent in the final stages on creating an accurate consistent bibliography.

Kerry — The other articles I had collected [i.e. other than those on information literacy, referred to on page 62] were filed under the relevant keywords I had identified, with sub-groups where necessary; these were my 'secondary' sources. Of course I highlighted passages of interest within these at the time of reading but filing them in subject specific categories actually helped me to visualize, in a physical form, how I would arrange the flow of conceptual arguments within my literature review.

Item No.	1
Year published	2006
Storage location	Boxes
Author	Orna, L
Title	No business without information products; how they can add–and subtract–value
Publisher/ journal title/ website address	Sage Publications, Business Information Review
Vol, part, pp	23 (2) 108–118
Organisation name	
Org. address. email, website, tel. Date	
Keywords/ notes	Added value Business value Information auditing Information design Information management Information products Knowledge management Negative value Stakeholders Subtracted value Value of infomation

Figure 3.7 An alternative, more comprehensive format

I also ... made the decision to record in an MSWord document, in the form of a bibliography, every document, book or article I had read during the course of my research, so that when it came to the final edit/write-up of my dissertation I wouldn't be worrying about digging out articles to reference them correctly or spending those last valuable days formatting references when I could be reviewing my report. ... It was also important to settle on one (relevant) referencing system e.g. Harvard and get to grips with it, because there was always the troublesome web page to cite!

Paula also took care of the references as she collected material; note her point about the time needed for mastering specialized bibliographic software – sometimes time saving has higher value than a fully automated way of doing things!

Paula Essential to keep an updated reference list as you go. Software like Reference Manager can be useful but you need to know how to use them and this takes time. Personally, I kept a reference list at the end of each draft chapter as I wrote. Then I could just copy and paste at the end and I didn't lose anything.

Also useful to keep careful records of articles you have ordered and received on a database.

My computer filing has also become more organized – small things like numbering or dating drafts etc. is very useful.

Karen's first approach involved noting the subject keywords on printouts of the materials she collected; but she moved later to the specialized software which she describes below.

Karen In the earlier stages I used to write them down on printouts of the material, in the margins, and then write down a summary in a word document in a full text. Now I use the software 'atlas.ti' which is a software for coding and commenting on qualitative material.

I transfer the (electronic) documents to the atlas software, creating what they call a 'heuristic unit' of all interviews and other texts. I then started by going through some of the key texts and creating 'code families': for instance, a family of 'information actions' consisting of seeking, distributing, storing information etc. I code the relevant parts of the texts with these codes, and I can relate the codes to each other in its family and get an output of all coded quotations in all texts for each code. I can also add comments, longer thoughts on specific parts of text or on how codes relate to each other, and attach them to either the code (then they appear when I create an output of all relating to this code) or to some of the text parts (then they show up when I'm looking at this text part, and I can get all relevant text parts to do with this comment). This might be something such as 'wish for rich information opposed by available tools for poor information', for instance.

When I've done that for the texts I want to study I make a lot of printouts, for each code, and for each comment, that I read over and summarize in another text, in Word. Slow, but a bit more sure that I don't forget any important quotes or instances.

Two industrial design researchers who answered our questions both set up databases to handle information collected in their literature searches (possibly because I give a talk about managing information to their course every year). Their experiences are interesting, and suggest that there are some points I ought to emphasize a little more next time.

Aragon started by 'categorizing data by date' and then found that wasn't quite enough. 'Because I had categorized my data by date ... sometimes it was a difficulty to find the information I wanted to adopt.' He solved it logically by adding 'classification of subject into my data base'.

Ismaril started with the aim of integrating textual information with material such as samples gathered during background context research in one place rather than storing them separately.

Ismaril The idea is to avoid storing different types of information such as images, texts and objects sounds and video separately but to integrate them all in one big omni database where all the material gathered can be accessed from one place.
Ultimately I guess that this requires a three-dimensional storage system. However the database could at least hold descriptions of objects and sound recordings etc. (and directions to their place of storage).

His explanation of what he wanted is an excellent example of what we have called a 'design approach to research' (see Chapter 1, page 23):

Ismaril The reason I wanted to do this is that the database then becomes a part of the design process providing links between concepts, knowledge and information found in texts and physical objects, images, product, material samples, etc. Seeing these links in front of you is useful I think for designers as it removes some of the boundaries between these two areas and helps to generate ideas, solutions and connections.

Rather than linking all of these different categories in an interconnected system I was only planning to link materials to texts, i.e. in Excel, put them in the same row as the text source but in a new column, so have one column for text, one for images, one for film, one for audio recordings, one for products and one for material samples.

So if I had a lecture recording from a seminar I could link it to a related text. Or if I had images from an exhibition (or of an object) I could link them to a related text.

This means that I could easily find the text references for my thesis and immediately also have access to any related material references such as film, audio recordings, images, material samples and products as well.

Naturally any given material reference would probably be linked to several different texts but at least they would be connected.

Maybe it's more of a Project Map than a database ... I guess it's a bit like making a great big website where images, sounds, text and video can all be easily interconnected.

We need a program that is like a cross between Dreamweaver and Excel.

He actually created two databases, but found some problems with both:

Ismaril 1 for literature only and

2 which contains literature and content of boxes and file path of images and file path of films, audio recordings. Tried to organize all these categories in relation to the literature category.

A database for recording literature sources has been very useful. But a bit problematic for containing large texts, specifically entering and editing them in Excel. Categorizing them by subject seemed difficult; just kept them in chronological order. Then search database by author or title. [The second database was] only partially successful and rather demanding to update, didn't last long.

I think the clue to the difficulties with entering and editing text lies in the choice of Excel. It is admirable for spreadsheets and tabulations, but the table format is not sufficiently flexible to handle unstructured text. The samples which Ismaril kindly provided suggest this is so; software specifically designed to handle text of variable lengths and structure would have helped avoid these difficulties. As for the problem of categorizing by subject – some initial thinking to establish a set of basic index terms, as recommended earlier (see page 64) would probably have helped both searching for relevant literature and integrating the literature collection with the material from video and audio recording.

If your research generates a lot of visual material – photographs, sketches, or down-loaded images from the web, for instance – you will need to think carefully about how you label and record them. If you want to include records of them in a database you will need to provide appropriate fields in the record for identifying the medium, subject content of the image, source, title, name of the maker, and date of creation and/or acquisition. Otherwise you will encounter the same problem as Mariana: 'I got really disorganized with the images and their time records. I didn't know which one was first or their chronological order.'

To end this section, here are two contrasting methods of dealing with the results of gathering information from people – Kerry's by questionnaire (you will remember her earlier observations about the questionnaire, pages 58–59), Kath's by interview. Kerry used a standard piece of software to prepare a tabulated format ready to input Yes-No responses, and word-processing to handle qualitative responses.

Kerry Information gathered from participants in my research was requested via email in the form of a questionnaire (MSWord). These were printed out and filed upon receipt and emails were backed up on my home PC as well as at work, just to be on the safe side, and because paranoia was beginning to set in at this point!

[For recording information from the responses] I had spent quite a bit of time setting up a fairly simple spreadsheet in MS Excel (not to perform any calculations, but merely so I could input responses in tabulated format) while I was waiting for questionnaires to come back. I'm glad I did this really as it saved quite a bit of time, especially as my anticipated response time slipped somewhat and I was waiting for some questionnaires to come several weeks after they had been sent out. Each question had a column in my spreadsheet and each participant a row, so I was able to input data in a consistent and reliable way. Having yes/no responses entered into Excel also meant I could export graphs directly into my Word document with a minimum amount of fiddling about. Where I had more in depth responses to questions, these were collated and recorded in a Word document under the heading of each question, which helped with later analysis.

Kath made audio-recordings of her interviews, and transcribed them onto the computer. From there on, after an unsuccessful attempt to use database software, her solution was manual and ingenious, and an object lesson in choosing ways of doing things which match what you need to do. The vast chart she describes made it possible to take a literal overview and to spot patterns in the responses.

Kath I recorded the interviews directly onto a laptop computer using a flat microphone and 'sound forge' software. I was then able to transcribe the interviews by playing them back on the computer and controlling the speed using foot pedals from a computer driving game set.

Initially I used a database but actually found it very difficult to deal with such a large amount of information in this manner. I ended up constructing a 'meta-matrix' (Miles & Huberman, 1994). They also call it a 'monster dog'. This consists of assembling summarized

> descriptive data from each respondent on a single chart. I used some old wallpaper as it needed to be quite long. This was much easier as I was able to see everything at once and was able to identify patterns across themes and across respondents. It was much more useful than any technology.

(For another researcher's account of experiments in visual interpretation – in this case of recorded group discussions – see Chapter 8, pages 164–167.)

Alternatives

Although I was using database software for my records, I went to a lot of trouble in the first edition of this book to describe a manual method, because I thought that the majority of readers might not have ready access to a PC. I have serious doubts as to how many people actually followed it for themselves; they would have to be pretty dedicated I suspect. Fortunately the everyday database software available to most researchers today allows us to get round all the problems, barring the initial thinking! You really need to understand the commonsense principles, and to think hard about the questions you'll need to answer from your store of information. Once you have done that, all you have to do is learn (if you haven't already) how to manage the relevant software, and get into the habit of dealing with material as soon as you've collected it.

Nevertheless, for readers who for one reason or another don't wish to use database software, or don't have guaranteed access to it, here are two alternatives, one just using word-processing software, and one wholly manual.

They both start with the same steps of numbering items sequentially as acquired, and labelling them with key terms and bibliographic data. After that ...

Word-processing solution:
Make an alphabetical list of your key terms as a word-processor file.

As you acquire items, input their identifying number and location under *all the terms* on which they have useful information.

When you want to search, use the 'Find' command in the word-processor package to locate potentially relevant items.

Manual solution:
Write each index term on a separate card, or sheet in a ring binder.

As you acquire items, write their identifying number and location under *all the terms* on which they have useful information. That creates an index to your collection.

When you want to find information on specific topics: search your index manually, just as you would the index at the back of a book.

Minimal solution for really small collections (e.g. <50 items):
Label each item with key terms and bibliographic data
File under main topic.

When you want to find information on specific topics: search by inspecting the labels on all items and select the relevant ones!

Putting things in their proper place

Now you can get the benefits from setting up storage in advance. Once you have labelled items and created records for them, put them in their proper place straight away! Don't let them pile up!

Put the physical items into suitable containers, for example: photocopies of articles, reports, notes you have taken about books or articles, print-outs from the web, etc. in folding boxes in numerical order; photographs in plastic sleeves in loose-leaf binders; word-processed files into suitably labelled folders (NB, keep your computer folders and files tidily nested and you will have much less trouble in finding the files you want. Classification comes into its own here; sound decisions about what things belong together and come under the same heading, and appropriate sub-divisions under main headings, make finding what you need much easier).

The next two chapters will look at two other aspects of research that both require and benefit from information management: project-managing your research, and keeping it up to schedule so that everything is done on time.

Summary

Managing information means: finding what we need; labelling and recording it so that we can find it whenever it's required; and storing it as we collect it. If we don't manage the information we collect and create during research, we can't get value from using it to create the end product of the research on which it is judged. If we organize from the start of research to manage information it will pay dividends right through the process.

The less experience of research, and the less knowledge of the research topic you start with, the more you need to help yourself to manage information.

Basics

- Whatever else you do, never forget to label any item of information you collect and store, with: the 'bibliographic details' that identify it; the topics on which it has useful information.
- The safest way of making sure you can find things in your information store is to give each item its own record in a simple database.
- If other people will be a major source of information for your research, e.g. as respondents to questionnaires and interviews, allow plenty of time for initial planning, and for analysing the results.
- *Don't let anything pile up!* As you collect information, label it and put it in its proper place.

References

Websites referred to in this chapter accessed on 18 March 2009

AYRIS, P (2006)
Moving beyond e-journals (Interview with Elspeth Hyams),
Library & information update, 5 (10) 18–20.

BATES, M E (2006)
'Save yourself! Free resources for organising, maintaining and sharing the fruits of your web searches', *FreePint Newsletter* 202.
http://www.freepint.com/go/newsletter/202

CAMERON, R (2006)
CiteULike.
http://www.citeulike.org/

CHASSEAUD, A (1993)
Transformations and the Hate object.
Unpublished MA dissertation.
London: Central St Martins College of Art and Design.

[CRESTADORO, A] (1856)
The art of making catalogues of libraries or, a method to obtain in a short time a most perfect, complete, and satisfactory printed catalogue of the British Museum Library by A reader therein.
London: The Literary, Scientific & Artistic Reference Office.

DEXTRE CLARKE, S (2006)
Guide to Meta-tagging with the IPSV.
London: Cabinet Office, e-Government Unit.
http://www.esd.org.uk/standards/
see under IPSV documents/guidance

FRY, J (2006)
Researchers migrate to search engines,
Library & information update, 5 (9) 5.

MACOUSTRA, J (2006)
Bar Orphans: Getting your questions answered at the FreePint Bar, *FreePint Newsletter* 199.
http://www.freepint.com/go/newsletter/199

MANTEX (2005)
Plagiarism.
http://www.mantex.co.uk/samples/plgrsm htm

MORGAN, J & BAWDEN, D (2006)
Teaching knowledge organization: educator, employer and professional association perspectives, *Journal of Information Science,* 32 (2), 108–115.

ORNA, E (2004)
Information Strategy in Practice.
Aldershot: Gower.

THE QUALITY ASSURANCE AGENCY FOR HIGHER EDUCATION (2004)
Code of practice for *the assurance of academic quality and standards in higher education. Section 1: Postgraduate research programmes.*
www.qaa.ac.uk/academicinfrastructure/codeOfPractice/

SHERMAN, W (2007)
'Are librarians totally obsolete?'
http://librarians place.wordpress.com/2007/02/02/are-librarians-totally-obsolete/

TODD, R (2006)
It's all about getting "A's", *Library & information update,* 5 (1–2), 34–36.

VERLANDER, P (2006)
'Beyond the library walls – establishing an information literacy programme for a dispersed user group', *FreePint Newsletter* 206.
http://www.freepint.com/go/newsletter/206

Other useful sources

BOOKS

ANDRETTA, S (ED) (2007)
Change and Challenge. Information literacy for the 21st century. Adelaide: Auslib Press.
For readers with a particular interest in information literacy, a helpful overview of current thinking, with theoretical and practice-based contributions.

BELL, J (2005)
Doing your Research Project Ed 4. Maidenhead: Open University Press.
For first-time researchers in education, health and social science; limited to small-scale projects taking 100 hours, 2–3 months start to finish.
'Reading, referencing and management of information' chapter gives good practical

advice; especially on references and software for managing them.

Useful advice in 'Literature searching' chapter on citing websites, radio reports, etc. Also has good advice on literature searching, and useful material in Part 2 'Selecting methods of data collection'.

Software and websites

BIBLIOGRAPHIC SOFTWARE

BIBME
Free bibliography maker. Facilities: search for books, websites, etc; item entry and addition to bibliography; alternative formats.
http://www.bibme.org

BOOKENDS
Reference management and bibliography software for Mac OS X.
http://www.sonnysoftware.com/

ENDNOTE
Thomson ResearchSoft, a division of Thomson Scientific (they also produce WriteNote, a web-based tool for importing references and formatting bibliographies, and RefViz which 'allows users to search multiple data sources simultaneously and visualize references to reveal major themes and topics.')
http://www.endnote.com/

LEARNHIGHER REFERENCING
Guide to academic referencing in Britain, supported by Bradford University School of Management.
http://www.learnhigher.ac.uk/

CODING QUALITATIVE MATERIAL

ATLAS.TI
'For the qualitative analysis of large bodies of textual, graphical, audio and video data. It offers a variety of tools for accomplishing the tasks associated with any systematic approach to "soft" data – i.e., material which cannot be analyzed by formal, statistical approaches in meaningful ways.'
http://www.atlasti.com/

FORMULATING QUESTIONS

ONELOOK
Index to a lot of dictionaries, with a reverse look-up facility - you describe what you want to find, and it presents you with a list of words that fit the request.
http://www.onelook.com/

INFORMATION LITERACY

CILIP Community Services Group Information Literacy Group.
Useful source on information literacy training, including outlines of what various institutions offer. 'Designed and developed by information professionals from key UK organisations actively involved in the field of information literacy ... news, case studies, examples of best practice and freely available toolkits.'
http://www.informationliteracy.org.uk

LITERATURE SEARCHING

ARCHIVES HUB
Single point of access to descriptions of archives held in over 150 UK universities and colleges.
www.archiveshub.ac.uk/searchhelp.shtml

BL DIRECT
'Our vision is to make the world's intellectual, scientific and cultural heritage accessible, and to bring the collections of the British Library to everyone – at work, school, college or home. British Library Direct is the first stage in this major programme. You can search the last 5 years' worth of our articles from the 20,000 most heavily requested titles at the British Library, covering most subjects, languages and places of publication. That's around 9 million records – all available to be delivered electronically!'
http://direct.bl.uk/

Also available from BL: free Research and Innovation e-newsletter
http://www.bl.uk/newsletter

EThOS (Electronic Theses Online Service Project)

Part of JISC's (Joint Information Systems Committee) Digital Repositories Programme, EThOS will maintain a UK database of theses, from which researchers will be able to find, select, access and archive e-theses that have been produced in UK universities and colleges.
http://www.ethos.ac.uk

The European Library

Project based at the National Library of the Netherlands; aims to give 'centralised access to the resources of the 47 national libraries of Europe.'
http://www.theeuropeanlibrary.org/

Open J-Gate

Electronic gateway to global journals in open access domain. Indexes articles from over 3K academic, research and industry journals. Search options include author, title, keywords, etc.
http://www.openj-gate.com/advancesearch.asp

IFLA Directories of Institutional Repositories

http://www.ifla.org/IV/ifla72/papers/151-Oliver_Swain-en.pdf
For a list of repositories of research material from this resource, see the very useful *Internet Resources Newsletter:* July 20 06 issue (Heriot-Watt University Library.)
http://www.hw.ac.uk/libWWW/irn/irn.html

InforM25: Find-a-Library

Directory of academic libraries in the M25 Consortium (London and surrounding area): searchable by subject and by institution.
http://www.inform25.ac.uk/AET/

Intute

Free online service giving access to Web resources for education and research, selected by subject specialists; also free online tutorials on internet research skill.
http://www.intute.ac.uk/
see also
Harrison, N and Place, E (2009)
'Intute', *Library & information update,* 8 (1–2) 48–51.

JISC Collections Catalogue of Online Resources

Covers subject areas of Arts & Humanities, Science, Engineering and Technology, Health and Life Sciences, Social Sciences, Multi-disciplinary resources.
http://www.jisc.ac.uk/Collections/catalogue.aspx

National Archives (UK)

Allows access to The National Archives' collection of digitized public records, including both academic and family history sources. Searching the index is free.
http://www.nationalarchives.gov.uk/documentsonline/

De Guire, E (2006)

Publish or perish: afterlife of a published article.
Article by an abstracting and indexing editor comparing effectiveness of approaches to literature searching of CSA Illumina and Google Scholar. Tips on abstract-writing to ensure published articles reach widest audience.
http://www.csa.com/discoveryguides/publish/review.php

MANAGING PERSONAL RESEARCH INFORMATION

Personal wikis

'Personal wikis allow people to richly link information on their desktop ... the same way a community wiki links information across the internet. Thus people who like the wiki philosophy of organizing information may find personal wikis useful.' Site lists several personal wiki systems, some with facilities for note-taking as well as editing and retrieval.
http://en.wikipedia.org/wiki/Personal_Wiki

PLAGIARISM PREVENTION

TURNITIN
http://www.turnitin.com/

TERMINOLOGY

TAXONOMY WAREHOUSE
Industry, region, subject and company taxonomies, from Factiva.
http://www.taxonomywarehouse.com/

WEBSITE EVALUATION

BEYOND ALGORITHMS. A LIBRARIAN'S GUIDE TO FINDING WEB SITES YOU CAN TRUST.
Karen G Schneider, Director of Librarian's Internet Index.
http://www.google.com/librariancenter/articles/0601_02.html

INTERNET DETECTIVE
Free online tutorial to help students develop critical thinking for using the internet in research. Developed 1998 with funding from European Union and translated into several different languages; original version withdrawn in 2005, but because of high demand, new version launched 2006.
http://www.vts.intute.ac.uk/detective/

HAMILTON-PENNELL, C (2006)
On the Verge of Revolution – Open-access Publishing. *FreePint Newsletter* 209
Useful questions for evaluating open-access publications.
http://www.freepint.com/go/newsletter/209

Keeping the record straight: documenting the research

Ch 4 Contents at a glance

'Research Management—to be able to:
Apply effective project management through the setting of research goals, intermediate milestones and prioritisation of objectives.'

Research Councils/AHRB (2004)

'Didn't know what order to do things in—wait for ethics, send access letters, etc, get writing'

'I would make more effort writing an analysis of the present, throughout the project—critical chronological journal.'

(Two recent researchers)

The researcher as project manager

The last chapter considered the role of researchers as information managers; this one is about another kind of management that involves a specific kind of information and some activities with which many researchers aren't familiar – project management. This is what the term as used in this book means:

Project management

- Identifying everything that has to be done in order to meet the objectives of the research, and to deliver on time [1] an end product that meets the required quality standards
- Setting up effective ways of doing it, especially appropriate systems and documents to record and report progress
- Communicating with other people concerned in the project, especially those to whom you are responsible, and those on whom you rely to provide you with information essential for the research
- Maintaining the systems and documentation, monitoring the progress of your research, and taking appropriate action to keep it on course
- Evaluating the project at completion and documenting what has gone well, what hasn't, and what lessons are to be learned.[2]

Figure 4.1 shows the activities involved in the project-management aspect of research.

Why researchers have to be project managers

The short answer is self-preservation; if researchers don't do it for themselves, nobody else will do the job for them. Remember that in doing research you enter into a contract; you may not have to sign any formal document, but there certainly are 'penalty clauses' for not fulfilling your part of it, and if you fall foul of them they can affect your future career. Project management is part of meeting the responsibilities that go with undertaking research.

If you don't act as your own project manager, it can lead to Bad Trouble; if you do it effectively, it can save your work from the consequences of injustice and incompetence on the part of others, as shown by this story from real life:

A few years ago, there was a change in course leader of an MA course on which I was a visiting teacher. The course was in an institution recently formed by a merger between two colleges in the same field of study, but with very different traditions. When the original course leader left to go to another

1 The time-management aspect is so import ant that we have made it the subject of separate chapter; see Chapter 5 page 105.

2 Other writers of research guides, for example Hunt (2005), extend this definition to cover all the activities which research projects involve, including what the present book calls managing information and writing. The first two chapters of Hunt's book deal specifically and comprehensively with the topics covered in the present chapter.

job, students were in the second term of a four-term MA which had been established some years before. He had been instrumental in developing it, and its clear structure and philosophy attracted students who found it congenial to their research interests.

His replacement came from the other college in the merger. He brought to the job an unusual amount of sheer incompetence, combined with determination to make his mark in this promotion by speedily overturning as much as possible of what he considered to be an out-of-date and fuddy-duddy philosophy, and replacing it with something more appropriate to 'modem trends' in the discipline concerned. In his eagerness to achieve this, he did not study the rules of the institution, so he did not appreciate that students already doing the course had entered into it under the terms set out in the existing 'course document', and were therefore entitled to complete it on those terms, and in accordance with the research proposals they had agreed at the start of their course.

So it came about that, within a few days of his arrival, he made it his business to interview each of the students; characteristically, he did most of the talking while they got little chance of explaining what their projects were and how they were progressing. The sequel was expressions of dismay on his part at the nature and quality of the projects, followed by almost total neglect of this group of students, while he busied himself with planning, off the top of his head, a new course structure and philosophy. Perhaps fortunately, it was expressed in such impenetrable language that nobody could make any sense of it.

Also fortunately, the existing students were mature and well motivated, so they kept on working conscientiously, but they were obviously anxious about what harm their new course tutor might do to their prospects. As the time for the assessment of the MA work drew near, their anxiety increased. They had not had the normal opportunity for a preliminary individual and group meeting with the external assessor of the course, and they feared that the course tutor might seek to influence the assessor against them.

In this unhappy situation, there were some positive points: the external assessor was an independent-minded person who had acted in that capacity for the course over the past two years, and the students worked well together as a group and supported one another. Perhaps most important, an 'assessment contract' had been introduced at the beginning of their research studies. It required them to set out clearly the nature of their projects, their objectives in doing the research, and the *criteria by which they considered it was appropriate to assess what they presented.*

The contracts were given to the external assessor in advance, and the students were able to base their preparations for presenting their work and answering questions about it on what they had stated in the contracts. In the event, although the course tutor was one of the internal members of the assessment panel, he was unable to muddy the waters and actually had to sing rather small, because the assessment contract constituted a reference point to which both students and assessors could address themselves.

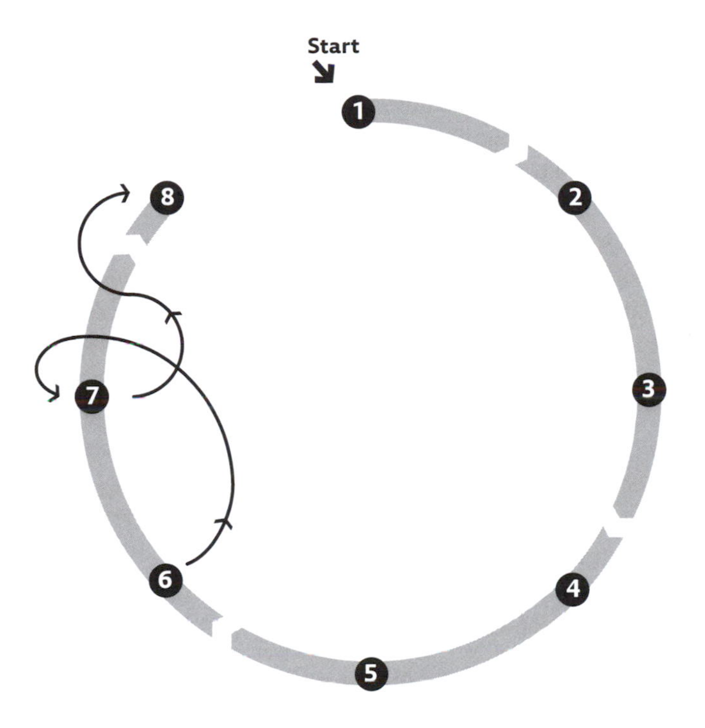

Stages 1 and 2 are done just once, 3, 4 and 5 are repeated procedural activities, but 6, 7 and 8 are cyclical activities that involve progress and learning each time around.

1. Identify essential actions
2. Set up systems
3. Collect/create documents
4. Manage communications
5. Maintain systems
6. Monitor/review progress
7. Evaluate
8. Learn and apply

Figure 4.1 Cycle of project-management activities

In this instance, the existence of a clear piece of documentation prepared by the students about their own research actually enabled them to defend themselves against the possibility of a damaging attack on their work, and unmerited failure.

It's not just a matter of self-preservation, however; good project management makes it possible, and comparatively easy, to take an overview of your research at any time from various perspectives, and that brings balance to the undertaking. It can be all too easy to dive into the serious business of gathering information and to forget about relating what you are doing to either the 'research map' or the timescale you established. Researchers who do that are not getting value out of the investment of good thinking time they put into the early stages of planning. They don't get the benefit of seeing how what they find relates to their first thoughts; and they miss the opportunity of redrawing and updating their research maps and making them into better guides for the next stages.

The discipline of project management can save you from that because built into it are points at which you deliberately pause to:

- Compare what you are doing with what you planned to do
- Check how you are keeping to the initial timetable
- Bring the 'research map' up to date
- Identify new questions and new directions to investigate.

If you do that, you can make good use of positive developments, happy accidents, and new thoughts, as well as taking timely corrective action. More than that, if you record the results as you go, you give yourself a 'chronological trace' (in some courses it is called a 'research diary') of the evolution of your thinking, and that can help you not only to evaluate what you are doing, but also to develop first tentative conclusions, and to get a perspective of the whole process as you approach the end of it.

Now let us look at the documents we need to manage, and systems to help us manage them.

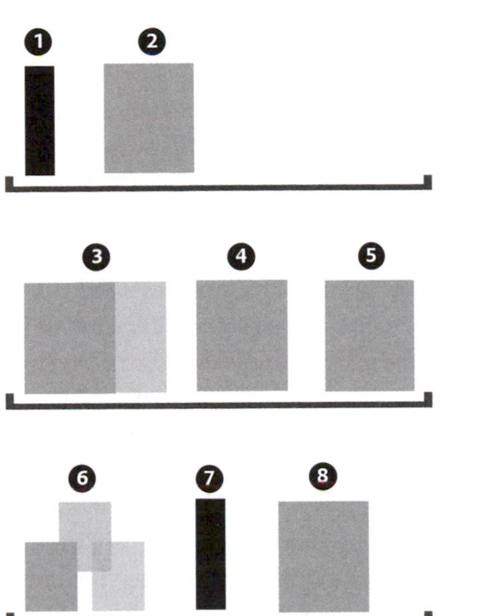

1 Research Handbook and Regulations
2 Research proposal

3 Research maps
4 Timetables and action plans
5 Tutorial reports

6 Research communications
7 Research diary
8 Incidental research products

Figure 4.2 Vital documents

Vital documents[3]

Figure 4.2 shows the essential information materials about your research that you need to have always accessible and to keep up to date.

The institution's documents on research

The first project-management file you set up should be for whatever documents your institution issues for researchers: regulations, guidance, etc, together with any correspondence you have with the institution about your own research.

3
It will be clear by now that researchers have to do a lot of writing long before they start 'writing-up' their dissertation: preparing assignments for supervisors, writing up notes, devising questionnaires, analysing interviews, etc; project management requires yet more. The preferred tool for most will be word processing using MSWord. As all the documents you write on the way contain potential material for your dissertation, it makes sense to establish a format for them at the start which will match the ultimate page layout of your dissertation, so that you can take passages from them and place direct into your dissertation draft. For instructions, see Chapter 9.2, pages 185 and 192–195. Save yourself time and do it now!

Experience suggests that it is often overlooked, or that the contents aren't referred to often. Research students have been known to reveal dangerous ignorance of the regulations at a late stage in the proceedings.

I am among them. Having often warned students of the need to be familiar with the institution's rules, when I was doing my own doctoral research, I duly set up my file, but didn't read the University's *Research Studies Handbook* carefully enough, and paid a price—fortunately only in cash and some embarrassment!

I was pleased with the Author's note at the beginning of my thesis (on re-reading, it looks rather smug), in which I took issue with the *Handbook's* recommendations about writing style and the use of the passive form of verbs as a 'way of conveying objectivity' and explained why I had departed from it. I also mentioned that rather than the consolidated bibliography mentioned in the *Handbook,* I had given the bibliography chapter by chapter, for greater ease of reference.

Unfortunately, I didn't pay close enough attention to the Appendix in the *Handbook* about physical format, and binding theses, and so failed to spot until my thesis was permanently bound that students were recommended to submit their theses for examination in a temporary binding, in case any amendments were required.

I got my just deserts for tempting providence; after the viva, the examiners said yes they would certainly recommend that I be given my PhD, but first, could I please just add a short section of evaluation, and while I was at it, could I also bring all the separate sets of references together into a comprehensive bibliography as well!

Research proposal

Whatever scale of research you are engaged in, from three-month undergraduate project to doctorate, before you can proceed with it you have to present and get agreement to a first statement (the level of elaboration required will vary greatly) of its purpose, the area of the research, the questions it seeks to answer, why they are worth asking and answering, how it will be done, and what you hope it will contribute to the subject area.

It constitutes the original 'contract' for the research and as such is a precious document. It may well go through more than one version in the preliminary stages—a provisional and then a final statement, for instance—and it may be amended at some later point; however many versions are produced, keep a copy of each, labelled with the date on which it was written and the date on which it was approved.

Not only is the proposal an essential point of reference; many other project documents will be derived from it at various stages in the research.

Research maps

The first maps of the research territory and of the route through it that we discussed in Chapter 2 are useful tools for project management. They will change as the work progresses; unknown territory will become familiar, blank areas will begin to be filled in, more connecting links will be added, and perhaps some territory will be abandoned in the light of increased understanding or recognition of the limits of time. The research 'itinerary' or route map will also become more detailed and less provisional in the light of experience.

As the scene changes, revise the maps to reflect the new point of view. Don't discard earlier versions; keep the complete series in date order, so that you can easily see – and show to other people – how the project has evolved over time, what has been done, and what is still to do. This is where graphic representation scores over all-text presentation; it is quicker to amend, and easier to show changes. My own maps (Figures 2.3 and 2.4, pages 40–41) changed over time – the map of the territory did not originally include web technology; and the research journey initially proposed action research in two organizations, which was replaced by a less time-consuming application in one organization of a new methodology to assess the value of information products.

Timetables and action plans

You also need an overview of the events and activities of the research, the relations between them which will affect the sequence in which they need to take place, and the fixed dates around which they must be organized. It makes a companion-piece to the research route map, and provides essential information for it on the timing of the stages.

Start it off with important dates or milestones when the institution requires particular things to be done, products to be delivered etc. As the research proceeds, you can feed in the results of your thinking about which activities need to be done before others can start, and which can run together or overlap; and this enriched schedule can be broken down into sub-schedules for specific periods, or particular activities as work progresses. (For fuller discussion of ways of doing this, see Chapter 5, page 109 – 115)

Tutorial reports and exchanges with tutors

Some of the contributions to this book from recent researchers show how valuable, and how much appreciated, their exchanges with supervisors and tutors have been to them (see Chapter 2 page 43). Not all researchers strike as lucky as this, but that is no excuse for not making the best of what's on offer – and that means:

- Knowing what the institution provides in this respect, and what obligations it expects supervisors and research students to meet

- Meeting your own obligations conscientiously by going well prepared to individual tutorials and tutorial group meetings, etc; taking note of your tutors' comments and what you've been asked to do, and acting on it; and keeping records of all tutorial exchanges and actions. (for reciprocal obligations of supervisors/tutors, see page 101).

Communications

This area of research project management is really standard office routine stuff, and in consequence is liable not to get much attention, except perhaps from researchers who have earned their living in that environment. It covers all the necessary communications that have to take place between researchers and the people whose help they need in the research: as potential/actual participants (see Chapter 3, pages 60–61); as suppliers of information about services, products or materials needed in the research; or as providers of essential authorizations for research activities (e.g. ethical authorization for interviews, permissions to reproduce copyright material).

You can make life easier for yourself if you start by making a list of all the people with whom you will need to communicate in these ways; record their *correct* name, organization and address details, and what you will need to communicate with them about (and put it in a contacts database or card index); and then decide what kinds of communication from you will do the job most effectively and economically. Next, you will save a lot of time and trouble if you establish and keep:

1 A standard brief description of your research project, to send/give to anyone whose help you need.
2 Standard letter(s)/emails requesting the various kinds of help you are likely to need—they can be customized for individual recipients, but it saves a lot of time having the basic letter on tap.

Then decide how you are going to store the ensuing exchanges, set up the necessary 'containers' (electronic or paper-based), grit your teeth and prepare to be conscientious about filing. It's a fairly painless process if you deal with it as things come in; it becomes a big black cloud only if you let it build up. And where you are dealing with people whose help and goodwill you depend on, you can't afford to take chances. Keep the exchanges up to date; answer questions promptly and accurately; keep them informed of progress; acknowledge their help courteously.

Kerry managed this side of the project in a straightforward way, using standard software tools:

Kerry — MSWord/MSExcel for both recording information gathered and for documenting receipt of participants' agreement to assist, tracking when questionnaires were sent out, received etc. Information recorded in tabulated form for ease of use.

Research diary

Some institutions encourage or require research students to keep a record of what happens in their research; either by compiling a written, or visual, 'research diary' of key events, significant changes in direction, major decisions, etc, or by using the institution's own 'research log' software.

Hamid UCL graduate school has a research log and we have choice to use online or print version and I use online version. It is a tool to help student to plan, keep the track of their progress etc.

Kerry We were also provided with and encouraged to use a template for a research log which I completed every time I met with my supervisor – a record of what we discussed, targets for next meeting etc.

An informal 'journal' can act as a vivid and personal complement to maps, schedules and the more formal paraphernalia; it makes a repository of memory, thoughts and feelings that can otherwise fade and be lost, taking with them insights that can support researchers when it comes to writing the end product. Karen took a characteristic approach to making sure hers weren't lost:

Karen I have a folder I call 'diary' that I quite seldom add a file to on what I've been doing. At my institution we are required to fill out 'individual study plans' each semester, and I keep these as well. Then I have some personal Excel documents, one where I put courses I've taken and 'points' I've gathered for my research, another where I have put down and numbered all empirical data-documents that I've gathered (interviews, observations, other documentation and such), with dates and where I keep them ... I started out by having a diary on paper, but I lost track of it and it was too much hassle to keep updating. Since then, I save all files where I put ideas and thoughts and half-finished projects, often with a date in the title, I can check over my thought process by checking on these.

Not all of us are natural diarists – Ismaril for one found that 'writing about experience at the time seemed irrelevant'; his solution was a visual one, appropriately for a designer, but there's no reason why it shouldn't be used in other fields of research too:

Ismaril using a digital camera was a great help in providing a visual diary particularly if the camera software stores images by date.

There's no excuse for not taking pictures of progress, as it costs nothing with a digital camera. I would also like to have recorded more short movies of prototype trials and have some opportunity to present them during tutorials, in my view movies are far better for communicating examples of interaction and events than still images.

Incidental research products

Researchers are required to create (or decide to create for themselves) various incidental products during their research: presentations to their fellow students, progress reports for their supervisors, dissertation plans, etc. Keep them as a resource for the final product; they can save time when you most need it, as Kerry discovered with a document she created to help her in devising questionnaires 'that actually asked the questions I wanted to ask, in a format that wouldn't make my respondents lose the will to live before they'd finished it.'

Kerry What helped me get the final questions sorted was a little exercise I took upon myself to complete prior to a meeting I had set up with my supervisor ... in order to try and get my rationale straight in my own mind ... I decided to actually write out the rationale behind each question. ... Writing down this rationale was a really useful exercise although, I didn't realize its full potential at the time of writing: not only in helping me come to terms with my ownership of the research ... and unwittingly developing my independent learning skills, but also because [it] ultimately enabled me to use some of this 'thinking out loud' material in my methodology chapter, so it was worth the time spent in the end.

Some institutions require researchers to create and agree with their supervisors, as submission time approaches, a formal document – sometimes called an 'Assessment Contract' – which goes to the examiners along with their dissertation or thesis (as referred to earlier in this chapter, on page 90). A kind of counterpart to the initial research proposal, it reflects researchers' judgement in the light of experience of the significance of the work they have done, and provides an opportunity of stating what weight they wish to be given to the various elements of the work they are submitting and the criteria by which they would wish it to be assessed. (It also provides an opportunity to state unambiguously what they have *not* sought to do in the research – which can save them from the embarrassing situation of trying to explain it in a viva, to an examiner who has picked up the wrong end of the stick.)

Of course in doing this, researchers are putting their judgement on the line, and drawing the examiners' attention to elements which may be found wanting, but that is a risk they should be prepared to incur by this point in their work, and it makes an excellent mental preparation for the examination.

(For more about the questions to ask yourself in this connection, as part of planning the end product of research, see Chapter 6, page 128.)

Systems to manage the documents

To complement the helpful information quoted above from recent researchers about how they managed this aspect of their research, this is what I would do if I were starting a research project now.

Create a set of 'Project Management' folders and files, covering the types of document discussed above, so that you have a place ready to store them before they start multiplying like mice and infesting your work-space! Here is a list, with suggestions about software, format etc:

1 The institution's research regulations
Files downloaded from its website/intranet, or hard copy of relevant publications

2 Correspondence with the institution
Hard copy of paper documents; word-processor files of email exchanges (I prefer to copy emails to appropriate word-processor files and keep them with the files to which they relate; I've tried setting up separate mailboxes on some jobs, but found it was less useful and took more time. Whatever you do, don't leave emails sitting in an unsorted in-box).

3 Research proposal
Word-processor file and/or printout

4 Research maps (see Chapter 2)
Whatever medium they have been created in—e.g. word-processor files with drawings, drawings created with drawing package; electronic and/or printout

5 Research schedules (see Chapter 5)
Whatever medium they have been created in; electronic and/or printout

6 Tutorial reports
Word-processor files and/or printout

7 Research communications and contacts
Word-processor files/folders—e.g. folders for different groups of people you have to communicate with, files for individuals within them; email exchanges with them saved as word-processor documents on files for individuals; database for all research contacts; word-processor files of standard letters, etc.

8 Research diary
Dated extracts from key documents, material collected, etc, that mark important turning points in the research; graphics, photographs, videos etc. of significant events, etc—to act as an aide-memoire for reviewing progress, and for writing the end product of research. Your Research Log if the institution provides one. Held in electronic form, and/or printout

9 Incidental research products
Copies of materials you have produced during research, in appropriately labelled files and folders; electronic form, and/or printout.

I find it most effective—and space-saving—to make the main repository of this kind of material electronic, and to print out relevant documents when I want to refer to them, think about them, discuss them with others, and use them in writing. That marks a change (partly brought about by the experience of being without easy access to a printer for a few weeks) from my earlier practice of using paper as the main repository, supported by electronic files. Whichever medium you use, it's critical to work out a clear system for deciding what goes with what (i.e. a classification) and for giving folders and files consistent names that mean something to you, so that you can easily and quickly get to what you want on the computer or among your hard-copy files!

Getting value from project management

Providing yourself with a straightforward system for managing the essential project information is the basis for getting good use out of it.

Obviously doing the things described above will help you in meeting obligations and responding to what is required of you. It will make it easier to: find relevant documents when you need them; be prepared to do things at the right time rather than being ambushed by them; know where you have got to on all the things you have to do; trace previous events and exchanges; and so save time to devote to creative research activities.

The greatest value from project management however—as suggested earlier (see page 92)—is that it allows *you* to take the initiative in reviewing what you're doing, and that is a really creative research activity. It can lead to new insights, bright ideas, spotting inconsistencies in arguments and ways of rectifying them. It goes beyond just meeting procedural requirements, and is an exercise of your autonomy as a researcher and your personal responsibility for something you're doing because you want to, not because authority has told you to do it. Make a regular appointment with yourself to review what's been going on recently. Sit down with the results of whatever you've been doing, together with the relevant formal documents.

The very act of bringing together the range of things you have been doing, and thinking about them in relation to one another, allows them to interact creatively. It is like a meeting of people who are working away separately at their own bits of a project, at which they can exchange news and negotiate useful joint action. Pausing to put your thoughts outside in the world and actually see them spread out before you on the desk relieves the stress of having it all inside the head, or in separate electronic containers.

And if you devote a session to doing nothing more than sorting documents and putting them into their proper place, that in itself has a calming and organizing effect on the mind at times when you feel under too much pressure to do anything more demanding.

Quiet sessions like this can indeed be a source of strength and reassurance at those awful times which most of us experience at some point in doing research, when we feel everything has gone out of focus, the original clarity of our intentions has disappeared and we no longer know where we are going. Such times are in reality potentially creative ones; the mental discomfort is likely to be the manifestation of rather more new experience than can comfortably be coped with at once, or of the conflict between the rational/analytical and intuitive/reflective modes of thinking mentioned earlier (see Chapter 1, page 23) as being part of the 'design approach' to research.

It is easy to lose nerve when what had originally seemed clear and certain starts dissolving into confusion. But if we can accept the inner turmoil and turn outwards to look at what we have recorded about the development of our thinking, we can find there clues to the changes and strands to follow that will gradually, given time, come together to form a new synthesis.

Questions for a review session:

Have I acted on all the points arising from the last session?
What have I done since last time?
What are the key things I've learned?
How do they affect the assumptions I started with?
Am I up to schedule? If not, what action can I take to improve the situation?

Record the results of review sessions, keep them where you will see them, and act on them. At each review, identify any documents you have created recently that could be useful in the end product of the research – for example questionnaire formats, which will show readers how you have done the things you report on – and put copies of them into a preliminary 'material for dissertation chapters' container. Similarly, assemble notes on significant insights and new developments in thinking, and ideas about appropriate criteria for assessing your work, for use in both the written end product and the oral examination on it. (See Chapter 6, pages 133–138 for more about using this kind of material in planning ahead for writing.)

Mutual responsibilities

Now a few words on the mutual responsibilities that are, or should be, part of the 'research contract'. On pages 95–96 we discussed researchers' obligations to their tutors and their institution. There are reciprocal responsibilities, which need to be made explicit, discussed, understood and committed to by both sides – so that there is a clear point of reference for everyone involved from the beginning, and no lurking ambiguities to cause trouble and dissension where they are least needed. (Some institutions embody the responsibilities in a 'Learning agreement' between supervisor and researcher.)

As the institution and its staff are the permanent parties to the contract, while the researchers are usually more transient, it should be their job to take the initiative in setting out and discussing the mutual obligations. If researchers find that this has been overlooked, then it is for them to take some initiatives of their own, to find out what's expected of them and what they are entitled to expect in exchange.

Today, in the UK, there is a welcome and growing insistence by institutions that staff who supervise research students should be trained for the job. As far as the aspects of research discussed in this chapter are concerned, well-informed supervisors will seek to meet these responsibilities to researchers:

- Ensuring that they are aware of the institution's rules for researchers, and reminding them of relevant ones at critical points.
- Being conscientious about regular tutorial exchanges, making clear what they expect, giving clear feedback on material presented by researchers, keeping notes of exchanges, checking that agreed action has been taken.
- Being sensitive to situations where researchers may under be under stress of various kinds, and in need of help.

(Other aspects of mutual responsibilities are discussed in Chapters 6 and 10.)

And finally ...

As I was finishing the first draft of this chapter, Karen mentioned that she had been preparing a lecture on 'doctoral studies as project management' for a distance-learning course on project management. She kindly agreed to let me quote from it, and to end this chapter here are some of her thoughts, arising from her own experience:

Karen *What is the problem?*
Problems [for research] aren't found – they are created, and that takes much time and effort. When helping students I tell them to expect to reformulate their problem formulation after the research has been finished. Also project aims can and do change – that is or should be accepted.

Scale down, scale down, scale down yet again
This seems to be a normal part of research ... and the result might be that there is very little result left.

Strategies to avoid project work
Motivation to work on research projects has its ups and downs. Feelings of isolation, insignificance, anxiety and uncertainty are among the more formidable obstacles when working alone on creative work for any longer period of time. Be nice to yourself, find ways to motivate yourself, and accept occasional dips ...

And for an insight into how researchers find ways of not getting on with the job, see: http://www.ling.su.se/staff/oesten/undvik/how-to-avoid-graduation.pdf – a fun text with a serious message. It ends with the 'scientifically proven' 'constant of Asp' that doctoral students spend exactly 29 minutes a day working on their dissertations.

Reference

Website referred to this chapter accessed on 18 March 2009

HUNT, A (2005)
Your Research Project: How to Manage It.
Didcot: Routledge.

Useful website

THE QUALITY ASSURANCE AGENCY FOR HIGHER EDUCATION (2004)
Code of practice for the assurance of academic quality and standards in higher education. Section 1: Postgraduate research programmes.
www.qaa.ac.uk/academicinfrastructure/CodesOfPractice/

Keeping on good terms with Time

Ch 5 Contents at a glance

Alice sighed wearily. 'I think you might do something better with the time,' she said, 'than wasting it in asking riddles that have no answers.'

'If you knew Time as well as I do,' said the Hatter, 'you wouldn't talk about wasting *it*. It's *him.*'

'I don't know what you mean,' said Alice.

'Of course you don't!' the Hatter said, tossing his head contemptuously. 'I dare say you never even spoke to Time!'

'Perhaps not,' Alice cautiously replied; 'but I know I have to beat time when I learn music.'

'Ah! That accounts for it,' said the Hatter. 'He won't stand beating. Now if you only kept on good terms with him, he'd do almost anything you liked with the clock. ...'

(Lewis Carroll, *Alice's Adventures in Wonderland,* 1865, Chapter 7)

create time plans and deadlines for yourself (and to show others) as if they were 'real' but accept that they will be broken because of circumstances outside of your control. Start from the end and the final product and work backwards. Assign a (flexible) chunk of time to each large activity and satisfice – do not strive for each part to be perfect but for the whole to be good enough.

(Karen, from a lecture on 'Doctoral studies as project management')

Problem or non-problem?

Mariana Time management wasn't a problem. I just respected deadlines, made changes to my proposal and the direction of my project every time they asked [me] to do it in the tutorials, and following the method I established in my proposal.

Wouter I was fortunate enough not to have any time-management problems. The reason is due to the fact that I was and still am the research assistant for my supervisor at the university where I studied. Part of my work was writing and presenting conference papers, and I also worked on a journal article. All of this work directly contributed to my master's dissertation. Being a research assistant for my supervisor also put me in a position to see my supervisor five days a week.

Not many researchers are as fortunate as Mariana and Wouter. In fact, few of us get through research – especially the closing stages when everything has to be brought together into the end product and delivered by the final deadline – without moments of despair, panic or acute anxiety about our ability to do what we have to do within the span available. When we are in the grip of those feelings, we can be our own worst enemies, so it's important to do whatever we can to avoid the situations that create them. That means starting early on coming to terms with time.

Many researchers, especially those undertaking research for the first time, haven't had the opportunity of developing the skills that can help them to do that. For them in particular, this chapter suggests experience-based strategies, starting with answering some questions, for maintaining good relations with time throughout the research process.

Making time visible in space

When you have answered the four questions on page 108, the next step is to get value out of the answers by making their meaning for using the time available clearly visible to yourself. Here, as elsewhere in this book, we advocate on the basis of experience trying to visualize the knowledge in your mind and to put it outside into the world in graphic form, where it can guide your actions.

Some (but not many) of the recent researchers quoted this book have sought to do this:

Paula Although a Gantt chart is useful in setting broad targets and timescales, a week by week timetable was more useful because it made the targets more realistic in terms of specific activities that needed to be completed.

Justin	I used very simple Gantt charts developed in Microsoft Excel for monitoring the progress of my work.
Aragon	I designed a time spool with date and names and tasks on it.

Since many researchers probably have limited experience of the range of visual methods available for this purpose, the diagrams in this book give a cross-section of techniques that are possible using Adobe Illustrator CS2.

Questions to help in managing time

In Chapter 4 (page 95) we said that researchers need:
'... an overview of the events and activities of the research, the relations between them which will affect the sequence in which they need to take place, and the fixed dates around which they must be organized. It makes a companion-piece to the research route map, and provides essential information for it on the timing of the stages.'

To make a start, you are invited to answer some simple questions in the light of your own research. We offer some ideas that researchers have found helpful in answering them, and some lessons they have learned from experience.

1 What are the deadlines and milestones for the work?
2 What are the most important things to be done in the research?
3 What's the best order for doing them?
4 How long are they likely to take?

Deadlines and milestones

They come first, because they set the fixed constraints within which you have to work. For a start: make sure you know exactly what they are (I have met a fair number of researchers who weren't too sure about them at a dangerously late stage in the proceedings); put a printout of them where you can see it every day and enter them in your diary in colour.

Some supervisors give researchers a good start on the process by insisting at an early stage on seeing a first timetable. In Kerry's two-year part-time MA course, work connected with the dissertation occupied the second year. Early in the first semester of that year, her supervisor required students to submit a dissertation plan and a schedule of associated activities, and strongly urged them to keep a research diary.

> 'The schedule should ... include activities undertaken during the class-based part in the first semester which covers October to December and the independent study stage covering January to August.'
>
> (Reproduced courtesy of *Susie Andretta*, Senior Lecturer in Information Management, London Metropolitan University.)

Kerry's schedule looked like this:

September	Initial literature review to establish potential dissertation topic.
October	Apply for prospectuses from the 18 institutions. View web sites and download information relating to these courses.
November, beginning of December	Continuing literature review using refined keyword search terms and further develop the scope of the proposed research from an analysis of the literature found.
Mid-December	Content analysis of prospectus/web-based course information. Participants identified and contact made with participants via telephone, where possible, to arrange a date/time for telephone interview.
Beginning of January	Formulation of interview schedule and questions. Pilot interview schedule with dissertation supervisor and work colleagues.
End of January	Postal/e-mail questionnaires sent to library and information studies subject librarians at the 18 selected institutions, and to those participants electing this method of data collection rather than a telephone interview. February 15 cut-off date. Telephone interviews conducted with programme leaders. Mail out reminders to non-respondents of postal/e-mail questionnaires.
Mid-February to April	Data analysis.
May/June	Write up and redraft.
July	Further redrafts.
August	Final submission.

In doctoral research there are comparatively few fixed points; in particular, the researcher has more control over the date of submitting the end product. That's a double-edged freedom, which accounts for many an abandoned PhD. It requires particular self-discipline on the part of the researcher, and it helps if there are any fixed points associated with work or career ambitions. As I was doing my research essentially to please myself, I decided that I wanted my PhD as a Millennium present. For Justin there was a natural deadline, set by the end date of a three-year contract on which he started work shortly after his research proposal was accepted. He treated it as a career-development opportunity, and took the workload in his stride, setting logical milestones within the three-year time-span.

Justin The critical point was when I decided to use the end of my contract with the FAO as my major target point. I was to finish work on the thesis and graduate before my contract with FAO came to an end. I had joined FAO on a three year contract and it was to end 15 January 2005. This would ensure that if I decided to go back to work in a university environment, a doctorate degree would give me an added advantage. Within this time frame, I set out the major milestones, i.e. when each chapter should be completed, when to conduct the questionnaire surveys, etc. Everything worked well and I graduated in September 2004.

On the evidence of the people quoted in this book, undertaking research in combination with working full-time on a job related to the research seems to have a 'Mark Tapley effect'; they certainly come out remarkably strong.[1] Here, for example, is Paula's laconic response to the question 'Was time management a significant problem?'

Paula Time management was a significant problem – During my studies I had a baby! Also I was working full time. I had to make significant changes to my writing / study habits.

Most important things to be done?

The methodology for my research on 'The role of information products and information presentation in organizations' was determined by the research topic: it depended on longitudinal case studies in 10 organizations, and that in turn set the framework for the essential activities, tasks and sub-tasks, which centred round:

1. The case studies
2. Reviewing the relevant literature on the subject areas identified in Figure 2.3 (page 40)
3. Bringing the findings together, interpreting them, and planning, designing and writing the thesis.

What order to do them in?

Making a list of things to do is a good start; but to get the full value from it, we need to sort out the most productive sequence. Are there things that *can't*

1 In Charles Dickens's *Martin Chuzzlewit*, Mark Tapley is a lively young man who longs to find himself in trying circumstances which will allow him to 'come out strong' under adversity. He gets his chance when he goes to America as servant of the hero of the novel, and takes it heroically.

be done until others have been done? Are there activities that require a lot of groundwork before they can begin? Are there jobs that can start at about the same time, and then run along together with work on them alternating?

As my research was going to depend for its validity on the results of case studies in a number of organizations over a long period, it was quite obvious that the first thing to be done was to find and persuade an appropriate sample to commit themselves to answering my questions at intervals over a period of five years – and I knew from past experience how much time and effort that alone would demand. However, I would at least be able to interleave it with setting up the basis for the literature review – starting with fishing out all the useful material I had already collected and entered in my database over a period of years.

For the first year or so of the research, case-study work would alternate with literature search and note-taking; after that, the case studies would go on alongside planning and starting to write the thesis, while the reading continued, but on a diminishing scale. Figure 5.1 on page 113, shows the sequence; the timescale is the one shown in a different way in the Chapter 2 'route map' for the anticipated research journey (Figure 2.4, page 41).

Other examples of the same kind of approach to the sequence and interleaving of activities come from Paula and Ismaril:

Paula	While waiting for ethical approval it is essential to start writing the literature review and make a start on methods and introduction – you can revise them later if necessary but this will free up time later on for data collection, analysis etc.
Ismaril	Making and testing very simple prototypes at an early stage was useful as these could pick up the basic issues and provide for further more detailed and accurate trials which could yield more valuable and precise information.

There are benefits that go beyond time saving in alternating two kinds of activity which demand different skills, and use energies in different ways. Boredom and fatigue are less liable to set in, and each activity is likely to prompt new ideas for the other.

How long will they take?

Before you can make realistic schedules for fitting all the things you have to do into the time constraints and milestones imposed by the institution, you need to know how long each job is likely to take you. This is difficult when they are jobs you haven't done before, but gets easier with experience. As cautionary starters, here are some discoveries that recent researchers made about tasks they hadn't had occasion to tackle before.

Things that take longer than you might expect

Lesson one is that anything that requires the participation of other people needs a long 'lead time' because you have very little control over the way in which they spend their lives, and they have plenty of demands on their time as well as their own preferences on what they do with what's left over. So start early – especially if you have to get any kind of official approval for what you need to do.

Paula — Critical points: Getting ethical submissions in early – some committees only meet every three months and if you are not successful first time, the delay on starting data collection could be six months.

Kath — The biggest problem for me was not realising how long it would take to get ethical approval. I left it until very late to submit my application for ethics. By the time I had made the required adjustments I had only four months to do my data collection, analysis and write up the dissertation. I would advise anyone to get to work early on this.

Justin — [If I were to start again] I would choose a research topic that would not require surveying a population that is scattered in so many countries. Some of the major delays that I experienced during the survey had to do with difficulties in getting in touch with agricultural research scientists in some of the target countries. In one country, Zimbabwe, I discovered that I could not distribute the questionnaires to researchers unless I got permission from the national research council. This process took quite a lot of time.

Be prepared to modify your plans for collecting information from people if it turns out they will demand more time than you have to spend:

Kerry — whilst I thought my research was important/interesting, clearly asking busy people to respond is the one element completely beyond your control and I learnt to accept that I wasn't going to get the kind of response rate I would have liked. ...

My original plan had also involved content analysis of institutional prospectuses and web-based course information to determine range and level of information skills training offered and qualitative analysis of data gathered via semi-structured telephone and one-to-one interviewing of programme leaders for each of the 18 institutions, but it soon became very obvious to me that I just wouldn't have the time to do this. ... Discussions with my supervisor made it obvious that I was being over ambitious in what I was proposing to do – especially trying to carry out this content analysis exercise as well as conduct and transcribe telephone interviews. ...

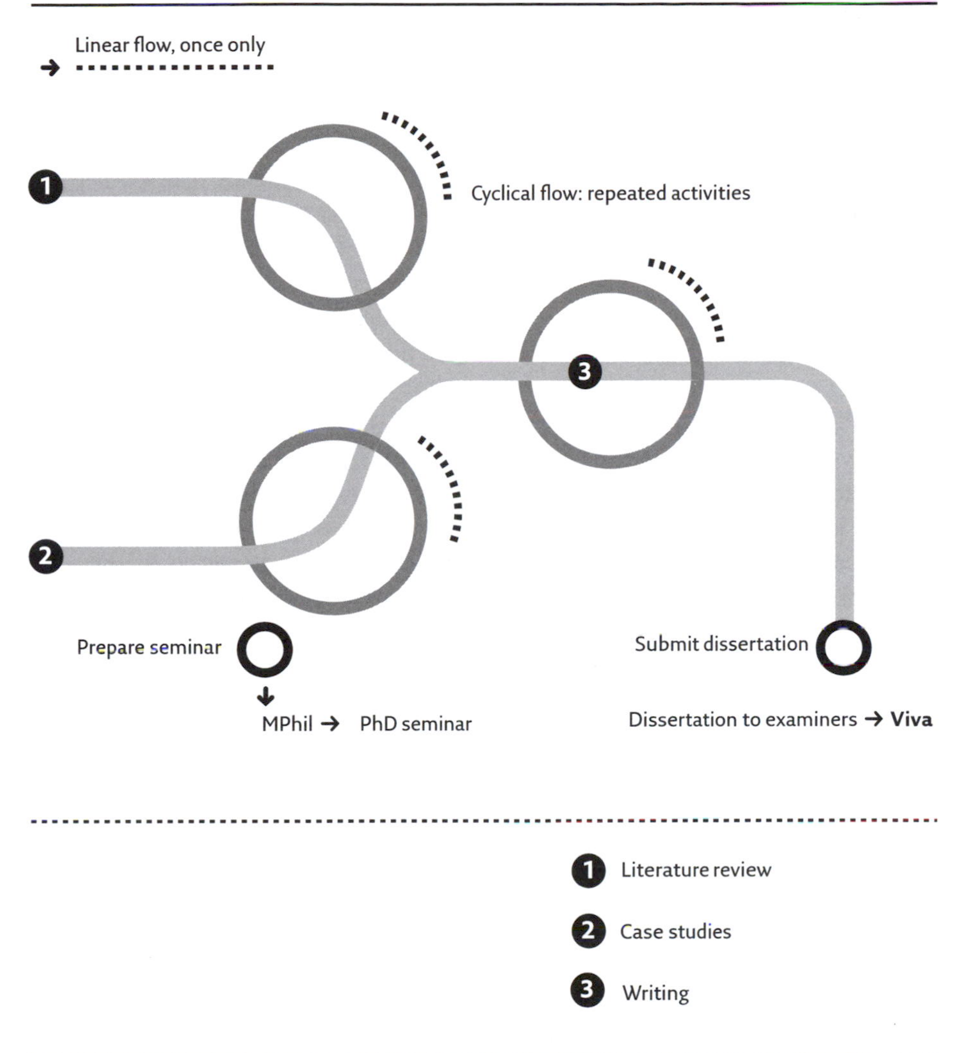

Figure 5.1 Breakdown of key activities into tasks; sequential and parallel working

Planning questionnaires and other instruments for collecting information from people in a form that will yield reliable material also takes more time than you might expect, especially if you are after qualitative information, as Kerry observes:

Kerry I was also surprised at just how long it took to come up with two questionnaires that actually asked the questions I wanted to ask, in a format that wouldn't make my respondents lose the will to live before they'd finished it. I think from anyone's experience of filling out questionnaires, if you've got to really work at it you get fed up and the resulting responses are not therefore going to be as information rich as the researcher would like. Saying that, I didn't want to just be dealing with quantitative data as I felt this wouldn't really get to the crux of the matter.

The activity that can surprise and dismay researchers by its demands on time and mental energy is the one they may dismiss in prospect as a kind of afterthought to the real business of research, as 'writing up'. As we'll see later (see Chapter 10, pages 237–238), there's good reason to believe writing is one of the most difficult tasks researchers have to undertake, and it merits a deal more attention than it usually gets – because for most researchers it's the only means of creating the visible end product on which their efforts will be judged. Yet some researchers defer all planning for the end products until they reach the 'writing-up stage' – which is usually not very long before the deadline for submission. Then it can come as a shock to find how much time it requires.

Laima Another problem was inadequate understanding about how much time the process of writing will actually take. The actual writing took more time than I expected. As I evaluate it now, I spent too much time on seeking information, but started writing the text too late.

Other tasks that take longer than you may think:

- Transcribing and editing from recordings of interviews and meetings
- Preparing diagrams and tables to a respectable standard
- Final checking and editing of text. (For more about this, see Chapter 10, page 264).

With those cautions in mind, let us look at ways of assessing how long jobs are likely to take.

Estimating times

As Karen put it: 'The problem is knowing beforehand how much time processes take – how much I can spend on analysing material, for instance.'

You can help yourself to master this essential survival skill by timing yourself on samples of the tasks that you will need to carry out in the course of your research. For example:

- Reading and making notes on a typical 10-page article in your subject area
- Doing a half-hour interview, and inputting your notes from it (or, if you intend recording interviews, transcribing the recording)
- Planning a brief questionnaire, testing that a small sample of the intended type of users can understand it, analysing their answers
- Analysing the content of a document type that you propose collecting, e.g. annual reports or college prospectuses.

Strategies for keeping to schedule

No matter how carefully you have planned the use of time, it's a common experience to find things don't turn out exactly as envisaged. Here are some stories about that.

'Cutting your coat according to your cloth'
Often it's because the reality proves more complicated and time-consuming than predicted. In that case, be ready to accept necessity and, like Kerry and Karen, turn it to advantage.

Kerry	I think the most important thing I learnt was to remain flexible. Although it did mean adapting my initial proposed interview questions into questionnaire form in hindsight this probably did me a favour as I was able to get straight yes/no responses to some questions, which made analysis and comparison of results easier.
Karen	[One of the most useful lessons for me is] always to be able to down-size my project at almost any step (less data gathering, less in-depth analysis, ...). I have managed to keep all my deadlines so far by 'satisficing' rather than aiming at the perfect article, paper, etc, and I believe that keeping deadlines is as important as writing a 'perfect' study.

In my own research, an initial plan of following up the case studies with action research in two organizations turned out to be over-optimistic. Fortunately, around the time I realized this, I found an article about a new and very relevant methodology for valuing information, and got in touch with the author, who had devised it. The upshot was that, with his support, I was able to undertake a small-scale application of his method to an information product in one of the case-study organizations – a valuable chance to combine a bit of quantitative methodology with the qualitative approach adopted for the main case-study work.

Setting modest targets

It's possible to prevent yourself from doing what you ought to do by setting targets that are too ambitious. The remedy, as Hamid found, was to break tasks down into bits that could be done within short spans of time.

Hamid I was not good at prioritising my tasks, not because I couldn't differentiate what was more important, [but] because sometimes I tended to avoid doing things which were of high priority but I didn't like doing them or I was stuck. To solve it, I took some courses to improve my time management and also chose some strategies like putting a deadline for myself and allocating smaller tasks for myself instead of intending doing something big in a short time frame. For example I tended to say for example tomorrow I will work on the that article but I never did; so I decided to adopt a different approach like saying tomorrow I will work on the introduction of that article (more likely to be done than the whole article) or tomorrow I will write 1000 words for that article.

Karen too recommends breaking tasks down:

Karen Do not think of your work as one big (overwhelming) task but plan for daily or weekly chunks and have a little reward or celebration when you've finished such a chunk.

Substituting alternative action

If you are thwarted from doing something on your schedule because of the action (or inaction) of other people whose actions you have no power over, use the time set aside for it on something else relating to the research. Never do nothing! There are always ongoing 'anytime' jobs such as reading, sorting out notes, drafting, or reviewing what you've done recently, that can be brought forward to fill gaps.

Circumstances beyond control

Sometimes it is impossible to keep to a schedule, for reasons – such as illness – that are wholly beyond your control. If you're struck down by the current virus, some things will inevitably slip. Don't try to struggle on in the face of feeling ill. Let your tutors know, and concentrate on getting better. When you feel you've rejoined the human race, reschedule and get on with it, as Paula did:

Paula There will always be a disaster that arrives that stops you doing anything for a couple of weeks – you just have to be prepared for this and accept it as inevitable (I had chickenpox about one month before hand-in!) – don't give up, don't ask for an extension – just get on with it, you can do it!

If it's a prolonged illness, your institution will have arrangements for an extension to make up for the lost time. Make sure they are notified and that they take the necessary action; accept the inevitable delay, take the time you need to recover, don't give up on the research, and resume work on it at a moderate pace to start with.

If you just feel frustrated, fed up, or temporarily lost, take it as a signal that you need to pause for a while, and let your mind alone. A quiet walk or some rhythmic exercise can help restore equilibrium and sort out tangled thoughts (dancing straightens my thoughts, and cheers my spirits).

Should you find that, without actual physical illness or external frustrations, you are getting seriously behind on your schedule, don't pretend to anybody – least of all yourself – that all is well; don't feel ashamed that you can't keep up; and don't keep the trouble to yourself. Tell your tutors, take advantage of your college's provisions for pastoral help or counselling if you feel they would help. Research can be a lonely occupation, especially if it's the first time you have done it, and if you have not previously had to take responsibility for managing your own work. Being able to talk it through with others, who understand something about both your project and the anxieties of researchers, should help you to work out a new approach to the research which will allow you to get to grips with it and to make friends again with time.

Supervisors and tutors can help greatly in this matter by keeping a watchful eye at the beginning of research projects on whether students are struggling with time. In taught courses particularly, it seems to be helpful in the early stages to set manageably small and relevant tasks to be done in a short period – and to insist that they are done to time, especially with any researchers who have difficulty in taking deadlines seriously. It's admittedly something of a bore having to spend time chasing up and reminding people of things they themselves should take responsibility for – but it goes with the job and with the obligations of institutions towards the research students they accept.

Time to reflect, time to play

One of the most important things you should build into your time-plan is spaces for the letting your mind alone to reflect, and for 'play'. The more demanding your schedule, the greater the need for these protected spaces, as Kerry and Karen found.

Kerry — In order to not let the whole thing consume my life, although it felt like it at times, I agreed with my partner that Saturday would be a 'play' day, while Sunday was my study day. The study door was closed and that meant do not disturb. That way it was fair on both of us and I got some time away from my studies over the two years I was taking the MA course. ... I deliberately tried to avoid late night sessions on the computer mid-week but the occasional Friday saw the candle burned to the very bottom.

Karen I think the most useful 'lesson' for me, is ... to keep my weekends free (if I don't I can get too stressed out and too close to burnout problems).

Rewards, small and larger, are another useful device for punctuating research

Kerry As I commuted to work by train I did have some 'protected' reading time. So I selected an article/chapter to read every morning and tried to make a few quick notes as I went along. The journey home I always had a novel to read as a) a treat if I had been a good girl and read my article in the morning and b) because after a day's work it was sensible to wind down a bit and not try to cram any more information in, especially if I was to continue working in the evening.

... my annual leave for that year did take quite a battering, as I planned long weekends based around significant dates in my research timetable. However, again I planned a treat in order to motivate myself and we had already booked our annual holiday to the Med for mid August, two weeks prior to the final date for dissertation submissions so I knew I had something to look forward to, but only if I got myself properly organized.

(The small reward I found really helpful was the prospect of a gin and tonic if I kept working until the finishing time I'd set myself!)

Timesavers

Each of us has an individual approach to work, and what helps one person to save time may look like self-imposed torment and a serious hindrance to others. The main thing is to be aware of your own natural ways of working – what makes you feel at ease, what constrains you and makes you unhappy. Then look for improvements that can save you time *and* support you in working in ways that you find comfortable. They may involve a bit of self-discipline, but once you find something that pays off, the necessary self-discipline stops being a burden and becomes an unnoticed part of your way of working.

Here is my personal list of timesavers, with additions from some of the researchers who have contributed their experience. They work for me, and some of them may help some readers – but remember they're not a prescription!

Interleave jobs: run different tasks concurrently, not end-on – don't just do one thing at a time! Alternate between different jobs so that you are going forward on two or more fronts at once.

Don't spend too long at a time on things that demand intense concentration and sitting in one place. Start in good time on the demanding ones (especially writing) and do them for the period of time you find comfortable, with different and less demanding activities in between. If you force yourself to go on working past the time when your stamina and concentration have declined, the work that results will be flawed – as an editor, I can recognize writing that has been done when the writers have pushed themselves to go on after the point when they were too fatigued to do the job properly.

Everyone has a time of day when they are most alert, and it varies from early morning to late at night. Save your best time for the jobs that demand most concentration and creative thought, and use the rest for the less demanding ones.

Keep everything relating to your research in good order, so that you don't waste time looking for particular sets of notes, or the phone numbers of essential contacts. Keep files on the computer in consistently labelled folders so that you can get quickly to what you want without scanning through a long list of file names.

Invest time (as suggested in Chapter 3) in giving yourself tools to help you to find relevant material among what you have collected; Ismaril found that this paid off:

Ismaril Continuously building up a collection of quotable material has paid off, particularly storing these in a database or collection of author-named files. Some sources, such as library books, have been difficult to keep for the duration of a project, so it has been worthwhile photocopying relevant chapters (plus cover and contents page) and storing these in lever arch files to read when time is available.

Otherwise to get an idea of the content of a book without trawling the library shelves a synopsis from amazon.com would prove useful as well as their 'look inside' feature which normally allows you to see the contents page of a book.

Once you've worked out the structure of chapter or section headings for what you're going to write, assign material as you collect it to an appropriate place in the structure so that it will be there when you are ready to write that bit. For example, in the course of writing this book, as answers from researchers to our questions came in, I printed them out and looked at them alongside my chapter synopsis. I marked answers up for the chapters they were relevant to and then I copied the extracts marked into the 'catch-all' files I set up for each chapter at the start of work, so that useful quotes were ready when I came to write the chapter. I did the same with details of useful websites and software, and references to relevant articles.

Before starting on any job, assemble everything you need for it, and follow the good advice passed on by Kerry (which I seldom manage to achieve!):

Kerry One good piece of advice I did receive was to make sure my desk at home was clear if I had a specific piece of work in mind, chapter to write, notes to read etc.

When you've finished a session of note-taking – from reading, meetings with people, or lectures – highlight the key points in the notes in colour while your memory is still fresh. It saves time later, when you need to use them as the basis for writing.

'When found, make a note of.' Follow the advice of Dickens's Captain Cuttle in *Dombey and Son.* Always make an immediate note of good ideas that come to you, things you suddenly realize you ought to do, etc, so that you don't lose them and then have to waste time trying to remember what it was you thought of.

Learn and use basic keyboard shortcuts for the computer operations you need to do most often.

Learn to type reasonably quickly and accurately, using all the fingers that nature has given you; it's about three times faster than pecking at the keyboard with two fingers. If you learn to type by touch as well, it's less tiring too, because you can keep looking at what you are typing from (or even shut your eyes if you are composing out of your head), rather than shuttling your gaze back and forth from copy to keys. (For more time-savers for writing see Chapter 10).

Instead of a summary...

A final observation, based on experience over a good number of years:

Time will, in the Mad Hatter's words quoted at the beginning of this chapter, 'do almost anything you like with the clock' to accommodate the things you have to do

If

You understand what you're doing,
Have thought thoroughly about it

And

You really want to do it.

Further reading, useful websites

Websites referred to this chapter accessed on 18 March 2009

ALLEN, DAVID (2004)
Ready for anything; 52 principles for increased productivity.
London: Piatkus Books.
Useful stuff; don't be put off by the US-style headings

MINDTOOLS
Information on time management, project planning, scheduling simple projects, Gantt charts, etc.
http://www.mindtools.com

SMARTDRAW
Drawing software: flowcharts, Gannt charts, timelines, diagrams, concepts, maps, mind-mapping, etc.
http://www.smartdraw.com

Planning the end product

The two chapters which make up Part 3 act as a connection and transition from Part 2, concerned with *managing* information, to the final part of this book, which deals with *using* the information and the knowledge gained in the course of research to design and create the end product. Their purpose is to help researchers lay a foundation for their work on that stage, which will allow them to concentrate their energies on it.

This is the point at which you have to start focusing on the people on the receiving end – first, the examiners, and then future readers who will wish to use it to enrich their own knowledge. You have to move outside yourself and try to see through their eyes, so that you can envisage what they need to find in your work in order to understand it, make well-founded and fair judgements of it, and do justice to you. Chapters 6 and 7 will help you to visualize the form and features of the end product you have to create.

Part 3

Thinking ahead: questions and decisions

Ch 6 Contents at a glance

Introduction

By the very nature of books, the matters treated in successive chapters look as though they represent a linear process in time, but this is only partly true in the present case. The questions we are now going to discuss do indeed relate to the end products of research, which can't be completed until a late stage in the process. But, as with all the activities discussed so far, we have to lay foundations. We have to ask ourselves the questions raised in this chapter early in the research, so that they form part of our awareness and help shape how we manage the other activities covered in earlier chapters. Then, as making the end product gradually moves from background to foreground, we can look at our answers again and consider them more deeply as our knowledge grows and acquires structure. This is when we start to benefit from whatever we have done to organize our information in relation to the structure of the end product, because it allows us to move naturally and without undue stress into creating whatever output we have to deliver.

A variety of requirements

It's evident from what recent researchers have told us on these topics that there are plenty of individual differences in approach, and that different institutions require varying levels of advance thinking.

As we've seen (Chapter 2, pages 31–36) some courses are planned to lead through such steps as a series of assignments and presentations, or preparing a research strategy, towards advance planning of the end product. Laima's experience shows the differing requirements in the two European countries where she worked on her research (Lithuania and Germany).

Laima — In Vilnius I had to present regular (end-of-year) formal progress reports in the meetings of my department. I didn't have to go much into the details of the content of my research, but only to report my progress: at what stage it is and what publications I have made.

In Berlin I was taking part in a doctoral colloquium where I had to present the concrete ideas of my research every half-year. In the beginning it was a detailed research statement, later it was chapters from my dissertation. This was where I had to go into more detail of my research methodology and it was more thoroughly discussed. The colloquium was useful since I really had to make progress in my research in order to be able to present new results for it, and benefited from the comments it evoked. In Lithuania, there is no doctoral colloquium in my faculty; despite continuous discussions on the need to introduce it (especially from those doctoral students who have studied abroad and have experience of colloquiums) it doesn't happen. ...Therefore a bigger responsibility for advising and controlling the doctoral student falls on the supervisor and the department which the student is attached to.

Other institutions in other places give research students a suggested standard dissertation structure and leave the rest to them. Wouter provides an example from his South African university, which sets out a conventional structure of introductory matter followed by chapters on literature analysis; research design and methodology; data collected and its analysis and interpretation; and ending with conclusions and recommendations for further research, references, and appendices.

And others again seem to leave it to individual researchers, some at least of whom may defer thinking about the questions until they arrive at something described as the 'writing up stage' – and then wish they hadn't left it so late in the day.

How researchers set about planning

When we asked researchers, 'How did you plan the end products? What questions and what readership did you take into account in writing?' we got a variety of illuminating responses. Two are very relevant here. Karen sensibly drew a distinction between the various situations in which products have to be presented, and what it implies for planning:

Karen [The final product will be a monograph.] During the process I will have written three texts on my project to present at research seminars – one at about a year into the five-year process, one about halfway, and one after around 80 per cent. ... Not required, but encouraged, are articles and conference presentations. ...

[Texts can be] less polished for the first two research seminars, where one does have to present a text that has to be readable and understandable, but where the loose ends and the questions I pose myself at the time can be included, as the text is seen as a work in progress, [whereas for articles and conference presentations they have to be] more general as well as more polished [and] ... there is a tighter limit on length too. For the seminar texts ... in one way, I started planning some three months before; in another I had kept them in mind during the whole process of writing smaller files.

(see also Chapter 10 page 240 for how Karen followed the process through into writing the end product.)

The Master's programme that Kerry undertook part-time at a London university required students to prepare a detailed dissertation plan. It had to embody: a short review of relevant literature, with references; a statement of the methods to be used in achieving the research objectives; a 'reflection on research issues' – such as ethical considerations, and strategy for ensuring the validity of findings; and a timetable for all the research activities envisaged. As Kerry explained, it was possible to develop a useful plan at this stage because she had also gained useful experience in another compulsory piece of work – the 'Applied Information Research' (AIR) module.

Kerry		If we hadn't had the opportunity to design research strategies in the AIR module this would have been much harder to do from a mere understanding of research theory/concepts.

The result was that she was thinking constructively from the beginning about content, structure and readership of the end product; those initial ideas were then able to evolve and change with experience, and when she was ready to begin actual writing, there was a long-familiar framework ready to 'write into'.

Paula found that she could save valuable time by making an early start on certain elements of the end product, including the literature review and the methodology chapter, as well as smaller jobs like the title page and contents page, which could be added to as the dissertation progressed.

Now let us look at the approach we suggest, on the basis of experience, for planning the products by which researchers make their findings and ideas visible and put them into the outside world.

The questions that researchers need to answer

A list of chapter headings provided by the institution is a useful start, but it's far from the end of the matter, and doesn't answer most of the problems most of us face when we come to this part of the business. As Hamid reflected at a point when he had started to think in detail about his dissertation, there are many other considerations:

Hamid		the general structure is well-established in each scientific field, so I have a clear idea of what a dissertation looks like in Library and Information Science, and what chapters I must certainly include (literature review, introduction, methodology ...). However the big challenge is how to present the results, which are normally structured on the basis of the objectives or questions of the research.

Although the readership is meant to be academics in my own field, I have to take into account that they may have different levels of know-ledge about the subject of my dissertation. So I have to write it in a way that people with different level of knowledge on the field can understand it.

The other thing is that it should be written as an stand-alone product. Although this sounds self-evident, it is tricky. It needs to have a logical structure and include all the necessary information and data required to understand the research presented. It also has to be written as a time-independent work. Of course people who read my dissertation 10 years later should see from the title page that they are reading a 10-year-old piece of research. But if they are interested in the content and plunge into reading the text, they may overlook the date. ... So whenever I refer to time-related matters I should clarify the time.

A list of chapter headings gives no guidance in itself on how to organize the content under the headings, or how to use the information created and collected in the course of the research to the best effect and in the best places, or how to present it – through words and visual means – so that readers can easily follow the reasoning and understand how the conclusions were reached. And these are all the things we need to think about if what we finally hand in is to do justice to our work.

That is why we make these questions the focus of this chapter. If you have followed the process of making a 'research map' and 'itinerary' discussed in Chapter 2, you will be well on the way to answering them.

1 Who are the intended users, and what are their purposes in reading the end products?
2 Are there others whose interests must be taken into account?
3 What are the most important elements in the research?
4 What do I myself want to achieve from the research?
5 What do the users need to understand about the researcher?

For each of the questions, we shall explain why we need to ask it, and the decisions about the end product that the answers will enable us to take; and we shall give cross-references back and forward to relevant discussions elsewhere, and relevant quotations from recent researchers, about how they approached making their decisions and what they were.

Users, and their purposes in reading the end products

If we don't take the users, and their reasons for reading what we give them, fully into account in planning the end product, it may not get a very warm welcome. It could, at worst, exasperate, bore, confuse or mystify its most important readers, and so provoke an unwelcome – and possibly unjust – judgement.

We need to answer the questions in order to make decisions on the content we present to the intended readers and the sequence in which it is presented, as well as the structure of the product, the style of writing, and visual expression. Vital decisions indeed.

The readers will certainly always include examiners and others who have to assess whether the research meets the standards set, and make pass or fail decisions. As Kath put it: '... issues were geared towards demonstrating a good academic style and receiving the best possible grade.'

Examiners and assessors

The end product has to make it easy for this readership to do their job quickly, fairly and without getting too cross! [1]

[1] As the author of the foreword to this book reminds us (see page 10) readers in other countries, whose traditions of scholarly writing differ from those of the Anglo-Saxon model, will wish to consider what *their* examiners will look for in dissertations, and what it implies for how to help them to do this.

What they want to be able to do	To enable them to do it
Grasp the objectives of the research – what it aimed to achieve (and what it didn't seek to do!).	Objectives must be clearly expressed at the start.
Get an overview of the structure of the product, so that they can quickly see whether it has all the required features.	Well-designed title page and contents list.
Assess how well the researcher knows the relevant background, as demonstrated in the literature review, and in the use of quotations.	Format for literature review with appropriate headings. Clear consistent style for citing references in text and in bibliographies. An entry in the reference list for everything cited in the text, and vice versa.
See how the research was carried out and judge the appropriateness of the methodology.	Clear heading structure. Statement of criteria for choice of methodology. Standards for describing how it has been applied, e.g. in setting up tests or designing questionnaires. Examples of materials designed for use in the research.
Understand the findings and assess their validity.	Effective and appropriate presentation of findings (e.g. tabulations, diagrams). Typographical standards for them.
Follow the arguments.	Writing which presents the steps in logical sequence, with cross-references to places in the text where evidence is presented, references to relevant literature. Internal consistency. Graphics where appropriate.
Check the evidence for conclusions (e.g. from references quoted, from results of experiments).	Visually distinctive standard for cross-references.

Table 6.1 What examiners want to be able to do; what will enable them to do it

So it has to meet the requirements set out in Table 6.1 above; each of them implies appropriate solutions in terms of information design, both visual and written—and these are the subjects of Chapters 9.1 to 10.

As well as all that, researchers also need to be aware of institutional guidelines and standards for this kind of product and to observe them as far as possible. (On occasion, the nature of the research may make it necessary to deviate from them; if that is the case, explain at an early point why you have not followed recommended standards.)

And if your research will be assessed by an external examiner, especially if that involves a viva, it is wise to learn in advance as much as you can about his/her academic background, field of expertise, publications, expectations, preferences (and prejudices) – see page 139 for a story that explains why. Forewarned is forearmed; if you know the background you can prepare for situations that may arise.

Other audiences, other products

Planning should also take into account other people who may consult the final product of your research, and the audiences for any other products you may have to deliver on the way – such as presentations and articles.

Future readers who want to use your research as an information source

Just as you have looked for relevant information in accounts of research on your topic, so too future researchers may well want to use your dissertation as an information source to extend and deepen their knowledge. And they are likely to consult the dissertations of other researchers in increasing numbers as making them openly available in electronic format becomes normal practice for institutions, through such developments as the UK EThOS (Electronic Thesis Online Service).

Whatever features you provide to help examiners will also help these readers. In addition, they will be grateful to you for especial emphasis on clarity of signposting, navigation, expression, argument structure, accuracy, and accessibility.

Audiences for other products

There is often a requirement to make presentations at various stages in research to audiences of academics (for example to gain approval to progress from MPhil to PhD research) or to fellow students and tutors. For academics in particular, the objectives of the research need to be made clear at the start, the arguments must be coherent (and the presenter needs to be ready for searching questions on the particular interests of those present). Hamid deliberately sought an opportunity for trying out his ideas on an expert audience:

Hamid — I planned to present a conference paper once I had some preliminary results, just to get some expert feedback and have my work assessed informally by referees and experts. I thought this would help me to know if I was going in the right direction or if there was anything terribly wrong with my research. I managed to have a paper accepted for a prestigious conference, my paper was reviewed by four referees, and I found that reassuring.

For fellow students presentations can be more informal, but they still have to be as coherent and as thorough as you can make it – that's a necessary courtesy to every audience.

In some cases you may have the chance to make a presentation to an audience who are professionals from the discipline in which you are researching but not necessarily academics, as Justin did.

Justin The first seminar presentation on *'Corporate information and knowledge management: a portal strategy'* ... was organized by the British Council, Lusaka, Zambia. ... More than 150 participants attended ... and these included information technology professionals, MBA students, library and information studies students, librarians and documentalists. ...

Holding it outside a university environment, ensured that all kinds of people ... with interest in information management, knowledge management and portals, attended the presentation. Their contributions in terms of questions and comments helped a lot.

For audiences comprising a mix of specialisms, or specialisms different from your own, clear careful explanations of purposes and findings, attention to terminology, and respect for different disciplines and their specialist knowledge are essential. If you do all that you should, like Justin, get good value from their contributions.

In all presentations, whatever visuals you use should be as good as you can make them—even if you are limited to PowerPoint slides you don't have to stick with the standard lists with bullet points to which so many of us have dozed off.

You may be required to submit articles about the research to scholarly or professional journals, either before submitting your dissertation, or as a follow-up to it.[2]

Either way, take it as an opportunity to bring what you're doing to an interested wider audience, and to learn more about presenting information in different kinds of 'container'. Study the journal's guidelines for authors, and the journals themselves, to get an idea of standard length of articles, style of writing, layout, heading structure, etc. It can be an interesting exercise to keep within those constraints, and to follow the conventions of scholarly discourse in the relevant discipline, while still writing like a human being in recognizably human language!

2
As Hamid points out, because articles 'are considered more serious works and more rigorous and they are supposed to last for longer, PhD students usually tend to publish their good journal articles after their viva because it is less risky, unless it is a kind of literature review or so'. A prudent consideration!

Other people whose interests must be taken into account

At an early stage we need to make a careful list of everyone who comes into this category, so that we establish contact at the right time, let them know what we seek from them, negotiate their contribution, agree when and how it will be made, how it will be used in the end product, arrangements for them to check and amend drafts, and the appropriate form of acknowledgement. The information we get from those exchanges will make it possible to decide how best to present and/or acknowledge their contribution in the end product of the research. Two main groups need to be taken into account in this connection.

Providers of essential information

In Chapter 3 (pages 58–61) we discussed dealing with people as sources of essential information on which the research depends: as respondents to questionnaires, interviewees, subjects for testing products, etc. When we start to plan the end product, we need to establish appropriate design standards for presenting data, analyses and descriptive text based on the information they provide – and to establish an appropriate format for acknowledgements. (See Chapter 9.2 pages 196–217.)

People without whose help the end product can't be created or delivered

We have already seen the unexpected delays that a number of recent researchers encountered in getting ethical consent to start approaching people as suppliers of information, and in extracting promised responses once they had got their sample together (see Chapter 5 page 112).

There are others whose help is necessary at the opposite end of the research process: the providers of essential services without which the end product cannot be brought out and delivered. Make sure you take their interests and their other commitments into account in time when you are planning.

If dissertations etc. have to be delivered in conventional print on paper, allow for demands on the reproduction unit, bindery, etc. Remember that they, and other technical services whose support you need, will have simultaneous demands from other researchers, be clear about what you will need from them, and get your requests in early to help their scheduling.

You need to know what format(s) the institution requires the end products to be presented in, and what medium they will be retained in for reference – whether paper or electronic, and to think about the implications for design decisions, and for the kind of essential metadata/labelling you need to provide to help future users to find your research, assess its relevance, navigate through it etc. (See Chapter 10, pages 250–252 and 256 for more about these elements.)

The most important elements in the research

We have to make a judgement on the most important features that have come out of the research, so that we can help all users of the end product to recognize them and understand their significance, and so to take from it at least some of the most valuable knowledge we have gained. Our answers will allow us to make design decisions on how to give those elements proper emphasis, to place them appropriately within its structure, and to present them in ways that match the nature of their content, and make clear the significant conclusions – using the verbal, graphic and typographic means discussed in Chapters 9.1–9.3 and 10.

For all readers, the most important elements will include:

- Anything that is ground-breaking about the research: a problem that hasn't been looked at before; a new approach to a question which has been the subject of other research; findings that differ significantly from those of other studies; new applications of existing methods or use of innovative methodology.
- Any changes of direction in the course of the research, and the reasons for them; key turning points; new syntheses of ideas. Potential value from applications of the research findings (see Figure 6.1 on page 135).

In Chapter 4 (see pages 93–100) we suggested how you could fairly painlessly, in the everyday course of research, assemble a useful resource of this kind of information from notes from review sessions, examples of materials created to collect information, diaries of new ideas and insights.

Using the answers to plan the end product

These are the answers I gave to the questions in relation to my own research on the role of organizational information products. I have to admit that I didn't actually set them out in this tidy format, but this is a fair representation of the thinking I did before starting to write.

Liz *The most important elements in the research*

A new approach

- Information products, and their design in the widest sense, have seldom been looked at, as they are in this research, in the context of the organizations which create and use them in the course of their business, or in relation to information management and organizational information strategies.
- There should be an opportunity for developing an innovative theory of information products on the basis of the findings.

Application of a pioneering methodology

While there are sound arguments for taking a primarily qualitative approach to the research, it is also desirable to complement it if possible with an approach that will yield relevant quantitative data. I was fortunate in meeting a professor of systems engineering who has developed a new methodology for expressing qualitative values in quantitative terms, and was able to benefit from his guidance in a small-scale application of the method in one of the case-study organizations.

Significant findings

- The activities associated with information products are diffused in most organizations; there is no overview of the whole range, and they are neither seen nor managed as a whole.
- They are not usually integrated into organizations' use of information to achieve their ends, in particular they are not seen as part of information/knowledge strategy and information architecture.
- There is little monitoring and evaluation of the processes by which they are created.
- The professional skills of information designers are not usually recognized or understood by organizations, and not often applied to their information products.
- The skills and knowledge of information managers and information systems/IT managers are relevant and necessary for the creation and management of information products, but are seldom applied in this context.
- The findings suggest that all three of the specialisms mentioned should collaborate on the creation of information products, but it rarely if ever happens.

Potential applications

The results of the research could be applied in various ways:

- Development of modules on the management and design of information products in information management/information science courses.
- Applications of the established methodology of information auditing by organizations to their information products, as a basis for up-grading how they develop and manage them.
- A follow-up information product to support organizations in man aging their information products.[3]

That bit of thinking was helpful for the decisions I made on structure, content and emphasis, and on appropriate forms of presentation. I had decided from the start on a primarily qualitative methodology, based on long-term case studies in a variety of organizations. This meant that, while the end product should

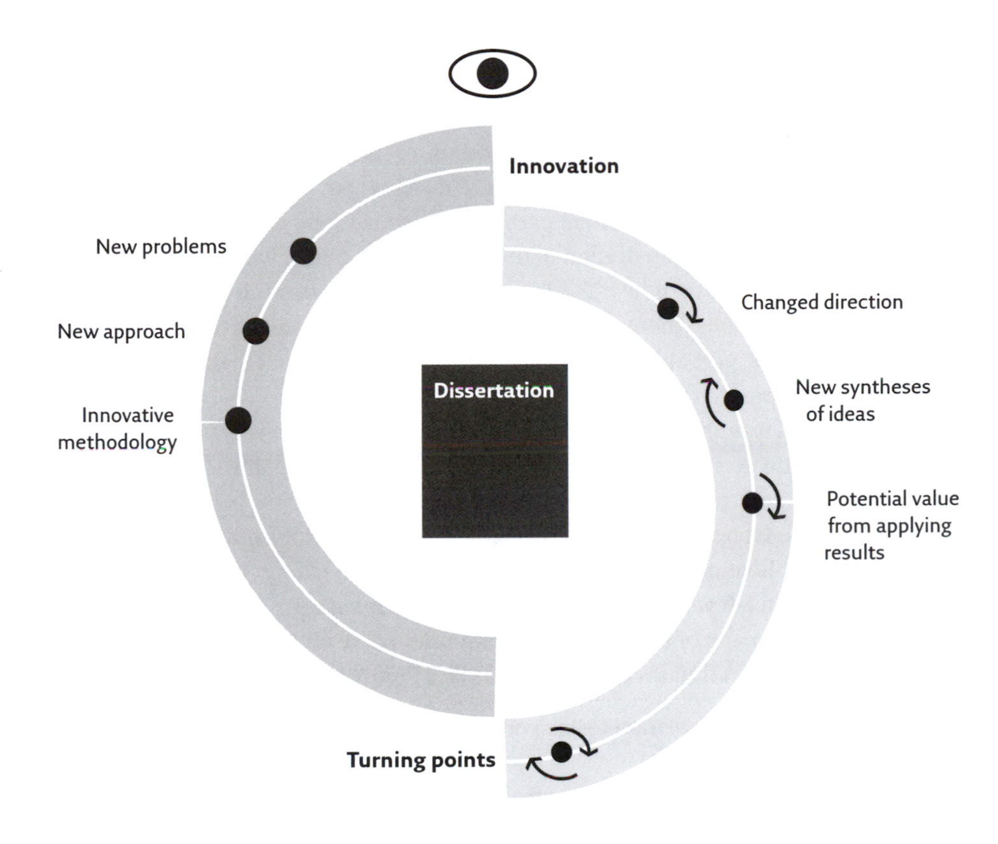

Figure 6.1 The most important elements in the research

fit the traditional thesis structure, some modifications would be essential in order to handle the case studies that were such a major feature of the work. It was part of the deal with organizations that I should provide them with a report to management, and these reports would make a basis for what appeared in the thesis. I decided that it would be best to put the case studies into a separate section, possibly separately bound, so that readers could get the full flavour and see examples of the products. The main text would have to present accounts of what happened in particular organizations under relevant headings, as evidence and illustration of the points being made, with cross-references to the full case studies. To allow read-across between the practice of different organizations, there would need to be standard headings for discussing the findings, probably those used in the interviews, which themselves derived from the research questions established at the start.

At that point, I was able to visualize the structure of the thesis very clearly, and to see the inter-relations of the various parts of it; I was also able to make a list of the kind of information elements it would need to embody to present the content for which typographical standards would be needed (for example, lists various kinds, bibliographic references, cross-references, heading hierarchies, tables, captions, etc). It was helpful at this stage to make myself an annotated picture of the main parts of the thesis, with reminders of useful things I had thought of while answering my own questions (see Figure 6.2).

There remains one final question to ask yourself ...

What do I want to achieve from the research?

It's an important question because research is one of the few occasions when you are responsible for making all the decisions. Even if someone else assigns the research topic, rather than the researcher choosing it, from then on the main responsibility is the researcher's.

So it is important to make the most of having that degree of control. As a researcher you will gain some unique knowledge from what you do, and you should make sure readers understand it, appreciate its value and as far as possible see it through your eyes in the 'silent conversation' with readers which takes place through the medium of the text. If the research has captured your enthusiasm – and it's a sad business if it hasn't done so at least at some point – then you should try to transmit that to readers.

Even if *you* take no thought about such matters, readers, especially examiners, will form their own view and it will enter into their judgement of what you present to them, so it's as well to try to make sure that the impression they take from it is both fair and favourable! This is not just a matter of presenting yourself in the best light to the examiners, though it is indeed important that they should form a proper estimation of the researcher as a person; more signifi-

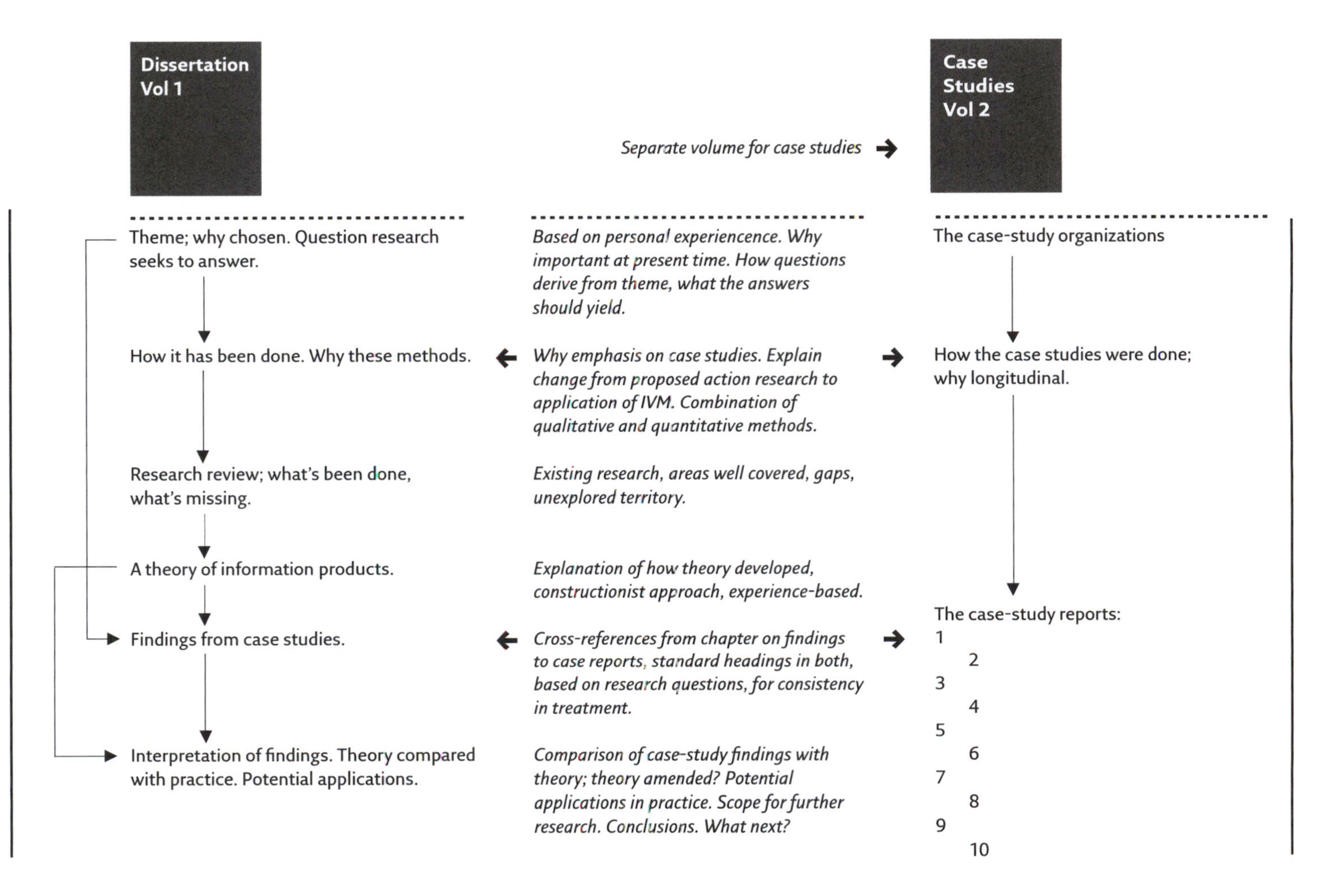

Figure 6.2 Annotated dissertation structure

cantly, it is a unique opportunity for self-realization, which can lay the foundation for further development towards taking control of your life and work.[4]

It's worth setting out your thoughts on this at the start of the research, returning to them at intervals in the course of it, and updating them at the end of the process as part of your evaluation of the research – which may in some cases be a required part of the final submission.

At the beginning of research it is important to consider questions like these, because the answers tell you what readers will need to know about you as researcher in order to understand what you present to them:

Why am I looking at this research question? What makes it important for me? A long-standing enthusiasm? Previous experience? A new discovery? Something in my background that makes me a particularly appropriate person to look at this?

As you near the end of the process and can look back over your experiences and what you have learned, the key questions to ask yourself are:

How effectively has my research done what I set out to do? What I have *not* attempted in the research and why not? What have I gained from doing it? What criteria would I wish my work to be judged on? (You will certainly need to consider this if your institution requires something like the 'assessment contract' mentioned in Chapter 4, pages 90, 92, 93.)

Your answers will help to shape decisions about what else you need to tell readers about yourself. They will also help you to consider the style of presentation that can express the person you are – and perhaps how to reconcile that with institutional constraints. (I have to say that for myself that when I read the work of researchers I prefer something that sounds like an authentic individual human voice, rather than an automaton conforming to convention.)

Researchers who, like some of those quoted in this book, have come to research after a number of years of work, which has shaped their decisions about their subject, tend to have thought about these questions and invest much of themselves in the work, as Paula did: 'This was a piece of work at the end of several years of study. It was a very precious piece of work and I wanted it to be perfect.' (But she added realistically: 'There has to be a level of acceptance towards the end that it will never be quite perfect!')

Support from supervisors

Supervisors and tutors can do a lot to help researchers as they approach this aspect of research. Continued support of the kind mentioned in Chapter 4 (pages 101–102) is very important – especially through well-maintained tutorial exchanges and awareness of situations for which the institution may make

4 And readers may be interested to know that one of the things tutors and supervisors sometimes complain about is students' passivity and lack of personal identification with their research, manifesting itself in timidity, unwillingness to take initiatives, and failing to find a personal voice. *It's yours, so make the most of the chance.*

special provision when it comes to preparing dissertations, such as dyslexia, working in a second language, or difficulties in vision or hearing. They will certainly be aware from experience that the stages of research associated with presenting the end product are liable to be stressful, and should be ready to spot signs of undue anxiety and to offer appropriate help.

It's particularly helpful at this point to encourage students in using their experience of the research as it develops – as expressed in research diaries for instance (see Chapter 4, page 97) – as an aid to planning the final product; and to check whether they are using whatever information-management systems they have set up in developing a structure for the end product, and assigning relevant content to appropriate places.

If the researchers face an assessment interview or a viva, this is also the time to start helping them to prepare themselves for it. It's an experience that many researchers don't look forward to, and it can produce some unpleasant surprises such as the one described in this cautionary tale:

A PhD candidate at her viva encountered a situation for which her supervisor could have prepared her, but did not. Her work had been commended all through her university career, but there were some aspects of academic life that she had so far not encountered. She was unaware that examiners who subscribe to a different school of thought from that followed by supervisors of the research they are examining have been known to use a viva as a means of settling scores with their opponent, and making the luckless candidate into an incidental sacrifice. And so she walked without warning into just such a situation at her viva: knowing nothing of the background, she found her thesis under ferocious attack by the external examiner – who had previously crossed swords with her supervisor. Not knowing what was behind it, she was too shocked to make an adequate defence, and was notified after the viva that there was doubt over whether she should be awarded her doctorate. She spent a very unhappy few weeks of self-doubt and distaste for her previous academic ambitions before the matter was resolved in her favour – the authorities having apparently recognized what underlay the events. Had she been made aware beforehand, she could have prepared to repel an unjust attack, and avoided the consequences.

Summary

If you answer the questions posed in this chapter, you will give yourself:

- Understanding of the people who will read the end product – especially examiners – and of how they will want to use it, and what that means for structure, content, sequence, verbal and visual expression.
- A list of everyone whose help you will need in creating the product and getting it actually produced, and what you need to do to ensure their co-operation.
- Recognition of the most significant and valuable elements of your research, that it's essential for all users to understand.
- Insight into how you as researcher wish to present yourself in the end product, and what you need to tell readers about yourself so that they can fully appreciate your research.

You will then be equipped to make sound decisions on the design of every aspect of the end product, and to give yourself a guide to using them in creating it.

You may be interested to know that the answers to the questions are the sort of information that information designers need from clients who commission them to design information products for them. It forms the basis for the 'Design Brief' they work to – a framework within which they can bring their skills to bear on designing a product that does the job the client wants. The next chapter will tell you how to use your knowledge of your own research to prepare a design brief for your own dissertation, research report, or thesis.

References

Websites referred to this chapter accessed on 18 March 2000

Orna, E (2005)
Making Knowledge Visible.
Aldershot: Gower.

EThOS service
http://www.ethos.ac.uk/

Further reading

Biggam, J (2008)
Succeeding with your Master's Dissertation: A step-by-step handbook.
Maidenhead: Open University Press.
Includes useful advice about helping examiners (and yourself) by understanding the marking schemes they use.

De Guire, E (2006)
Publish or perish: afterlife of a published article.
http://www.csa/discoveryguides/publish/review.php

Phillips, E M & Pugh, D S (2005)
How to get a PhD. Ed 4.
Maidenhead: Open University Press.
Treats the form of the thesis at an early stage, and emphasizes the importance of self-evaluation as part of it.

A design brief for your dissertation

Ch 7 Contents at a glance

7

Introduction

The last chapter introduced the idea of a design brief for the end products of research. In this chapter we shall explain what designers mean by design briefs, and show how researchers can use their unique knowledge of their own research to build a brief that they can use in planning an end product that does justice to their work, and enables readers to do justice to them. The brief can be built up over time, starting early in the research, and developing with it.

A design brief starts with an outline specification by a 'client', for a required product. This initial specification consists of something like this:

- Description of product and purpose
- Features it should possess
- Constraints to be met (e.g. cost, wordage, materials, etc)

Sometimes it is very helpful—and sometimes not.

Ideally, the client's first outline is added to in the course of developing the brief—by the designer and any others commissioned to deliver the product (e.g, providers of content, writers)—through exchanges with the client. The resulting final brief then embodies the application of the specialist knowledge of the designer and others to the client's initial statement, and forms an invaluable basis for examining relevant options for meeting the requirements, and finding appropriate solutions.

In the case of research, the client who provides the initial brief is the institution where the research is being done, and the researcher fulfils the roles of designer and everyone else responsible for developing the final brief and delivering the product.

The development of a design brief

Designers often complain that the briefs which clients give them both lack the information they really need, and specify too precisely what the end product should be like:

> *'Designers frequently find themselves having to work with a brief which imposes the client's preconceived view of the end result.'*
>
> *'Clients seldom understand that the essence of the designer's skill is constant visual analysis, which can lead them to investigate what lies behind the brief as initially presented, and to find that the real design problem is quite different from what was presented.'*
> (Two designers, quoted in Orna, 2005)

Readers may be interested to know how the design brief for this book was compiled. It was agreed on after a synopsis for the new edition had been submitted and a contract signed, and when work had started on the writing and exploratory design work. At this point we had an informal meeting at the publisher's headquarters with the editors responsible for the book and the production manager, to discuss the work submitted and get some feedback on the outline design proposals.

As designer, I showed examples of the proposed page design, based on what had been written so far. The most important considerations at this stage, however, were to establish how, and where, this academic book was to be printed and produced, what production constraints would be imposed, and what quality of printing we could expect to see. Designers can deal with some of the problems of printing quality by studying example material from the printers concerned, but if you neglect to get answers on the production constraints that will operate, you will have to suffer the consequences, and this is why it is so important to establish a clear design and production brief.

The design brief as given by the publisher

This is a summary of the brief as given by the production manager at our meeting, and elucidated through a series of questions and answers.

1. Format (book size): Either 229 x 152mm or 240 x 170mm
2. Paper: a standard stock paper of 90 gm^2, frequently used for similar textbooks. Print colour: black; tints will have a screen ruling of 130
3. Maximum number of pages: 272
4. Location of printing: at present uncertain; 90 per cent chance that it will go to a printer in Europe, 10 per cent that a printer in the UK will get the job. If printed in Europe the book would be thread sewn, if in the UK it would be notched bound. From the point of view of the designer a thread-sewn book is preferable to a notched bound one. The reasons are technically straightforward: in thread-sewn books, batches of folded pages, known as *sections*, are joined together by a continuous thread, and then a thin layer of glue is applied to the spine. In notched binding, the folded sheets are notched during the folding operation and the book is held together by 'stitches' of glue, penetrating the notches. The glue holds the sheets together, but the glued sheets are prevented from opening flat to the spine. Notched binding is less functional, because the glue restricts the natural opening mechanism, whereas the much older method of thread-sewing books does not.
5. The uncertainty over the way the book is to be bound affects the width of the back margins. In notched bindings you have to allow for wider margins, a) to compensate for the folds being cut off, and b) to allow for the fact that the book can never open completely flat because of the binding method. This demands additional design work in finding an appropriate solution to the page structure.
6. Cover: soft cover, with the design printed in three colours
7. Target audiences:
   Primary readership: Postgraduate researchers for master's and doctoral degrees. Other readers: undergraduates doing smaller-scale research projects; supervisors and tutors of research students.

Questions still needing an answer

This brief is technically far from complete, but most of the detail concerns the typographical specifications that deal with the micro and macro level. As the designer I now know what the format is, and in addition I have all the technical background information necessary to begin the preliminary design work.

As co-author, having worked with the other author on developing the proposal for the new edition, I also have information about the structure of book, the number of parts and chapters into which it will be divided, the nature of the text – which is complex – and the number and levels of the subheadings.

There are, however important questions still unresolved. Most significant is the choice of paper, which will depend on the printer selected. That in turn influences, among other things, what typefaces to use, and in what point sizes, and how to design the numerous illustrations. This question can be answered only by arranging with the printer, when chosen, to run one 16-page backed section on the actual paper that the publisher intends to use, closely examining the finished result, and making design decisions in the light of it.

Building your own design brief: a framework for action

It is important to realize that the primary process of writing and designing a short-run dissertation is exactly the same as writing and designing a mass-produced academic book printed in hundreds of copies; the only differences are in the processes that follow page origination. Much of the information in the brief quoted for this book has a close parallel with what you need in assembling your own dissertation brief, in particular, the institution's requirements regarding paper size and weight, maximum length, binding and cover, together with any other stipulations affecting the visual appearance and structure of dissertations.

Most researchers are unlikely to have the specialized knowledge, based on lengthy education and experience, which professional designers bring to their work, so Chapters 9.1–9.3 provide guidance and models designed to ensure that the dissertation they present will meet appropriate standards. Unfortunately, the general lack of attention to this aspect of research means that very often the visual presentation of dissertations does not match, and may actually conceal, the quality of the work they report on.[1]

As explained earlier, a final design brief often embodies a range of knowledge besides the kind discussed above, including that of the people who will be responsible for the content – and that of course is the case when the end

1
Many higher degrees today are for 'practice-based research', in which made objects of various kinds – from textiles to books, recordings of performances, installations, films, etc – are a major part of the work presented. In that case, one of the main things researchers need to do is to plan their written submission to complement the artefacts, by commentary and explanations that can be conveyed only in words – another aspect of design.

product is a dissertation. These are the questions researchers need to ask and answer about their own research in order to produce a design brief that will be a reliable reference source for all the things they will need to do in designing and creating a worthy end product.

1 The research: its subject, purpose, and objectives?
2 The audience(s) to whom dissertation is addressed: Who are they? How will they want to use it?
3 Rules to be met? Options to be considered?

- Physical features, medium, format, etc.
- Content and how it should be organized
  Obligatory content features for dissertations
  Options to consider
- Style of presentation required
  Obligatory house style elements, e.g. style for references
  Options to consider
- Time constraints affecting delivery of dissertation.

To complete this chapter, here is an example of a design brief compiled by a researcher (the co-author of this book) at a point when the research proposal, with details of objectives, subject, methodology, etc, had been accepted, and the research had begun. It sets out the researcher's answers to the questions, and her comments *(in italic)* on the implications as she saw them at that point for the visual, conceptual and verbal design of her thesis.

Design brief for thesis

Title: The role of information products and presentation in organizations

Q The research: subject, purpose/objectives?

A This research looks at how organizations manage that area of their activities whose function is to give essential information to their inner and outside worlds, in the form of 'information products', print on paper or electronic, through which information is presented for use. It sets them in a context in which they have not commonly been considered – the organizations which create them – and it seeks to illuminate them with relevant research and practice from the disciplines of information science and information design.

The questions it seeks to answer:

1 Does the way organizations manage the processes of creating information products and presenting information affect how well they do in achieving their strategic objectives in such matters as information flow, communication, cost-effectiveness, efficiency?
2 If investigation suggests that it does, is it possible to raise awareness of the relevant issues and achieve positive change through action based on principles from the disciplines of information science and information design?

Comment
This will form part of the Abstract, and the ideas will need to be expanded and discussed, with definitions of essential terms, in the Introduction.

Q Audience(s) to whom dissertation is addressed: Who are they? How will they want to use it?

A Examiners: for assessing quality, deciding on award of degree.
Comment
An unusual subject, which involves extending the territory of information science a bit! Information products and information design will probably be unfamiliar areas to the university examiner (let's hope the external will be selected for knowledge of them!). So I need to give particular attention to defining them at the start, and to arguments for their relevance to organizational information strategy and information management. Literature review will need to be very thorough and well organized, to show both what exists – especially in the unfamiliar areas – and what has been little discussed so far in the literature. Given the subject of the research, the end product will have to be a good example of information design in all respects.

A Future researchers/practitioners in this area: for purposes of their own work.
Comment
They need all the above, and maybe an evaluation from the researcher's point of view.

Q Rules to be met? Options to be considered?

1 Physical features, medium, format, etc?

A Institutional requirements (set out in the university's *Research Studies Guide)*

- Medium: has to be submitted in hard copy
- Format: A4, double-sided; high-opacity paper
- Length: maximum 100,000 words; if over 300 pages, to be presented in two volumes of equal size.

Comment
These don't raise any particular problems.
Case studies will probably require a separate volume.

2 Time constraints affecting delivery of dissertation?

A Not specified by university.
Comment
I'm answerable only to myself on this, so I have to set time limit for myself. Five years from start date should permit longitudinal rather than snapshot case studies (which can be argued as an advantage), and allow interleaving research with other work.

3 Content and how it should be organized?

A Institutional requirements

- Organization of content:
  Obligatory: title page, contents page, lists of tables and figures, abstract.
  Suggested structure: Introduction (reasons for research on this topic, summary of previous work on it, research intentions, propositions to be examined/tested, definitions); Methods; Results; Discussion (interpretation of results and significance, relation to previous knowledge of theoretical framework); Conclusions.
- References/bibliography: suggests Harvard system
- Ethical implications: to be considered if research involves interviews, questionnaires, surveys, observation of people, etc.

Comment

Guidelines for thesis structure are OK, but in this case better not to put so much into the Introduction as they suggest; in particular the literature survey will be extensive and should be a separate chapter. And there should be an index!
Key features to emphasize will certainly include:

- *The innovative approach taken of looking at information products in the organizational context, in relation to information strategies and to the role of information management and information design*
- *Use of researcher's relevant previous experience to help shape inquiries in case-study organizations*
- *Potential for applying an information-auditing approach to evaluating how organizations manage their information products.*[2]

Things users will need to understand about the researcher's qualifications for doing this research:

- *Why I chose to undertake it at this stage in my working life*
- *Topic and method allow drawing on a range of relevant experience of working in and with a variety of organizations, and with people from different disciplines*
- *Background of finding innovative ways of looking at subjects: e.g. initiative in looking at how museums manage information and writing a book about it in 1980, maintaining this interest, and using it to include a museum case study in present research*
- *The researcher's enthusiasm for the subject of the research and intention to make practical use of the findings.*

2
Case studies will involve interviews, so it will be necessary to agree ethical requirements to be met with each organization in matters of confidentiality, reading, amending and signing off drafts, and providing final report to management.

Q Style of presentation?

A The Research Studies Handbook doesn't say much about this.
Comment
I don't think I'm going to be able to observe what they suggest about using the passive voice! In which case I guess I'll have to add a note to explain why. There's hardly anything about such typographical elements as headings, spacing, line length, treatment of tables, etc. I'll need to define all those it's likely to require, and establish standards for them for reference – which will need professional advice!

Reference

ORNA, E (2005)
Making Knowledge Visible.
Aldershot: Gower.

The final transformation

The aim of this final part of the book is to show readers a practical and manageable approach to the final stages of creating the end product. It is based on experience: our own and that of the recent researchers who have contributed to the book.

The chapters that make up Part 4 apply the design approach to the second main theme of the book: creating the dissertation which embodies the results from gathering information and transforming it into knowledge throughout the research process.

Chapter 8 explains how to design the visual treatment of the end product and the actual written words as complementary parts of a single process. This is an approach that can take a lot of the stress out of writing.

Chapters 9.1 to 9.3 give practical and very professional advice on designing a coherent visual framework for the dissertation. If you follow it, it will free you to concentrate on writing without other distractions, and help your readers to find their way about the finished product without confusion.

The final chapter explains how applying the design approach to writing can help overcome the difficulties that so many of us encounter when we set out to write. Practical strategies that the authors and the researcher-contributors have found useful are gathered together in the section on 'Tips, time-savers and troubleshooting'.

Part 4

Integrating design and writing

Ch 8 Contents at a glance

‘We must acknowledge that the reader is doing something quite difficult for him, and the reason you don’t change point of view too often is so he won’t get lost, and the reason you paragraph often is so that his eyes won’t get tired, so you get him without him knowing it by making his job easy for him.’

Kurt Vonnegut, quoted by Donald Norman (Norman, 1992)

Introduction

This chapter is about the first stages of using a design brief of the kind described in Chapter 7. Like that chapter it is jointly written by both authors, each contributing from the point of view of their own professional background – in one case typographic design, and in the other writing – and in the light of many years of shared work and discussion of the subject.

On the basis of experience, we suggest designing the visual treatment and the actual written words as complementary parts of a single process, because it allows the end product to develop organically. If you have done the kind of thinking about your research recommended in the earlier chapters, you will be well equipped to apply this approach.

The context for the ideas put forward here is the difficulty that most of us experience in transforming three-dimensional dynamic knowledge inside our heads into a two-dimensional static and linear organization of information which we can put into the outside world. It is truly one of the most remarkable and distinguishing achievements of human beings, but few of us can accomplish it effortlessly and spontaneously.

We recommend taking it in stages, working from the outside in, from large-scale down to finer detail, starting with visualizing the overall structure of the end product.

Visualizing a structure for the end product

It's not surprising that one of the problems many researchers speak of is making a structure for the end product that will accommodate everything they've done and learned in the process, and allow them to show all the connections they've found, which are the basis for the interpretations they make and the conclusions they present.

While, as discussed in Chapter 6 (see page 126) some institutions provide researchers with a list of the main parts of a dissertation or thesis, it's only a start, and the real problem lies with how to organize what goes inside them. One thing that's noticeable, in fact, about many of the end products of research is the lack of headings and sub-headings within chapters. (It's curious that it should be so, because when you ask research students, as I did when writing the first edition of this book, what are the things that most turn them off when they are trying to read material that looks as though it's relevant to their research, the top one is always 'Acres of grey text without headings to give clues to the content'.)

This may be because the kinds of writing required at school and later – especially essays – don't demand much in the way of headings; perhaps they should! The lack of them in dissertations certainly deprives users of valuable indicators of where they are, and worse, the writers deprive themselves of focal points round which to structure what they write. So it's important to understand how to develop a consistent scheme of headings. Here is a visual metaphor that may help.

Progressive sorting

Try thinking of each chapter as a container for content of a given kind. Then imagine throwing into a 'holdall' folder for each chapter everything that looks as though it belongs there, without any attempt to sort it; and then visualize turning out the holdalls one at a time and sorting their contents into a set of smaller ones. If you apply that to the material you have collected and created, you will be on the way to an arrangement of the content that will tell whatever is the 'story' that each chapter has to impart. See Figure 8.1 on facing page.

This book was planned in much that way. As described in Chapter 7, it started off with a synopsis as part of the proposal for a new edition which the publishers had requested. When the proposal was accepted, I set up a 'holdall' folder for each chapter and into it dropped material as it came to hand or into mind – articles to refer to, downloads from useful websites, relevant answers from the responses of our researcher-collaborators, extracts from email exchanges with the designer/co-author, notes of ideas, relevant quotations. When we reached the stage of visualizing a framework to write into, a first tipping out of the contents (which sometimes caused me to wonder how and why they got there) made it possible to identify main themes for the chapters, and, as described below, to see what kind of standard features would be needed in the design of the book. Chapter 10 presents the further stages of the process in detail, taking the writing of that chapter as an example (Figures 10.1–10.4, pages 244 to 247). Those stages will give you:

A logical sequence for the material, from which it's possible to work out:

  A set of main headings for the contents, which in turn make the framework for:

  Sketch layouts, showing how the contents might be arranged and presented on the pages.

A useful return on the initial bit of sorting.

I find the metaphor of sorting things into appropriate containers is more concrete than that of hierarchies or family trees. Unless readers are acquainted with theories of classification – they will be if they are librarians, botanists or palaeontologists, but they account for only a small percentage of researchers – telling them to arrange what they write under an appropriate heading hierarchy isn't likely to make much sense to them.

Linear sequence and 'moving sideways'

Going through a process like the one just described helps to get the 'forward flow' of the content organized. That still leaves the occasions where a kind of 'sideways move', as shown in Figure 8.2, is necessary. That's one of the classic difficulties of transforming three-dimensional knowledge inside the head into two-dimensional information presented in a linear structure, and it often gives trouble to researchers when they are writing, because they are aware of so many lateral connections among the things they have been investigating.

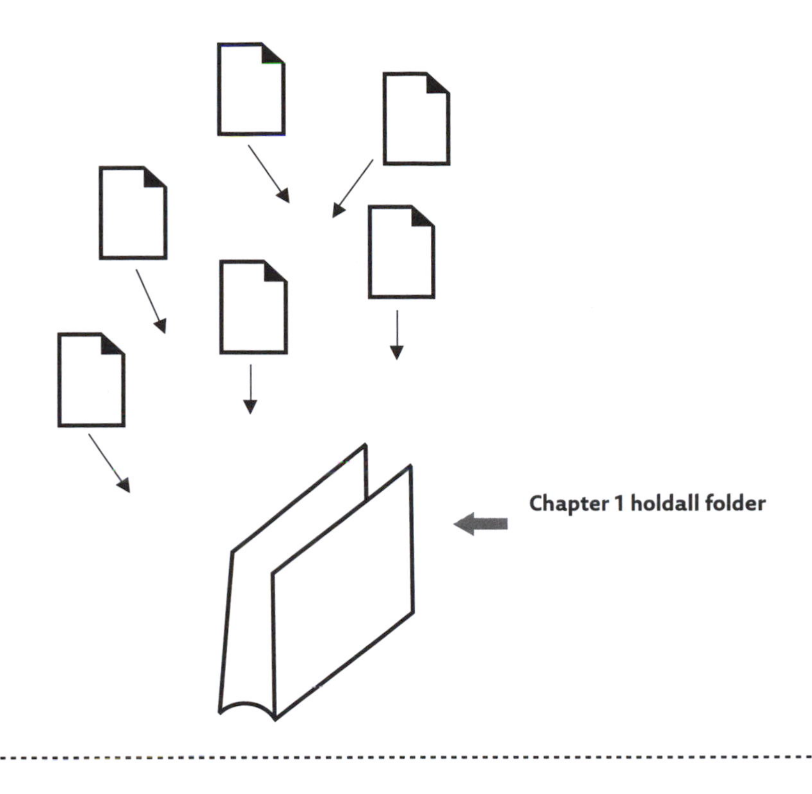

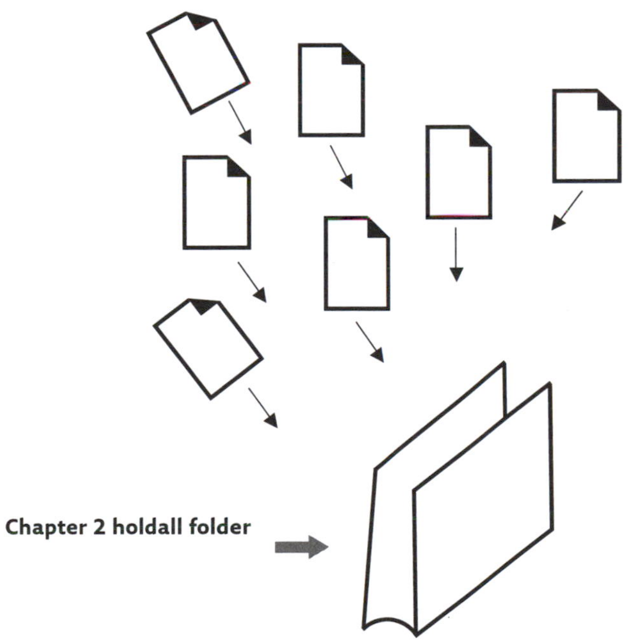

Figure 8.1 A holdall folder for each chapter

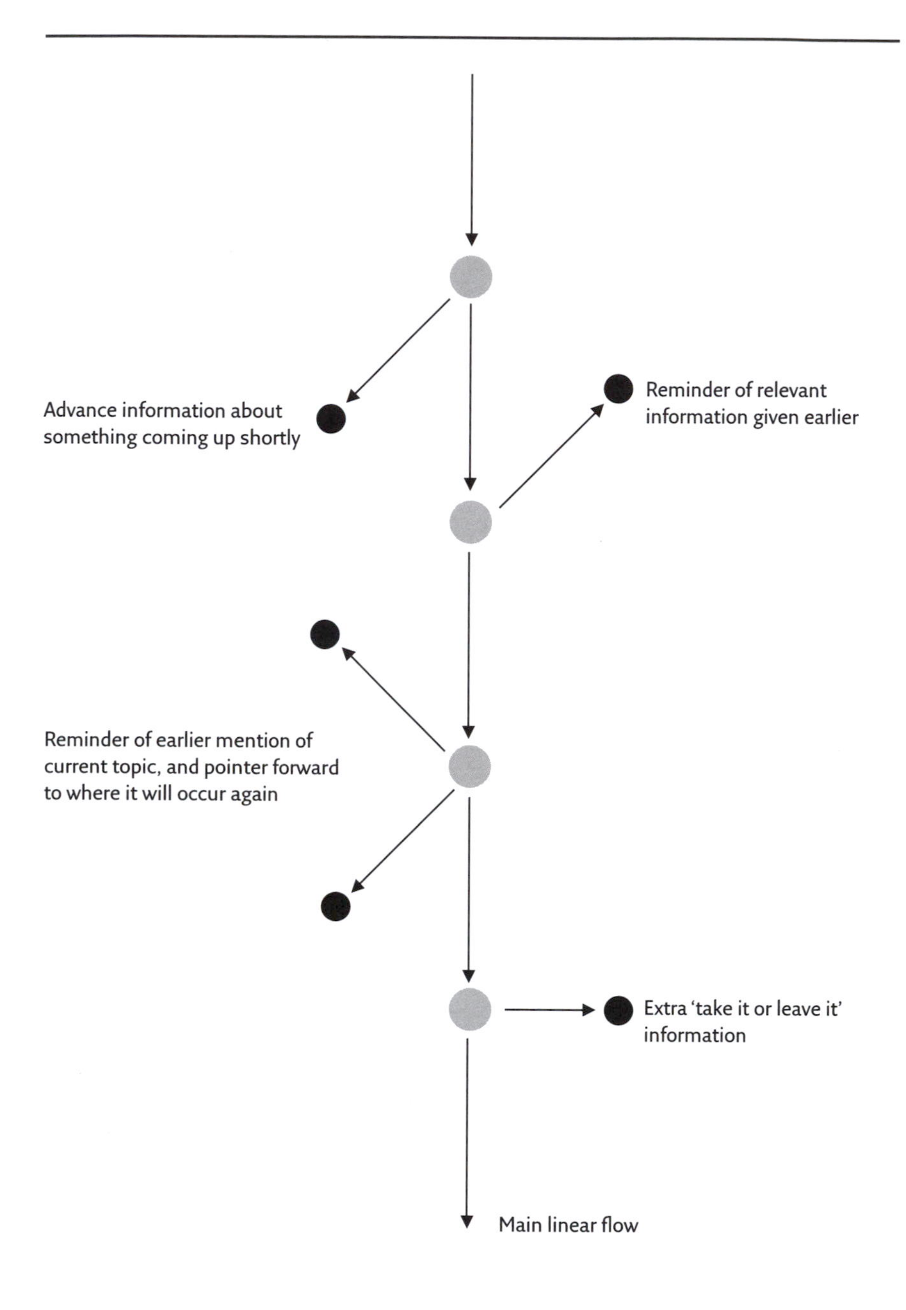

Figure 8.2 Two kinds of progress: linear and moving sideways

Examples:

- When the readers have to be given some advance information that they will need in order to understand something you haven't yet told them but which they will meet shortly.
- When readers need to be reminded of relevant information about the current topic, that they have been given earlier.
- The cases where the writer wants to offer a bit of extra information on a 'you can take or leave this' basis – perhaps something that will be useful to some, but not all, readers.

Showing linear sequence and sideways movement both entail using appropriate 'information elements'; so let us now introduce those.

Identifying information elements

What are they? They are features that will or may be required in the finished product, and they all have a role in helping readers to see where they are in texts and to find their way around them. Every information element used in the end product of research needs a design standard to ensure that it's treated consistently whenever it's used. If you identify the ones you need and create a set of standards for them first, it's one thing less to bother about while you are writing. The relevant obligatory and optional ones for dissertations are listed, with detailed advice on design, in Chapter 9.2 (pages 196 and 198–217).

The information elements which are helpful in dealing with the situations mentioned above, by the way, include footnotes (in the bottom margin of the page), 'sidenotes' (material presented in the outer margin) or text starting at a different point from the normal left-hand margin, and cross-references (forward and backward).

Don't forget the users!

Having mentioned that the information elements listed above are essential as a help to users, this is perhaps a good place to remind readers of what we said in Chapter 6 about how researchers should consider in the first place (and we mean *consider* in every sense of the word) those users who will decide whether or not the end product of their research will earn them whatever reward they are aiming at. It *should* be pretty obvious that their own interests coincide with those of the examiners in this matter, and that they had better give them all the help possible. But one does wonder sometimes if that elementary message has been grasped. As the writer and designer Donald Norman (1992/2004) puts it:

> *'What I find most peculiar about this business of writing and design is that these activities are presumably done for the benefit of others, so shouldn't the needs and abilities of those others be considered? A good writer and a good designer share many things in common. They need to understand the needs and abilities of their audience, and they must consider just how the product will be used.'*

He also points out something that researchers are not always aware of:

> *'once a person has worked hard on a design or writing project, they then know too much about the material to be able to step back and look at it with a neutral eye. Unintelligible sentences seem perfectly reasonable. Even misspelled words or only half-finished sentences can be overlooked. Awkward or dangerous design features can be passed by if the designer is too familiar with the work.'*

He concludes that before products reach the eyes of the end users they need the help of typical readers or users who can put them to the test, and be 'willing to speak of any difficulties they find'. This kind of 'diagnostic testing', based on collaboration between information designers and users, has been developed by the Communication Research Institute in Australia over a number of years, and, as described by Shrensky and Sless (2007), applied to many of the 'every-day' products we need to deal with in daily life. But it is hard to find people both willing and able to undertake this necessary service for the end products of research.

This makes a good point to introduce one more recent researcher, who has not previously appeared in these pages. Jane is a knowledge- and information-management specialist with long experience in local government; her job includes writing many 'information products' and, unusually, responsibility for a professional design team. I had the pleasure of working with her on an information audit for her authority (described in Orna, 2005), at a time when she was starting on part-time study for her Master's degree, and the audit became the subject of her thesis. Given that background, I asked her specially for her observations on the questions considered in this chapter, and, in spite of having more than enough to do at work, she kindly provided this response:

Jane — The majority of research papers I prepare require a draft report for consultation and agreement with sponsor and stakeholders. This version is then amended and a final version prepared and presented. My recent thesis followed a similar pattern and was submitted to my supervisor by chapters, draft and final version. Comments on chapters and the draft were provided and necessary changes made.

Planning
In preparing my thesis I followed the route I would normally take with any other publication or research paper. Planning the product starts before writing commences. It is vital to know who your audience is and to write in a style this audience will both expect and understand.

House style
All work products are prepared according to set guidelines and I used these in the production of my thesis. From a document's inception, house style is adhered to. This helps to ensure consistency through-

out the document, something which is not always easy if decisions have not already been taken on aspects such as capitalization, word form and use of abbreviations.

Having a house style also informs on use of fonts and other typographical issues. It provides a framework which again aids consistency in layout and presentation. It helps to prevent overuse of design tools which can so easily lead to a document in which design hinders readership.

Content and structure

The content, style and structure of the document will affect the way the audience responds to the message you are trying to relay to them. Does the structure aid this aim? Does the structure aid the reader? Will the reader need an executive summary, a list of contents, an index, a glossary? Should the content be arranged in chapters? And if so, what should the order be?

These were some of the questions I had to answer and take decisions on. The format for the thesis was laid down as to what it had to contain, such as methodology and literature review, but it did not stipulate the inclusion of items such as indices and glossaries. And ordering a great deal of information into logical chapters which flowed seamlessly into a coherent whole was not as straightforward as I had thought it would be.

To get the structure right, decisions had to take into consideration the order in which a reader would need to know something. Subjects could not be mentioned before they had been introduced. This ordering process helped to form both the introduction and the document structure.

Design

Normally, all research papers I produce would go through the design process. A design team transforms documents produced in Word into professionally produced products. However, for my thesis, I though it would be taking unfair advantage to make use of this team so I submitted it in its Word format. I did take care though to ensure all the headings, spacing, page layouts and page numbering were consistent and helpful to the reader.

If I had to start again, I think I would have asked my supervisor if I could use a professional design team. The finished product, despite all my efforts, would have looked so much better.

Jane's observations about design remind us that where writing/design integration happens in practice, it's usually done through collaboration between people from two different specialisms, like the great Czech designer Ladislav Sutnar and the architect and writer Knud Lönberg-Holm in the 1930s, who are described as working as 'two halves of one mind' (though the two halves had their disagreements, as when they didn't speak for a month after an argument about wording) and 'merging verbal and visual into a seamless whole' to produce the innovative building-products catalogue they created, and the books they wrote and designed. We recognize that we are doing something unusual in asking the same person – the already heavily burdened researcher – to use both halves of their mind on the task in hand. Our justification is that experience shows the attempt to do so pays off, as the next part of the chapter exemplifies.

How visualization can help in developing ideas

Using visual metaphors and other forms of visualization can help us not only with sorting out a logical arrangement of content, but also with critical intellectual tasks that are difficult to manage only by thinking and verbalizing. In research, particularly important tasks of this kind include interpreting the meaning of findings, developing new theory, or extending or questioning existing theory.

The whole subject of using visual means to help interpret observations, express the resulting ideas, and communicate them to others is today often called 'Knowledge Visualization'. Applications in various domains are discussed by researchers from a range of disciplines, and many techniques and software tools for applying them are on offer (see the list of references and further reading at the end of this chapter). Eppler & Burkhard (2004) in particular give helpful definitions and discuss the concept of knowledge visualization.

In the context of this book, it is particularly interesting that scientists have been among the most frequent and creative users of knowledge visualization since at least the 19th century and possibly earlier. They include those who, like James Clerk Maxwell, reached epoch-making insights into hitherto insoluble problems through visual metaphors that bring into play what he called 'a department of the mind conducted independently of consciousness'. When trying to develop a comprehensive theory of how electrical and magnetic fields interact with one another, Maxwell approached his aim by making 'an imaginary mechanical model of the combined electromagnetic field' which would visually account for all the effects observed in experiments (Mahon, 2003). The result was the well-known visualization of tiny spinning cells interspersed with even smaller particles acting like 'idle wheels', which resolved all the observed effects, barring electrostatic forces. At that point he was able to write up the mathematics; in the resulting paper (Maxwell, 1861), he was careful to explain that his visual model was not brought forward as 'a mode of connexion existing in nature' but as something that something that would help rather than hinder the 'search after the true interpretation of the phenomena.' After that, while he was on holiday in Scotland, the 'department of the mind conducted independently of consciousness' took over again, and provided him with another visual metaphor (of the cells being made of a material with a degree of elasticity), which solved the outstanding question of how electrostatic forces were transmitted.

In our own time, Richard Feynman was probably the greatest exponent of 'physical intuition' as the essence of creative insight in physics. By that he meant, as James Glieck (1992) puts it, 'not just visual but also auditory and kinesthetic' images, which were for him part of a process of 'putting oneself *in* nature: in an imagined beam of light, in a relativistic electron'. As Maxwell had done, he too found that what he expressed, in typically Feynman terms, as 'a half-assedly thought-out pictorial semi-vision thing', was an irreplaceable step towards the point where 'the mathematics can take over'. And he told his colleague Freeman Dyson (in a conversation quoted by Glieck), that when Einstein stopped creating it was because 'he stopped thinking in concrete physical images and became a manipulator of equations'.

Drawing on other capacities of the human mind than the verbal or mathematical ones isn't limited to scientists of genius grappling with the laws of nature! Researchers taking a qualitative approach to interpreting observed human behaviour sometimes do it too, and creating visual models is indeed something that many human beings do to try to explain the world to themselves and others. The experience of two of the researcher contributors to this book is an example.

Karen included in her original reply the intriguing remark that she liked 'using models of my own, and those I spend a long time creating in the "draw" function in Word, which is a quite annoying function really'. That interested me because it sounded like what I do myself when trying to sort out ideas so that I can express them clearly, so I asked her for more information. Her answer confirmed that we were doing the same kinds of thing:

Karen — I mostly have drawn models to sort out my theoretical framework. Since I use bits of several theories I try to draw their relations to one another and to my own study, or also I try to draw what I see happening in my empirical study – relations between different aspects, hypotheses about what I think is happening and such. I do this mostly to help my own understanding but I will include some of the final versions in my dissertation as well.

We are also fortunate in being able to present an extended account by a recent researcher (a university teacher, who also taught two of the researchers quoted in this book) of how she used knowledge visualization to solve a critical problem of interpretation in her own research. It shows how it can be a step to unlocking meaning that has so far defied interpretation and then communicating it to readers.

Using visualization to interpret the meaning of data
by Beverley French

Beverley — My PhD was about how nurses use information from research. I wanted to know how they decided what to do about particular problems in clinical practice, and how they used information from research to do that. I was particularly interested in their practical reasoning from research and its implications for clinical practice, so the method I chose was participant observation of nurses in clinical workgroups. These were a series of meetings of nurses from multiple hospitals and community health services across a Health Region. ... In all, I observed five clinical workgroups on different types of topics, such as how to manage fluid infusions, or how to promote self-care in children with asthma. ... In the main study, I taped group discussion from three clinical workgroups, each attended by 15–25 nurses, on 31 different clinical problems.

In observing, my concern wasn't with individuals, nor was I much concerned with the topic they were talking about. My interest was in *how* they talked about the topic, and where their information about it came from. That meant the focus was on analysing the *process of reasoning* that nurses might go through in considering information about topics, rather than on the actual content discussed. Clues to the processes involved were 'hidden' in the data: they lay in the types of statements or questions, the order things were said in, which points were debated and which were not.

Initially, I found it very difficult to separate out process from content, and to recognize these different layers of analysis. I found that drawing helped, however. What follows is an account of how I used visual methods of presenting data in my own study. It isn't offered as a model of a method, more as an illustration of how a visual approach might help in working though the process of analysis for particular types of studies.[1]

In my own study, although process was my primary interest, it seemed clear that I had first to try to approach it through understanding the *content* of the nurses' discussions. I tried different ways of modelling it.

In the first example, I took a specific problem (deciding how to change an intravenous infusion line) and tried to map not only the content of the reasoning – all the factors the nurses mentioned that they had to take into consideration in deciding – but also how it seemed to fit together, and where it came from. I used arrows of different colours to represent something about the type of relationship between the factors they talked about, such as whether it had a positive or a negative impact, and added words in colour to indicate information from different sources.

As well as that, the resulting 'factor map' showed features about the patient groups considered, details about the elements of the process, and interactions among them. Its 'movement' was from left to right, and it felt as though it captured some of the process of the nurses' reasoning, but it still illustrated more about the *content* of their discussion, rather than *how* they were reasoning.

A second attempt captured another aspect of their reasoning: the debate over different methods of tackling a clinical problem, in this case whether to use anaesthetic for urinary catheterization (putting a tube into the bladder). At this stage of the analysis I focused on how information from different sources contributed to the nurses' reasoning about whether or not to use anaesthetic. The form of the diagram was a flowchart with a succession of questions; the YES and NO answers were displayed in different colours according to the source of the information used (practice/personal experience; theory/ethics; or research). This told me what factors contributed to a decision outcome, but still didn't capture *what they were doing*.

The third map was another attempt to capture how the nurses expressed their reasoning about factors influencing a decision in practice – this time about how to assess the competency of parents for managing their child's asthma treatment. This one was a decision map, which showed the factors that nurses took into account in making their decision (such as severity of the asthma, and parents' feelings, knowledge and attitudes). It, too, allowed me to progress in my analysis, this time in understanding how the nurses 'fitted together' information from different sources, how they understood a problem

1

A combination of visual and technical considerations makes it impossible to reproduce the original figures described here, with the exception of the final one. The visual considerations arise from the fact that the original figures were designed for an A4 page whereas the size of the finished book is B5. Although in direct proportion to A4, B5 is considerably smaller with regard to the page size and text area, and that makes the surface area too small to accommodate the drawings in any sensible way. The technical reasons centre round the fact that the visual sizes of the typeface in their original form were either too small or the stroke of the typeface too fine to reproduce with any clarity; and, although experimental black and white and greyscale scans were carried out, there was no guarantee that the printer producing the book could reproduce the image with any degree of clarity on the paper being used.

All the figures – apart from the final one – really needed to be redrawn, changing the typefaces so they would reproduce well and removing the three colours and substituting black; but most importantly the visual complexity of the original designs needed simplifying and that entailed major changes in configuration and overall structure. This, however, was not possible, on grounds of time and cost.

and how they arrived at a decision. But it still didn't tell me the *process* by which they were doing all that.

At this stage, I felt as if I was drowning. I had represented the data every which way I could think of, and still I hadn't got to what I was really interested in – the process of reasoning. I couldn't think how to do it.

Then I decided to go back to the drawing board and map out each and every statement from the transcript on a time line through each of the meetings. The drawing that resulted gave me a plan for analysing four broad stages of practical reasoning that I had noticed in the data – description, analysis, evaluation, and application to practice – in order to see if I could recognize any similarities between the way in which the different clinical workgroups progressed through them in the course of their meetings. I made the analyses on an Excel spreadsheet, and then printed them out in a long, long sheet!

In their final version, these 'stages of practical reasoning' maps developed the four simple stages of reasoning I had started off with much further, into a series of questions relevant to each stage. The method of visually representing the analysis, however, was much the same as it was in the plan, with a graph of the sequence in which participants discussed questions over time, accompanied by relevant quotations. This was my breakthrough. When I laid out all 31 of these maps on the floor, I began to notice similarities in the way that each workgroup moved through their reasoning on a topic. From here, I had finally found a way of visually representing the hidden concept of 'a process of reasoning' that was enough to allow me to work with it.

The final drawing (shown in Figure 8.3 on page 167) – a comparatively simple one emerging from the complexity of the earlier drawings – shows three main stages, with sub-stages corresponding to the questions the nurses were asking about research and whether to use it in practice.

I don't think I would have arrived at the last stage of analysis if I hadn't had the thorough grounding in analysing the content of the nurses' talk beforehand, because it was while doing this that I was comparing how the nurses talked about different topics and noticing the broad stages they moved through. However, the maps weren't just useful in moving me through the process of analysis. They were also useful in illustrating that process for an external auditor, who checked both descriptive and interpretive validity. And in the final thesis they helped me to illustrate for the reader how I had analysed and interpreted the data. In that version, the process of practical reasoning

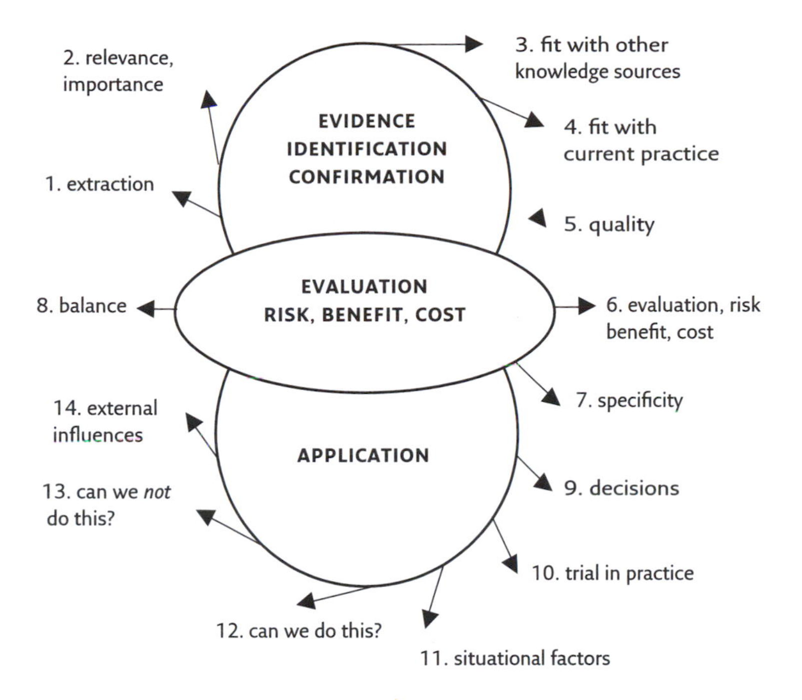

Figure 8.3 Final illustration of stages in the process of practical reasoning

is represented by three main stages, with sub-stages corresponding to the questions that the nurses were asking about research, and whether to use it in practice.

While it looks simple, it took a lot of work to get to it! As a novice qualitative researcher, I think the main value of the visual methods was that they gave me the confidence to defend my process of analysis, and, indeed, their thoroughness was commended by my examiners.

I don't think that visual representation is necessarily suitable for all forms of qualitative research. It could be argued that it is quite reductionist, in that it abstracts out certain features of the data from context. But I would argue that qualitative data are sometimes more closely related to image than to linear text, particularly in the representation of complex concepts and the relationships between them. It is to be regretted that as yet there is little guidance for qualitative researchers on the use of visual conceptual tools and the principles underlying their effective use in either the analysis or presentation of data.

Support from supervisors

The approach suggested in this chapter follows logically from what we have advocated throughout: treating research as a continuous process – rather than one chopped into different disconnected activities – in which the emphasis gradually changes and transitions are gently prepared for. Observation suggests that when the deadline for submitting the end product comes in sight, researchers are liable to start 'writing-up' without building an adequate scaffolding or framework to support them in the intensive, risk-filled and stressful job of writing. There are two possible reasons: either they are so eager to get on with it that they jump straight in, or so reluctant that they avoid it until it's too late to do anything but scramble through. Neither is likely to do much good for either their own comfort or the quality of the work they produce.

Supervisors and tutors can help them protect themselves against the uncomfortable experiences that result from these strategies by:

- Insisting on seeing a detailed structure plan at an appropriate point, not too early and not too late
- Introducing the ideas about information elements discussed in this chapter, and encouraging researchers to make their own list of those they will need, and to decide on and document the standards they will follow for them (Chapter 9.2 gives more help on this)
- Encouraging researchers to experiment with visual ways of showing structures, expressing relations between ideas, or making sense of observations.

Help from the software

Our research on software established that Microsoft Word is the universal choice for researchers when writing and designing their final dissertation. In university departments offering design research degrees probably 25 per cent of research students will use professional DTP packages for text design. That small percentage is not surprising when you know the steepness of the learning curve associated with these higher-level software packages.

Analysis of the content of an average dissertation will show that text is the predominant factor, with a small number of diagrams supporting the text. Photography doesn't seem to be used, except in dissertations dealing with some aspects of medical research.

Researchers appear to use the drawing facility of Word, but don't venture to use specialist drawing packages such as Macromedia Freehand or Adobe Illustrator, which again require extensive work to master their features.

Getting into Word

The advantage of using Word is that, compared to DTP packages, it is relatively easy to use, once you have discovered how to get into the various features. With some basic typographical knowledge you can achieve some very good basic page designs; while not sophisticated, they can be far better than anything produced on an electric or manual typewriter.

To attain this, you have to be prepared to spend some time understanding the extent – and the limitations – of what the software can do. To help readers with this, Chapter 9.2 offers a basic toolkit, which includes a set of templates for all the design elements commonly found in a dissertation, plus grids for A4 and US letter size, with accompanying notes and explanations. There is also a set of pages on the features available in Word for setting up the page design and composing continuous text. Chapter 9.3 offers help on choice of appropriate typefaces.

Summary

- It's hard for most of us to turn ideas inside our minds straight into written words. It helps if we take a 'design approach' through making mental and actual pictures in various ways.
- The first thing this visual approach can help with is planning the structure of the end product – from the broad divisions into chapters, through to finer divisions by appropriate sub-headings, and using a range of 'information elements' that will make the story of the research clear to readers (who don't have the researcher's close acquaintance with it), guide them through it, draw their attention to what's most significant, and make clear the evidence for the conclusions presented.
- If you do that successfully, you will be showing understanding and courtesy to those readers whose understanding of what *you* write is vital for you – the examiners.
- Visualizing can do more than just help us to sort out structure. It can be the key to interpreting the meaning of findings from the research, developing new theories to account for them, or questioning existing theories.
- And we can use the pictures we make to explain things to ourselves as a powerful means of making our ideas clear to readers.

The next chapters provide practical examples and help in using the design approach, by establishing visual standards for expressing the elements of structure. The final chapter deals with how to use the resulting framework as a secure scaffolding that will support you in writing, and allow you to concentrate without distraction on the hard thinking which it involves.

References

Websites referred to this chapter accessed on 18 March 2009

EPPLER, M J & BURKHARD, R A (2004)
Knowledge Visualization, Net Academy. University of St Gallen.
http://www.knowledgemedia.org/modules/pub/view.php/knowledgemedia-67

GLIECK, J (1992)
Genius. Richard Feynman and modern physics.
London: Abacus.

MAHON, B (2003)
The man who changed everything. The life of James Clerk Maxwell.
Chichester: Wiley.

MAXWELL, J C (1861)
'On physical lines of force',
The Philosophical Magazine, Part 1, March 1861; Part 2, April & May 1861.

NORMAN, D (1992)
Turn signals are the facial expression of automobiles.
Cambridge, MA: Perseus Publishing.
Chapter available on the author's website:
http://www.jnd.org/dn.mss/chapter_11_turn_sig.html
© 2004 Donald A. Norman.

ORNA, E (2005)
Making knowledge visible.
Aldershot: Gower.

SHRENSKY, R & SLESS, D (2007)
'Choosing the right method for testing'
http://www.communication.org.au/htdocs/modules/smartsection/item.php?itemid=64

Further reading, useful websites, etc.

STANDARDS AND MANUALS

BRITISH STANDARDS INSTITUTION (1972)
Recommendations for the Presentation of Theses,
(BS 4821, 1972).

SPINK, J E (1982)
A Manual for Writers of Research Papers, Theses and Dissertations.
(First British edition of Turabian, 1973).
London: Heinemann.

TURABIAN, K L (1973)
A Manual For Writers of Term Papers, Theses and Dissertations.
4th ed. Chicago: University of Chicago Press.

THE CHICAGO MANUAL OF STYLE ONLINE
http://www.chicagomanualofstyle.org/

VISUALIZATION

vizNET (UK Visualization Support Network). JISC project (2006–2009) to spread knowledge of visualization technology in the UK academic community. While its focus is on computing to achieve outputs, especially 3D, rather than on the thinking that precedes them, it does, however, aim to 'allow users to harness the phenomenal visualization resources that are available in even the most modest personal computer.'
http://www.viznet.ac.uk

Design is more than cosmetic: background and observations

Ch 9.1 Contents at a glance

On a hot summer afternoon in the summer vacation of 2006 I was visiting the library of a South London University where I was carrying out a visual audit on a selection of dissertations produced over a 10-year period and from a range of disciplines. At some point in the afternoon a student sat down at the desk opposite. He had a couple of bound dissertations in front of him and he was casually flicking through the pages in a random way and didn't appear to be stopping at any particular spot.

After a while I asked him what he was doing, and he explained that he was an MA criminology student and his personal tutor had advised him to visit the library and look at a few dissertations so he could learn the principles of how to design a dissertation.

I asked him what he was looking for, he replied 'I don't really have a clue, I suppose it's a matter of copying from one of these, once I start typing-up'.

Background to Chapter 9

In reply to the student who didn't have a clue' about how to design a dissertation, I commented, 'if you don't know what you are looking for how do you know how to progress? There are actually some fundamental rules about designing dissertations – or any products that are meant to be read.' I asked him if he would like a quick lesson in designing a dissertation. He answered yes, so I started doing rough drawings on A4 sheets of plain paper and went through the primary stages of designing a dissertation. What you will find in this chapter is an expansion of that impromptu lesson.

That means the strategy in this edition for helping researchers design their dissertation is very different from the one adopted in the first. There, I took a broad-brush approach to the subject of typography, which emphasized the primary knowledge that underpins the discipline. Each example given to illustrate the basic principles was carefully selected from sections of a first-year full-time BA design syllabus, which was based on established teaching methods used to introduce the subject to students of graphic, typographic and information design. These teaching methods, developed over a period of forty years, were based on a mixture of formal lectures, one-to-one teaching, workshops and tutorials. Their success in imparting this specialist knowledge was greatly helped by the regular contact which students had with their specialist tutors.

With the luxury of hindsight, it is probably true to say that the approach in the first edition was over-complicated for non-designers (that is, researchers without a formal design training), and that it would have been more helpful had it focused more directly on the design of dissertations. Readers new to typography who attempted to use it to design a dissertation – without the help of a specialist lecturer with whom they could discuss the issues – must have found that trying to select and absorb the appropriate pieces of knowledge from it to apply to the task was a slow and daunting business. This judgement is supported by the thoughtful comments provided, in preparation for the present edition, by academics who have used the first edition in their teaching.

A more focused approach

So in this new edition, the focus is primarily on the typographical knowledge and associated techniques for designing a dissertation. As before, the information is presented by means of a mixture of text and explanatory diagrams.

Chapter 9 is divided into three sections, reflecting three distinct aspects of the subject: how dissertation design is usually approached (or, rather, not approached); appropriate techniques and processes which non-designers can apply; and advice on avoiding poor design decisions.

This first section, Chapter 9.1, is entirely text-based and describes the background and findings of the visual audit specially undertaken for the purposes of this book in order to establish how average researchers go about designing their dissertations. This looked at the overall handling of individual page design, awareness of navigational aids, and how successfully the different kinds of text material were combined to form a connected whole.

Chapter 9.2 deals with visual planning, and explains what constitutes best practice in the design of dissertations. It provides smaller-than-actual-page-size printed examples – similar to a template – of all the basic elements that go to make up a dissertation. Each of these pages is given a part name and classified according to whether it is an obligatory or optional element of dissertations, in order to help researchers in the initial stages of design planning.

Chapter 9.3 presents some of the basic rules of typography that, once understood and put into practice, can help researchers to avoid submitting to the examiners work that makes the process of reading visually stressful for them.

How do researchers set about designing their dissertation?

In the summer and autumn of 2006, as designer as well as co-author of this book, I spent some time carrying out a detailed audit of how individual researchers went about designing their dissertations. The sample of dissertations was drawn from a number of universities in London; their subjects included visual arts, humanities, science, technology, criminology and medicine. The dissertations were mainly PhD or MPhil, with a small number submitted for the MA.

The overall purpose of the audit was to make observations on how effectively researchers deal with design issues in writing and presenting their dissertations. Its specific aims were:

1. To make a close study of the design and visual organization of dissertations completed in the last six years
2. To establish at first hand just how researchers were using PCs and word-processing software in the present educational environment
3. To observe whether there was any evidence that researchers had acquired any basic typographical knowledge while studying in higher-education institutions
4. To look at the overall design standards of dissertations produced before 1980 when the technology was simpler, and from the end of the 1980s onwards when PCs were becoming more commonplace.[1]

1
The technology of the manual or electric typewriter was the method used to design dissertations in the 1980s. I was also aware of the potential that this now obsolete technology offered to designers of documents.

Questions asked	Recorded answers
What is the overall structure of the document?	This recorded each individual part of the document, and was ticked off against a checklist. It covered the following parts: title page, abstract, acknowledgements, contents page, list of figures, individual chapters, use of hierarchical headings in text (A, B, C), footnotes, notes, appendices, bibliography, index.
How is the overall page organized?	This was concerned with the way the document had been set up: What were the dimensions of the margins; had single or multiple columns been used; what mode of typesetting had been selected?
What typefaces and specfications for text setting have been chosen?	This looked at: What typefaces (fonts) had been used. Was the text typed with a justified right-hand edge, or an unjustified (ragged) right-hand edge? What was the number of words in a line of text?
Is the finished dissertation easy to read?	Did the text use hierarchical headings as a navigational aid to the reader? Were the basic typographic rules about how to achieve comfortable reading applied? How much understanding was there about spatial page organization as a method of grouping and separating elements of text information? Did the dissertation contain any graphic material?

Table 9.1.1 Questions asked on the 2006 audit

Asking the questions, and recording the answers

Table 9.1 shows the detail which the audit looked at. The observations were recorded on specially designed A4 forms and checked against Microsoft Word default parameters. The results have informed the content of this chapter as well as the design and content of the typographical models. See pages 199–217.

Observations on the findings

The findings are very similar across the whole range of dissertations, apart from those of researchers who had studied graphic, information or product design and a few notable exceptions from other disciplines. They suggest that the majority of researchers lacked the necessary typographic knowledge for designing pages which are easy and comfortable to read; they seemed to be unaware of how to avoid placing obstacles in the path of their readers, and in many cases produced documents that could be described as visually illiterate, rather than achieving visual clarity. The main manifestations of this are:

1 Pages with acres of grey and monotonous text and very little to relieve the monotony. (An interesting observation, because, as noted in Chapter 8, page 155, when researchers are asked what features hamper their search for information in texts, this is the feature they mention as the worst obstacle to finding it)
2 Excessively long reading line with too many words, making it far more difficult to read
3 Frequently an absence of headings in the text to help the reader to navigate and follow the story
4 Little appreciation of the importance of using horizontal and vertical space as a technique of grouping and separating elements of information to aid navigation.

Why spend time on designing your dissertation?

The short answer is 'Self-interest and/or self-preservation'! As we pointed out in Chapter 6 and Chapter 8 (see pp 128–129 and 159–60), if we don't take account of the examiners who will pass judgement on our work and of what they need to help them do their job, we harm our own chances. It is unfortunate that, as the opening story reveals, so little help is given to researchers in this direction, and the nature of the help required is so little understood.

Unless you are a researcher with background or qualification in graphic, typographic or information design, the idea that the final dissertation needs any particular design consideration will probably strike you as being unnecessary. After all, today the final typing up of any document using a PC is such a commonplace activity – and the software appears to be so intelligent – that there seems no good reason for any design intervention or even an outline specification. And if that is the case, writers will just let the inbuilt default settings of the software remain in place, instead of consciously using forward planning to achieve better designed products, and making their own settings to reflect it.

My own experience of teaching typographic and information design in higher-education institutions suggests that most researchers – as well as their supervisors – regard the final stage of typing up a dissertation as having nothing to do with design. The origins of that view probably go back to the time when the final handwritten draft of a dissertation would be handed over to a trained and qualified woman to be typed up as master pages using a manual or electric typewriter.[2]

2
Typing was still seen as 'women's work' as Tilghman Richards wrote in 1964, '... today we are so familiar with the part taken by women in commercial life that one may overlook the very important part played by the typewriter in their so-called "emancipation".' The first successful commercial electric typewriters were developed by (IBM) International Business Machine Corporation and introduced commercially in 1959.

This was at a period before the present expansion of higher education, when there were fewer students studying for higher degrees, and the technology was far simpler.

It is often forgotten that the personal computer has been with us only since the mid-1980s, and even if these earlier machines found their way into universities or polytechnics, they were not designed for text setting or word processing, and by comparison with the PC used today, were fairly primitive. At that time many university students didn't have easy access to typewriters and had to produce their final drafts as handwritten texts.

It is only in the last 15 years that the PC has become the primary method of originating and designing documents. Although this technology is now the norm, the particular skills and knowledge that professional typists brought to their work are still relevant, but they have now been lost to today's users and this loss of knowledge is part of the problem.

Is writing a text the same as designing a text? [3]

First a distinction should be made between the *ideas* expressed in a piece of writing and the *visual/spatial organization* of it on the printed page made by typographers.

The ideas and the content of a piece of written text are set down in accordance with certain rules of grammar and structure. Individual units of words are organized in sentences, then into paragraphs; and in many cases the text is also organized into larger units of chapters or sections. In languages that are read from left to right, the final written text appears as a series of orderly lines, separated by ribbons of white space, which start at the top left-hand corner of the page and continue down to the foot. These formal grammatical and structural rules are observed every time we write prose text, whether it is hand written, typewritten, or typeset using word-processing software such as Microsoft Word or sophisticated publishing software such as Adobe InDesign, or QuarkXPress. The ideas expressed through the use of the rules, however, are different for each individual piece of writing.

3
While there is indeed a distinction between the conventions to be observed in writing and typography, the two activities can both be rightly called design, and writing is a part of the totality of information design. Chapter 10 (page 237) makes the argument for the claim that 'writing is a design activity'.

Typography has its origins in handwriting, as can be clearly seen in handwritten books produced in Europe before Johannes Gutenberg, a German goldsmith, invented movable type around 1450.[4]

Typography is a visual language

While the reading process and the rules of structure, syntax and punctuation are the same for the writer and the typographer, when you enter the world of typography a different set of conventions applies. The move from the world of writing to that of typography can be successful only if the fundamental laws governing the craft are understood and consciously put into practice. Typography, as defined at the start of this book (see page 15) is often described as 'visual language'. The typographer requires knowledge and skill in these areas:

1. The insight to analyse a document and recognize the writer's overall plan, and to identify each of the separate text elements that needs design attention. In particular, the typographer needs to be able to identify elements in the original document that could better be communicated in a different mode from the one its writer has used; for example, quantitative information conveyed in continuous prose that would be more readily understood if treated as a table.
2. Asking appropriate questions about the overall production requirements, starting (if it is to be presented in print) with the paper on which it will be reproduced, and its suitability for the nature of the product
3. Finding appropriate typographical answers to the problems identified, and then designing the individual pages, having regard to the overall document plan
4. Choosing the most appropriate type (font) design, and making decisions on the size of the types to be used, and the spacing between lines and words, as well as on the software package that will be used.

4
A full account of Gutenberg's invention can be found on the Gutenberg Museum website in an English translation by John Burland, which explains how 'The genius of Gutenberg's invention was to split the text into its individual components, such as lower and upper case letters, punctuation marks, ligatures and abbreviations, drawing on the tradition of medieval scribes. These individual items were cast in quantity as mirror images and assembled to form words, lines and pages.'
http://www.mainz.de/gutenberg/english/erfindun.htm

For a typographical designer with this range of knowledge, finding a solution to designing an A4 multi-page dissertation – even one with a complex written structure – is straightforward, but if your experience is restricted to less complex problems then clearly it is far more of a challenge. The deepest problem that non-designers face is lack of the internal design models which are laid down in the memory of typographers as a result of hours of practice and hard work, and which can be brought into consciousness at a moment's notice and used to solve design problems. That raises the question 'Can we help the novice typographer or the researcher to produce an acceptable-looking dissertation, without the investment of time that the skilled typographer has to make?'

Templates – the building blocks for designing a dissertation

The English typographer and historian John Dreyfus (1991) asked a similar question about how the early printers might have acquired their skills to design, produce and print the first books, using what was clearly the new technology of the time. His answer was:

> *'My impression is that book design at the outset of printing was dominated by the instructions given to printers by their powerful and self-confident patrons in the church or in the universities. The earliest printers were often itinerant workmen practicing a new craft which had not yet acquired any standing. Printers were grateful when patrons supplied texts in book form, carefully written by an experienced scribe, which would serve as a design for the early printer to follow. In such cases he had virtually no more design problems to solve than would nowadays arise with a reprint, except that the earliest printers had to create types that would suit the taste of their patrons.'*

This seems to indicate that early printers were often guided in their decision-making by the use of templates[5] that set the standards for the different elements of the books they worked on. The next section of this chapter follows that tradition in providing researchers with practical guides to creating dissertations that meet sound standards of design.

5
While today the word 'template' is most often used in relation to documents, both printed and electronic, (for example 'A set of predesigned formats for text and graphics on which new pages and webs can be based', www.javaworkshop.sourceforge.net/glossary.html). It has a long history, going back to the patterns that master masons would produce for shaping and cutting stone for Gothic cathedrals.

References

Websites referred to in this chapter accessed on 18 March 2009

Tilghman Richards, G (1964)
The History and Development of Typewriters.
London: Science Museum, HMSO.

Dreyfus, J (1991)
Who is to design books now that computers are making books?
In: *Classical Typography in the Computer Age.*
Papers presented at a Clark Library Seminar 27 February 1988.
Los Angeles: University of California.

Gutenberg Museum
http://www.mainz.de/gutenberg/english/erfindun.htm

Further Reading

Febvre, L and Martin, H-J (1990)
The Coming of the Book. The Impact of Printing 1450–1800.
London and New York: Verso.

Design is more than cosmetic: a basic toolkit for dissertation design

Ch 9.2 Contents at a glance

An overview of the basic toolkit

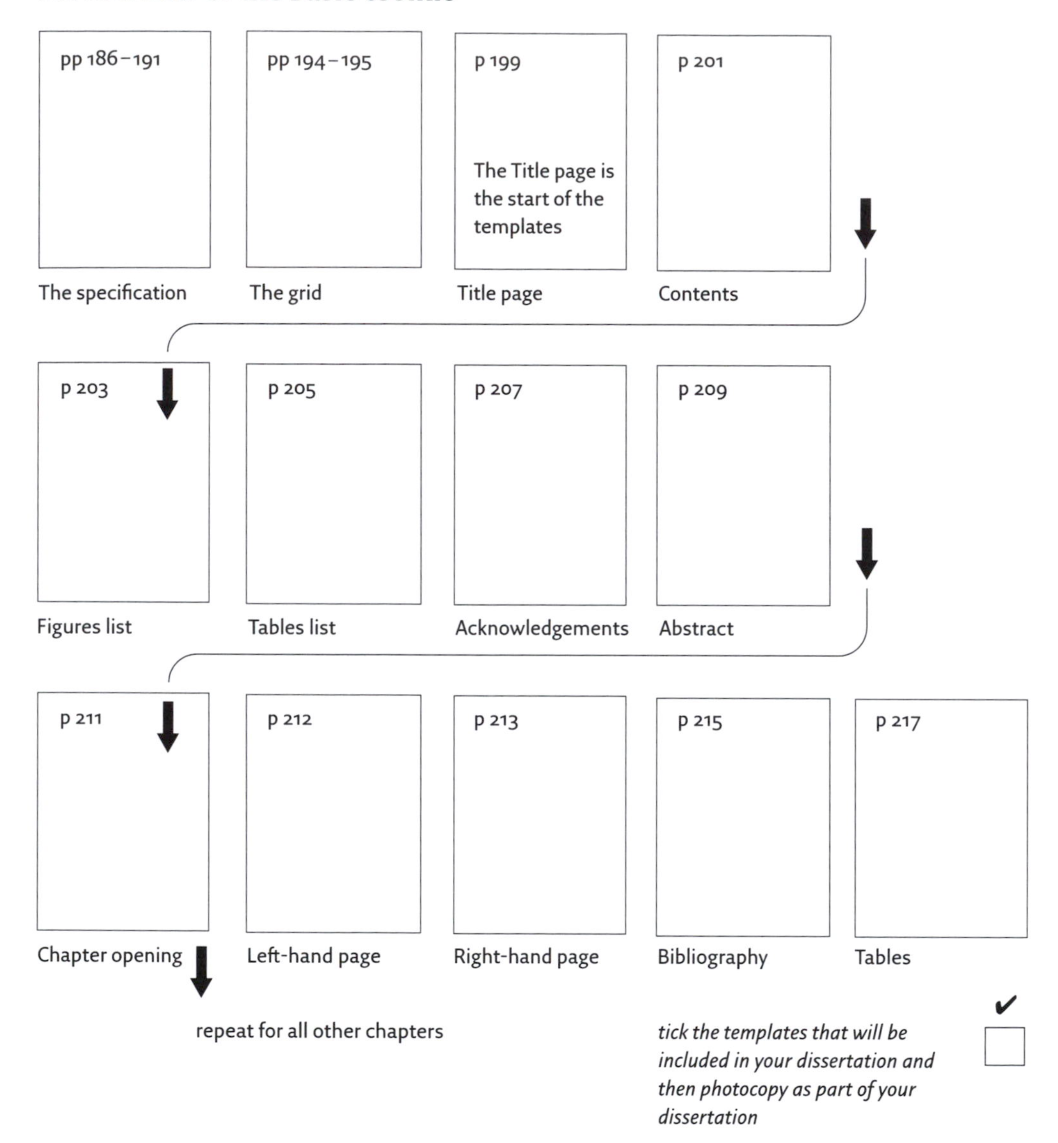

Note

The text used in the models in this chapter comes from Liz Orna's doctoral dissertation. There are two reasons why it is used in this way: first, it was available in electronic form; and second, before starting to write it, Liz asked my advice about typefaces and layout, and the advice I gave her was a brief version of what you will find in this chapter. The final design is a well considered example of what can be achieved by an outline set of instructions.

Introduction

The visual analysis of recent dissertations described on pages 174–176 made me acutely aware that researchers without formal training in typography or graphic design face really difficult problems when they have to make design decisions – probably for the first time in their lives, and with nothing in their previous or current education to prepare them for it – for a multi-page document, embodying many different elements.

The help offered in this chapter is based on these principles:

1. Simplicity in appearance and consistency in placing all page elements, based on an underlying page plan (grid), with numbered reference points
2. Minimal number of typefaces (fonts) and type sizes
3. An electronic specification that is as straightforward and uncomplicated as the software will allow
4. Respect for the users – helping them to think about the reasons for the actions they are asked to take, and to understand the process they are engaged in rather than requiring passive mechanical obedience to complex unexplained instructions; minimalist instruction.

It comes in the form of a 'dissertation design toolkit', see opposite page for the constituent parts.

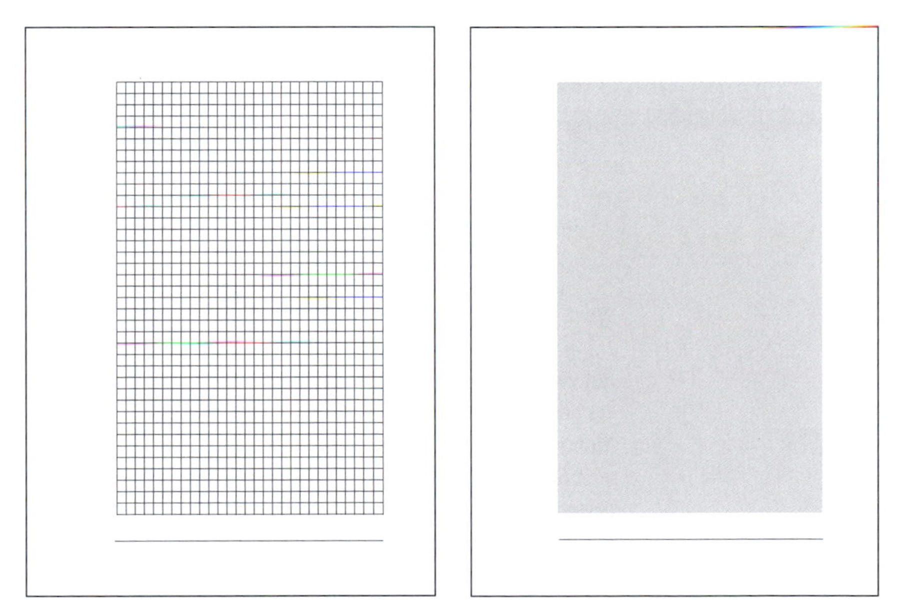

Figure 9.2.1 Left: reduction of the A4 dissertation grid for a right-hand page. Right: the text area on which the grid is superimposed

A dissertation design toolkit for researchers

The toolkit consists of:

1 A basic grid (see Figure 9.2.1), which readers can set up on their own PC using the full version of Word or other professional software

2 Templates (see pages 174 & 179) based on the grid, for all the standard dissertation elements, together with an outline typographical specification, for photocopying.

What is a grid, and how does it help researchers?

Put simply, a grid is a master page plan, made up of horizontal lines, on which the page text is constructed. The grid for the dissertation pages shown in Figure 9.2.1 is a text-only grid – rather than one for text and pictures. Vertical lines, which can be used as tabulation points, have been added on the grid. The advantage of using a grid is that it allows you to see the underlying design structure of the document while working on screen and monitor how the design work is progressing. That gives very useful feedback on how many lines of text the page is making and where headings and footnotes are positioned, as well as allowing you to make sensible decisions about where and how to end the page (see page 192). So, without any guesswork, it is possible to see how each page is taking shape as you write, as well as making any visual adjustments.

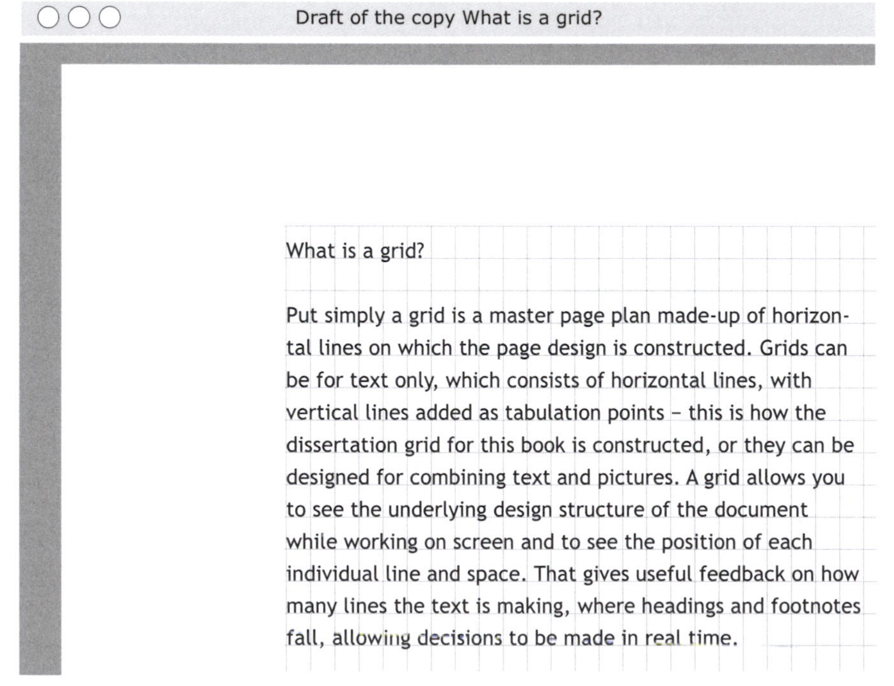

Figure 9.2.2 If you use the dissertation grid at all stages of writing, the visual feedback you will get will save you time on designing the layout of pages.

The technique of using underlying linear plans to help the designer structure a document is not a new invention; it was actually used in handwritten manuscript books well before the invention of printing. As Michelle Brown (1994) notes, 'Before the eleventh century, ruling was generally executed with a hard point, producing a ridge-and-furrow effect. Thereafter lead point was used in the layout of individual pages.' Without this visual help, the scribes would have found it more or less impossible to write a straight line of words, let alone decide where to start, where to finish, how long the lines should be on each new page. Figure 9.2.2 opposite shows how this piece of text looked while I was writing and typing it, with the Word document grid turned on. See pages 187 to 191 for instructions on setting up the grid and master document.

Division of labour

The two sets of skills described below are required for designing a dissertation. I am providing the first of them, in the form of a toolkit, because they are unlikely to have been part of the education of most researchers. It will be up to the individual reader, with help from me, to supply the second.

1 A developed feeling for appropriate placing of words and lines on a blank A4 space reproduced on a flat computer screen. This skill in placing of words, lines and shapes is sometimes called 'graphicacy' in the educational context. But the school education of today's researchers, at any rate in the UK, has not specifically attempted to teach the required skills; and children still seem to be expected to 'pick it up as they go along'.

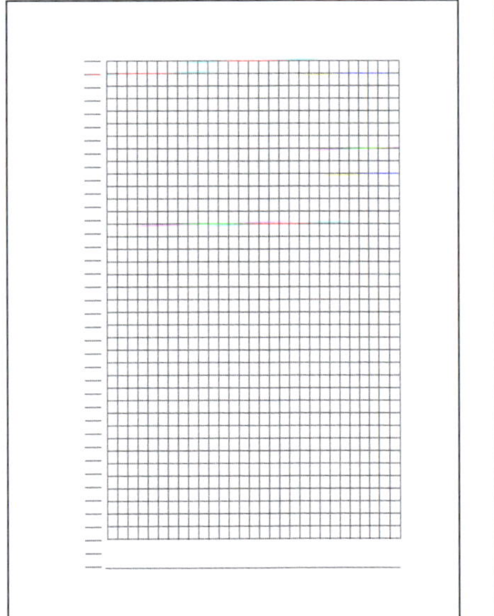

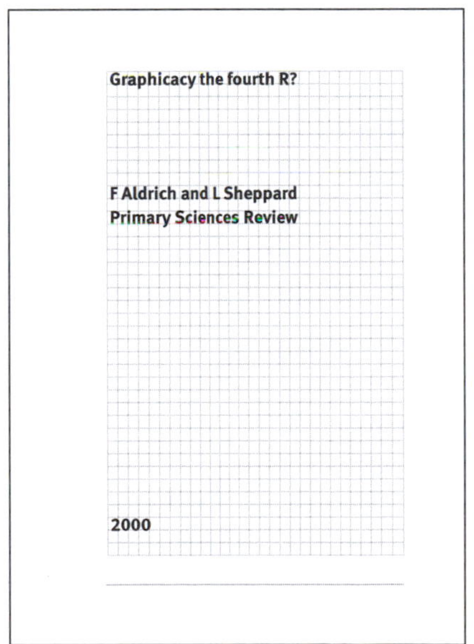

Figure 9.2.3 **L:** The basic grid **R:** The grid underlying the templates makes the framework for typing the dissertation text. The combination of grid and templates is the foundation for well-designed pages

2 Skill and patience in exploring the software so as to gain control of the full range of the program rather than being forced to work entirely in default mode. Some readers may already be in the habit of exploring whatever software they use, and may just need to extend it to the features required to use the toolkit; others will need to develop the necessary skills, and to be aware of the issues discussed on the following pages.

We still have to do our own thinking

Gaining the level of mastery over the word-processing software referred to above is an essential preliminary to setting up the typographic specification for your dissertation, for which specific parts of the software have to be opened and activated. In Word on a PC, or on the Mac, for example, to access the grid feature you have to open up the Drawing Tools – hardly an obvious connection to organizing text. But placing grids in the drawing program is not unreasonable, since grids are a system of x and y coordinates and have a part in designing some forms of diagrams and tables. Grids in text designing are fundamental in placing text, and date back thousands of years.

And it is worth reminding ourselves here of two important factors about software. Firstly, in using word-processing software, unless you 'declare' each of your design decisions (that is actively instruct the software to do what you want), all the design and typographical decisions will follow the default settings and values built into the software. These determine everything from the measurement units used, to the width and proportions of the margins, to the font (typeface) and the point size and line spaces selected. Secondly, while word-processing software makes many design activities easier to perform, of itself it can't confer any typographical skill or knowledge (see page 43).

The fact that the software can't do the thinking for you is a problem for all who have to design and deliver a dissertation on time. The design models in the templates from page 198 on should help, though readers still face a learning curve; I have tried not to make it too steep.

The design specification

From the facing page through to page 191 you will find step-by-step instructions for setting up the page that will be used in conjunction with the grids and templates. The instructions are for Word 2007 with Windows Vista.[1] The pages can be photocopied onto A3 or US Letter sheets according to the paper size you will be using (see page 193). As you work through each stage you are producing an outline specification (see page 220 for a complete checklist).

1 The decision to use Word 2007 on a PC using the operating system Vista rather than Word 2007 on a Mac was deliberate. I appreciate that many researchers will be using earlier versions of Word – and possibly the new operating system Windows 7. While it is impossible to show every version of Word, keep in mind that all the features you require can be found even if the routes to them are not as transparent as one would like.

1 Changing the measurement system

Click on the **Office Button** on the extreme left hand side of the **Taskbar**

click on **Word Options** panel

click on **Advanced** panel

cursor down the sublist and find **Display**

find: Show measurement in units of: **Millimetres** ▼

units are available in: Inches, Centimetres. Millimetres, Points, Picas

Click OK *tick box when completed* ✔

2 Setting up for single-sided right-hand pages

For facing pages go to 3

Click on **Page Layout** tab found on **Ribbon** just below the **Title Bar**

click on **Margins**

click on arrow ▼ cursor down to **Custom Margins...** click to open **Page Setup** window. *Alternatively* click on the **Page Setup Dialog Box** ↘

This will also open the **Page Setup window.** Leave: **Orientation** as **Portrait,** and **Multiple pages** on **Normal** ▼

Set margins to:

Top:	27 mm	Bottom:	38 mm
Left:	44 mm	Right:	27 mm
Gutter:	0 mm	Gutter position:	Left

open **Paper** leave as **A4**

open **Layout**

change Footer to **28 mm**

Click OK *tick box when completed* ✔

❸ Setting up for mirror or facing pages

Open the **Page Setup** window. leave: **Orientation** as **Portrait,** change **Multiple pages** to **Mirror margins** ▼

Margins terms will change as below:

Left becomes **Inside**

Right becomes **Outside**

Note: If you use mirror pages the single sheets of paper have to be printed on both sides. This will halve the thickness of the bound and finished dissertation.

back to 'Set margins to' **in** ❷

Click OK

✔ *tick box when completed* ☐

❹ Setting up the grid

To use the grid, the grid icon has to appear on the **Quick Access Toolbar**

If it has not been activated:

click on the **Office Button** on the extreme left hand side of the **Taskbar**

click on **Word Options** panel

click on **Customize** panel

click on **Popular Commands** ▼

click and cursor down the list and find **Drawing Tools | Format Tab**

find and highlight **Grid Settings...**

click on the **Add >>** button to transfer the grid icon to the **Quick Access Toolbar**

tick ✔ **Show Quick Access Toolbar below the Ribbon**

Click OK to close window

✔ *tick box when completed* ☐

Before you go on to the next page, do this:
Go to ❶ Change units of measurements to **points**.
Now continue with ❹

❹ Setting up the grid *(continued)*

Click on **Page Layout** tab. Click on the grid to open the **Drawing Grid** window. Check the boxes and type the dimensions exactly as shown here.

Object snapping

☐ Snap objects to other objects

Grid settings

Horizontal spacing 13.6 pt — Type in13.6 pt: this is the exact space

Vertical spacing 18 pt — Type in 18 pt: this is the exact space

Grid origin

☑ Use margins

Horizontal origin: 124.75 pt

Vertical origin: 76.55 pts

Checking the **Use margins** box changes the units from mm to points, and ensures that the grid appears only on the text area.

Show grid

☑ Display grid on screen

☑ Vertical every: 1

Horizontal every: 1

Check the two boxes under **Show grid** and type in each the numeral1. If this is not done the grid will not display accurately

☐ Snap objects to grid when the gridlines are not displayed

Click OK to close window

✔ *tick box when completed* ☐

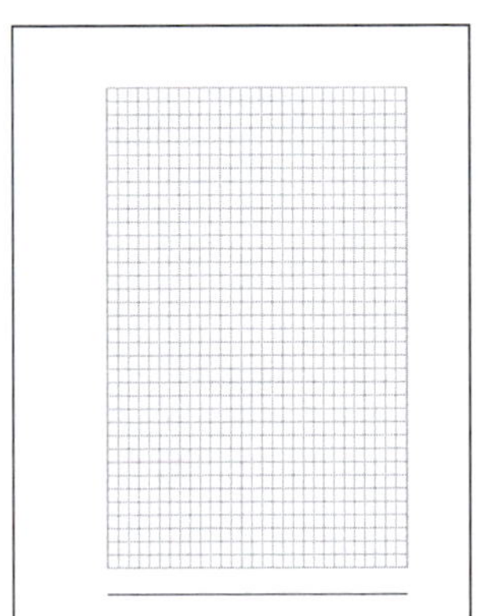

The grid

Is constructed out of 1044 units, each measuring 13.6 x 18 pts. There are 29 vertical rows and 36 horizontal rows; 29 rows can be divided into two equal columns of 14 units which can be used for two-column pages.

The whole grid can also be divided into six squares, each made up of 11 horizontal units and 14 vertical units. These can be used in combination for diagram or picture boxes.

You have now completed the basic page layout and the grid. The next step is to set up the style sheets. Stage ❺ tells you how to do it.

❺ Setting up the style sheets for typesetting. Stage 1: Paragraphs

It is important that you set up style sheets to help with the setting of text and headings. Setting up a style sheet is slightly complicated, but once mastered it makes the designing of pages easier. Individual styles will be displayed in the **Styles** section. Highlight the text and click on the style to activate.

Click on **Home** tab, navigate to the **Paragraph** section, and click on the **Dialog Box Launcher** ↘ to open **Paragraph** window and then do this:

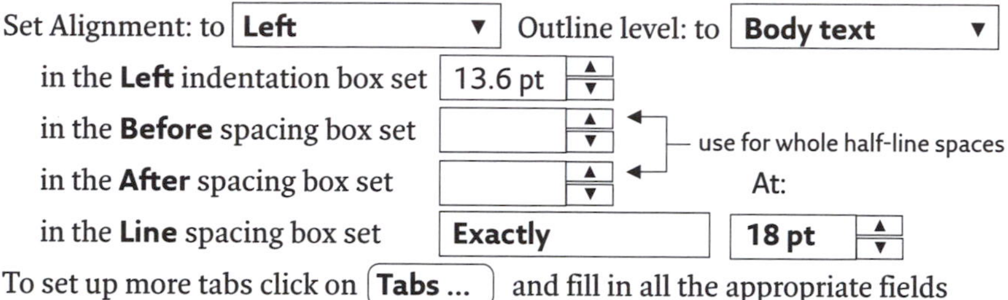

Click OK to close window

Stage 2: Creating a typographical style sheet

Click on **Home** tab and navigate to the AA panel at the right-hand side and then click on **Dialog Box Launcher** ↘ to open the **Styles** window.

Navigate down to the first AA button at the bottom of the window, click to open **Create New Style from Formatting** and do this:

in the **Name:** panel type this **Text setting for dissertation** ▼

in **Style type:** leave as **Paragraph** ▼

in **Style based on:** click to open **(no style)** by clicking on arrow ▼

click on **Format** ▼ button and click on **Font** to open and choose the Font

Font	Font style	Size
Cambria	Regular	12
Brush Script MT	Regular	8
Calibri	Italic	9
California FB	Bold	10
Calisto MTBold	Bold italic	11
Cambria		12

Cursor up and down to select the font name, the style of type, and point size you want to use. Click on each to highlight and Click OK

The individual style will be transferred to the **Styles** section as well as the **styles** list.

✔

tick box when completed ☐

6 Inserting symbols that are not on your keyboard

Click on **Home** tab and navigate to the Ω panel at the right hand side and click to open small **symbol** window. Navigate to Ω **More symbols** click to open full size window showing the full range of the individual symbols available in the highlighted default Font: (normal text) ▼ window. Cursor down to find the **text font** you have chosen (in our example it was Cambria) and highlight the font. That will open all the symbols available for that font. Navigate to **Subset:** **Basic Latin** ▼

If you cursor down from the Basic Latin subsets you will find a list of 16 individual sets of symbols (or glyphs as they are called). Cambria has a total of 992 individual glyphs. To insert a glyph in your text, place the cursor in the text, highlight the individual box and click on **Insert** to copy it to the text. Close the window when completed.

---

7 Visual marks

When designing and writing, as well as using an underlying grid, it is always worth getting as much visual feedback as possible when working on screen.

Word allows you to display the following formatting marks on screen:

Tab characters	►	Hidden text	abc
Spaces	···	Optional hyphens	¬
Paragraph marks	¶		

To show these marks return to stage 1 on page 187, open Word Options, click on **Display** and cursor down and find **Always show these formatting marks on the screen.** Check the boxes.

✔

Click OK

tick box when completed ☐

Other useful typographical information

Turning over a new leaf, ending and beginning a page

It often happens when designing a page that you discover the last line turns over to make a new page. This happened on the 'A4 Abstract' template – see page 209 – where the last line falls outside the text area by three words.

If this line of only three words is taken over to the top of the next page it will cause a certain amount of visual uncertainty and hesitancy on the part of the reader.

The most intelligent solution is to take over the line before the short one as well, leaving the page at 34 lines. This rule would apply not only to continuous text, but also to lists, footnotes and headings. It is perfectly acceptable to allow pages to fall short of an exact page depth.

B and C heading using half-line spaces

This is dealt with in more detail on the relevant A4 size example dissertation page: see pages 218–219.

The grid for placing text elements

A grid is an aid to designing and writing. This is particularly so when the writing/typing and eventually design are carried out on identical page sizes, thus achieving what might be called a 'seamless process'. But this can't be achieved with any degree of accuracy unless the grid exactly matches the document specification. As shown on pages 194–195, the horizontal lines of the grid which correspond to lines of text are numbered, and the most important lines – where to start and finish, and where the drop [2] is to appear on all the templates as line **7**. When the grid and the templates are enlarged to **159%** they can be checked against each other.

One further factor has to be taken into account in relation to the grid: the size of the paper on which the dissertation is to be printed. The implications are discussed and illustrated next.

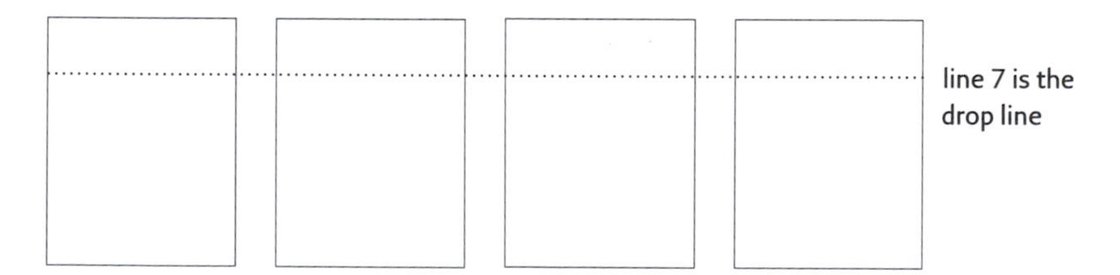

2
The drop is a line that shows the position where text starts on pages with 'A' headings (chapter openings, prelims and indexes).

Grids for A4 and US Letter paper sizes

The first edition of this book didn't take account of the fact that, while most countries have gradually adopted the ISO 216-series of paper sizes, and use A4 when designing documents and writing letters, the US and Canada have retained non-metric measures. Letter and Tabloid sizes for documents and stationery are still in common use there, as can be seen when selecting a document size in Microsoft Word or other DTP software – a fact that is not surprising given the dominance of the United States in computers and computer software.

Although A4 and US Letter sizes do not differ greatly in overall dimensions, (see the diagram below) you do have to take the differences in width and depth into account if the finished size of your dissertation has to be US Letter. To give North American researchers a choice, there are master grids for both sheet sizes.

The internal document structure remains identical for both sizes; the only difference is that the Letter size has 34 lines to the page – against 36 for the A4, and the left-hand and bottom margins have been modified slightly.[3]

A4 proportion

US Letter proportion

A4

mm	inches
297 x 210	11.69 x 8.27

US Letter

mm	inches
279 x 215	11 x 8.5

3
It is, however, possible that at the time of writing some researchers in the US and Canada are using A4 sizes, for as Brian Forte mentions in his 2002 paper on A4 vs US Letter 'I understand A-series paper – especially A4 – is slowly becoming the norm in US and Canadian universities, if for no other reason than making it easier for students and staff to photocopy articles from (inevitably A4-sized) journals'.

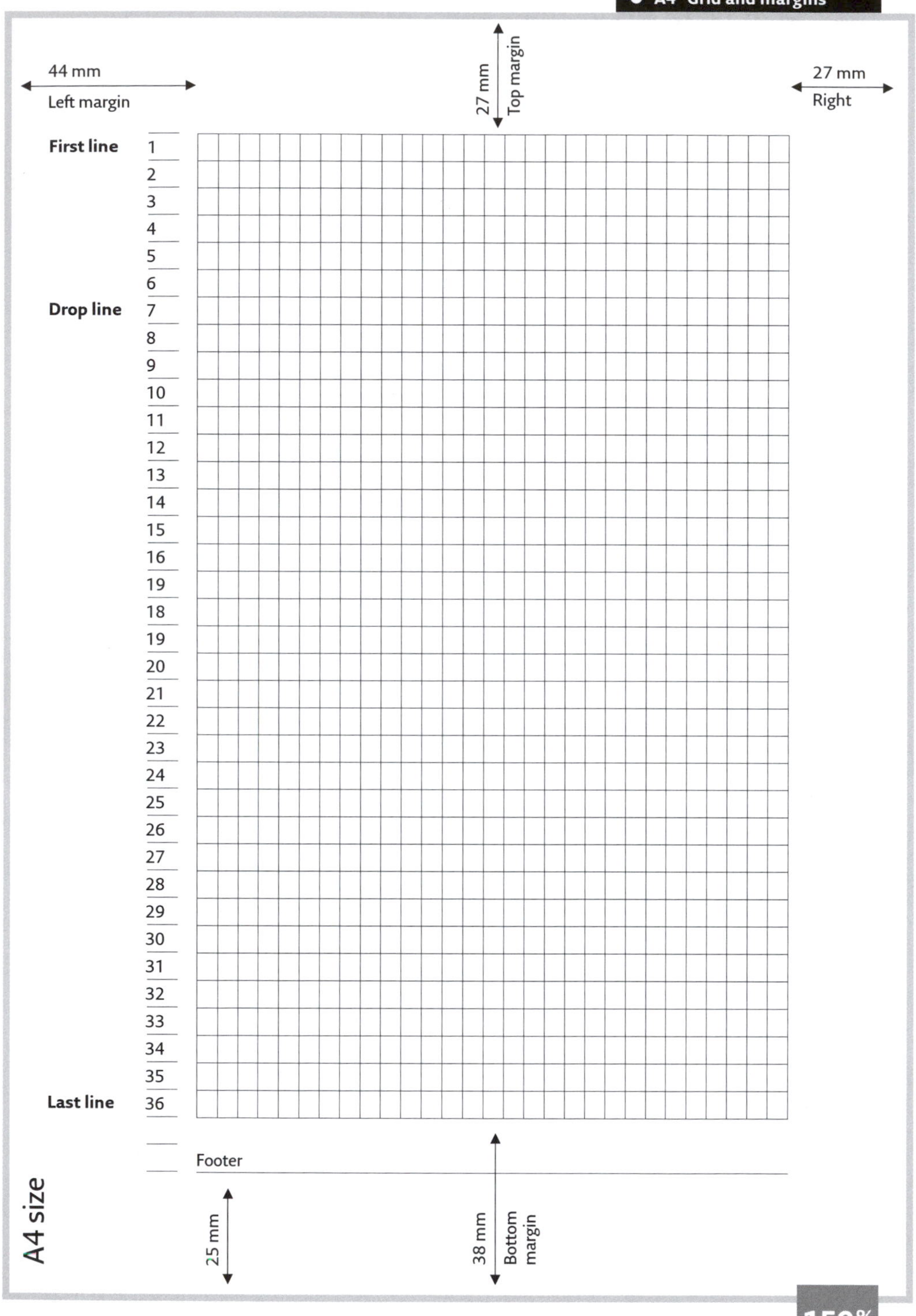
A4 Grid and margins
44 mm
Left margin
27 mm
Top margin
27 mm
Right
First line
1
2
3
4
5
6
Drop line
7
8
9
10
11
12
13
14
15
16
19
18
19
20
21
22
23
24
25
26
27
28
29
30
31
32
33
34
35
Last line
36
Footer
A4 size
25 mm
38 mm
Bottom margin
Enlarge page to
159%

● US Letter Grid and margins

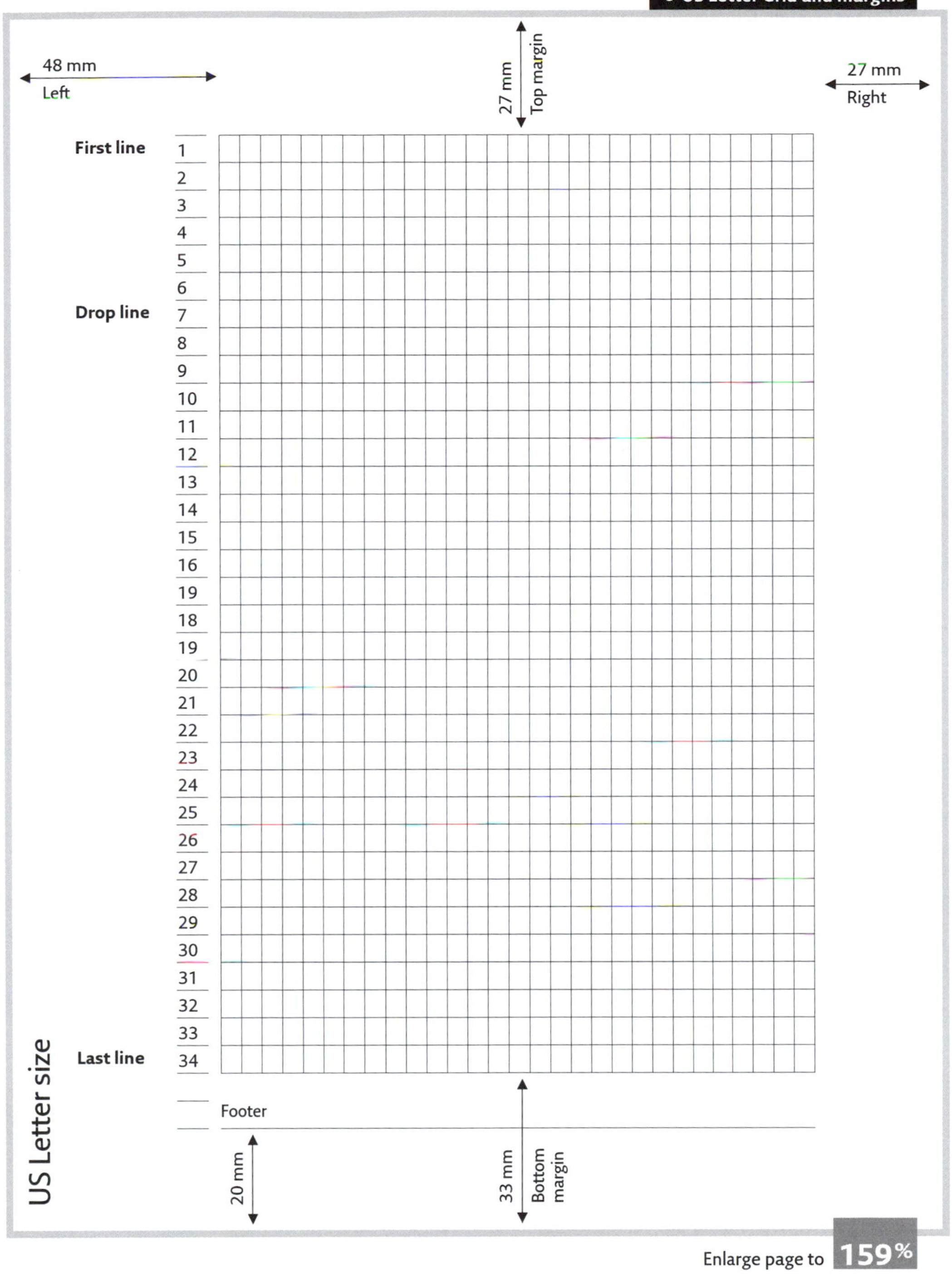

Enlarge page to **159%**

The typographical templates

This section offers researchers practical help in designing, planning and putting together the elements that make up a dissertation. The elements are based on the published research guidelines of UK institutions, and on my own visual audit (see page 174) and standard ways of dealing with them are presented in the templates.

They are arranged in the order in which they appear in an actual dissertation. Presenting the pages in this way gives a more realistic picture of the part each separate element plays in telling the story and in the communication process as a whole. A dissertation built up in this way is more likely to be a coherent synthesis than a collection of fragments.

How the templates are classified

The templates are identified by a combination of background tone and name, as shown below. They are always positioned at the top right-hand corner of the template.

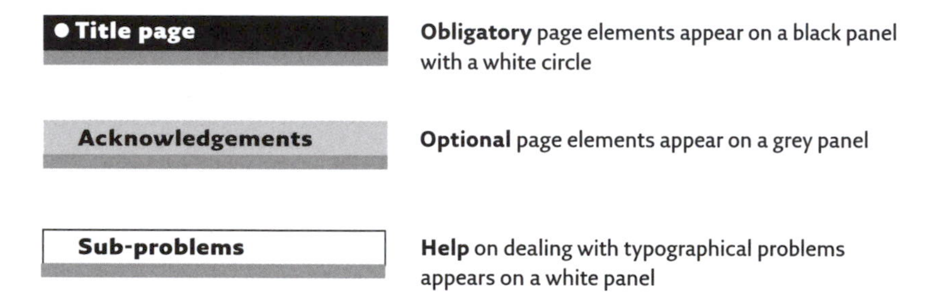

The *obligatory* pages are those most UK institutions consider to be an essential part of a dissertation. The *optional* pages are elements found in well structured dissertations – and more formal academic texts – and if used will give a richer picture of the content, and help the examiner navigate the contents with greater ease. The *sub-problems* are those design issues which don't fit into the category of continuous text – problems such as quotations, bibliographical references, tables – which nevertheless require a design answer.

How the templates are designed

The templates are designed as *single right-hand pages*, printed only on right-hand pages, with the left page remaining blank. It is feasible to design your dissertation with *facing pages*, (see pages 182, 212–213) so that the pages are printed on both sides of the sheet of paper, a decision which will reduce the number of sheets used, as well as the thickness of the bound volume.

Specifying facing or mirror pages requires a modification to the inside margin only; see page 188 for how to make these changes.

To print off the individual A4 page templates:

1. On the overview on page 182, tick off those typographical elements you have decided you will need in your overall dissertation.
2. Select the first template page, and place the open book face down on the photocopier glass. Make certain the head margin of the book is positioned as shown in the diagram below:

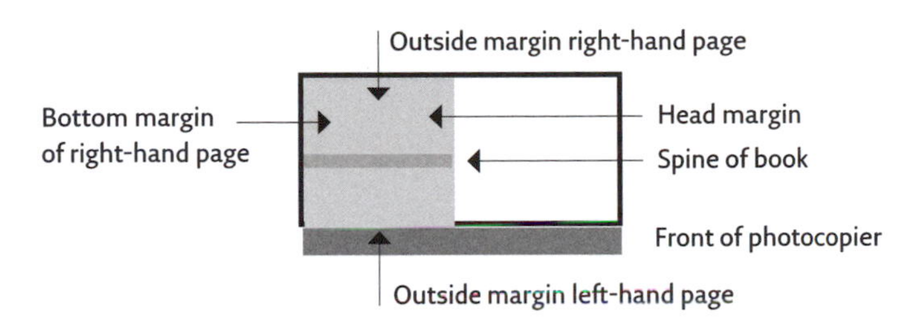

3. Select the **A3 paper size**; select **159%**
4. Press the copier button and when printing is complete check that the entire area of the template has been printed.
5. Check the inside template measurements and make sure the inside of the template frame measures **297 x 210 mm.**
   Note: In the initial experiments to enlarge the book to achieve an exact A4 page, I discovered that different photocopiers would give slightly different measurements. The differences were a millimetre or two, which will have no significance when putting the pages together in Word.
6. Repeat for rest of the templates you need.
7. Check the order of the pages before you staple them together.

To print off the individual US Letter page template:

If you are using US Letter as a finished sheet size, follow stages 1 to 7. The same enlargement of **159%** still applies. The only difference is that you need to select **US B (Tabloid)** paper size.

Note
That completes the introduction to the templates for all the dissertation elements shown on page 182.

Title page A few lines of type on an A4 page. The title page of a dissertation is the first thing the reader sees; it contains essential information, and should set the design tone for the whole dissertation. Although it contains only a few lines of factual information, the way they are organized on the page is critical for understanding the content. My visual audit of dissertations found many title pages that gave little help to readers in that respect; they were frequently designed with the lines arranged on a central axis, while the rest of the dissertation was designed asymmetrically. The two methods are shown below.

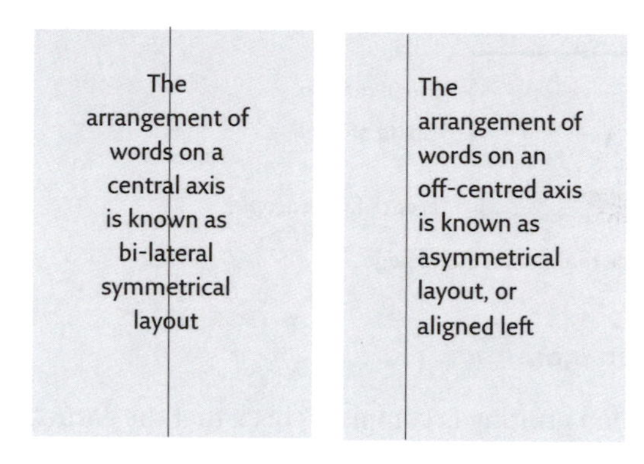

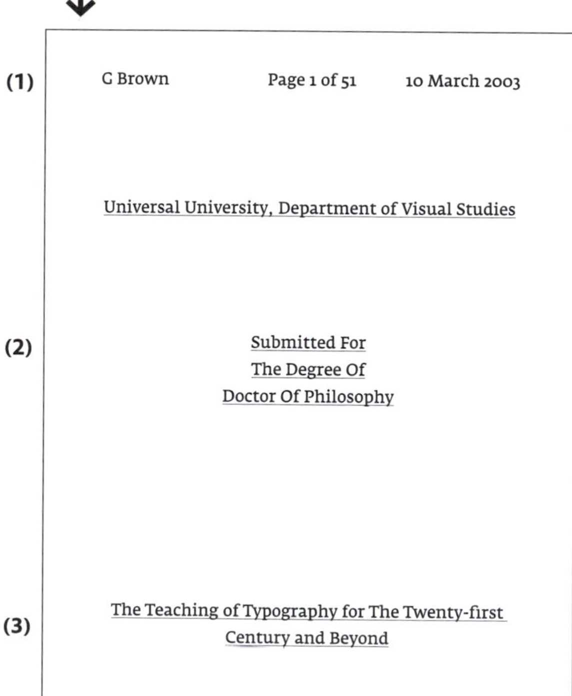

Placing items in the order of their importances

Here is an example of a title page where the individual placing of lines has no overall relationship with the whole. The the top line **(1)** has no business to be there at all; the group of lines **(2)**, in the centre of the page, forms a unit and that makes them the focal point of the whole page, but the information they contain is less important than the main title **(3)**, which is isolated in space and visually hidden away low on the page; while the author's name is part of what in Word is termed a 'header', and more or less hidden from sight!

It is a misconception that underlining gives words more importance; in fact the line usually touches that part of the type known as the *descender*, and it is better to find other answers.

For the novice designer asymmetrical layout, as shown opposite, is easier to handle, not only for title pages but for all the features of dissertations.

● A4 Title page

The numbers refer to specific line positions on the grid

1 **The role of information products and presentation in organisations**
Elizabeth Orna

line drop **7** Submitted for the degree of Doctor of Philosophy
City University, Department of Information Science

July 1999

36 © Elizabeth Orna 1999

Choosing typefaces: see pages 218–219 and 228–229 Enlarge page to **159%**

Contents list A reference page that is often designed as continuous text. The practical value of a contents list in a dissertation is that it gives users a quick and concise overview of the entire piece of work, with its main features and overall scope clearly indicated.

Dissertation contents pages often fail to provide this easy access, because they are visually muddled and lack a clear typographic structure that reflects the structure of the content. The root cause is often failure to appreciate that a contents list is essentially a *list,* which can't do its job if it's treated like continuous text by filling the text area from edge to edge.

If each separate item in a contents list had exactly the same number of words, the problem would be relatively easy to solve. But lengths can vary from single words to twelve and above, and this variation, plus the necessity of attaching a page number at the right-hand edge, creates the problem.

Many of the issues in typography for books and dissertations concern the arrangements of units of words, lines, and graphic material, where visual clarity is achieved by the use of *proximity*, *separation*, and *grouping*, which collectively are concerned with visual literacy. The contents list below is an example of not finding the right degree of *proximity* and *grouping* between, on the one hand a list of words placed in the centre of a page, and on the other, two adjacent groups of numbers floating either side.

Avoid this configuration

CONTENTS

	Introduction	
	Glossary of Symbols	
1	Matrices	1
2	Elementary logic	10
3	Calculations with four-figure logarithms	23
4	Matrix multiplication	40
5	Boolean algebra	58
6	Quadratic equations and factorization	74
7	Vector spaces	95
8	Comparing statistics – position	102
9	Algebraic inequations	123
10	The straight line	133
11	More inequations	144
12	Patterns in numbers	152
13	Matrix algebra	167
14	Further logarithmic calculations	172
15	Quadratic functions and their graphs	179
16	Transformations and matrices	194
17	The slide rule - some other scales	210
18	Areas under transformation	221
19	Logarithms and roots	235
20	Polynomials	240
	Index	246

The use of dotted lines

In my visual audit, I was struck by the number of contents pages that used dotted lines to help link page numbers to chapter titles. They all used rows of single full stops (or periods) to create each line, but in doing so created a heavy-looking visual line. See the entries '20 Polynomials' and 'Index' on the left.

Dotted lines are rarely used today, but when they were more common, the convention was to use widely spaced single, or paired dots. The dots *aligned vertically* regardless of the space to be filled and they didn't visually intrude.

The message is don't use dots; instead treat the page numbers as shown in the template model opposite and place them nearer to the entries.

The recommended example on the opposite page is both clearer and simpler to construct.

The numbers refer to specific line positions on the grid

┛ ┗ tabs

➡ 1 **Contents**

line drop **7**

36

Setting up tabs: this page uses right ┛+ ┗ left tabs separated by a 13.6 pt space

Enlarge page to **159%**

Figures list A figures list page is similar to a contents page; the difference is that it usually links figures to the chapter as well as the page. The example below gives only figure and page numbers, whereas the template opposite shows the chapter and the figure numbers combined. This system provides a far more accurate way of referring to figures. The issues of vertical alignment apply whatever figure numbering system is used.

In the comments below I draw attention to the apparent uncertainty that besets researchers in deciding where to place text when the overall number of lines varies from page to page. There is an aesthetic tendency to 'balance out' the page by moving the first line down when there are fewer lines or up when there are more lines, or simply forcing the lines apart to make full depth.

The simple answer is to recognize that – apart from text pages – neat packages of even numbers of words and lines don't exist, and forcing lines into a fixed text area is never been possible. The solution is to use a fixed starting point, and let the material make its own natural depth – like washing on a line – as much of Chapter 9.2 has been designed.

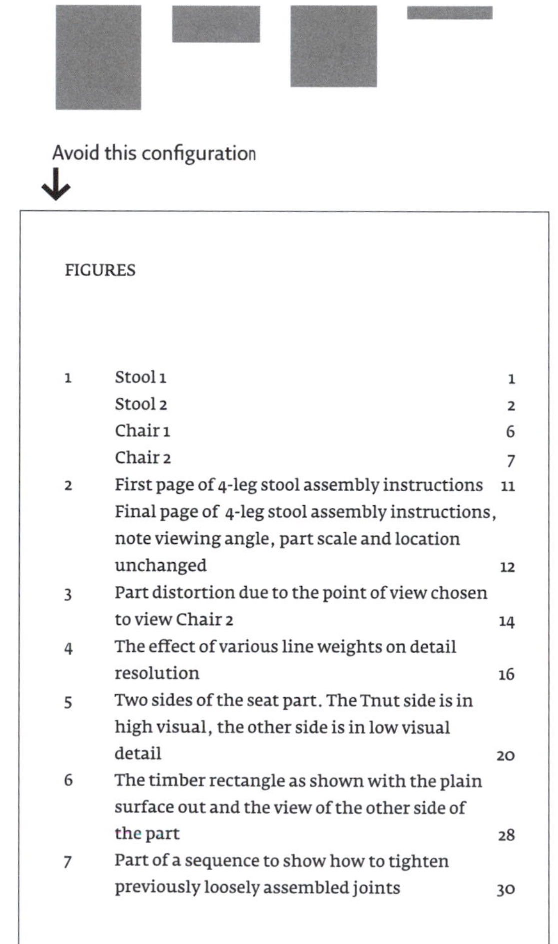

FIGURES

1	Stool 1	1
	Stool 2	2
	Chair 1	6
	Chair 2	7
2	First page of 4-leg stool assembly instructions	11
	Final page of 4-leg stool assembly instructions, note viewing angle, part scale and location unchanged	12
3	Part distortion due to the point of view chosen to view Chair 2	14
4	The effect of various line weights on detail resolution	16
5	Two sides of the seat part. The Tnut side is in high visual, the other side is in low visual detail	20
6	The timber rectangle as shown with the plain surface out and the view of the other side of the part	28
7	Part of a sequence to show how to tighten previously loosely assembled joints	30

Issues of rapid scanning

The starting point of the figure numbers and titles is identical to the contents page on page 201, but the distance the eye has to travel is too wide for comfortable scanning.

In addition, the baseline to baseline distance between one line and the next, known as the 'leading', is too wide, making it more difficult to see where each group of words begins and ends.

The practice of increasing the leading to fill the depth of the text area is adopted in the cause of balance and neatness – which is not worth pursuing. It is better to let all pages find their own depth.

And finally there is a lack of clarity in the text. It is not clear that Figure 1 consists of two pairs, and that Figure 2 refers to one pair, and Figures 3 to 7 to single objects.

The numbers refer to specific line positions on the grid

1 **Figures**

line drop **7**

36

Setting up tabs: this page uses right ┛+ ┗ left tabs separated by a 13.6 pt space

Enlarge page to **159%**

Tables list Like the figures list, the tables list page usually appears as part of the preliminary pages and consists of a column of text sandwiched between two columns of numbers. But for all practical purposes the example below is identical in most respects to the figures list on page 202.

In my visual audit, tables – as well as diagrams – didn't feature very prominently, and if tables were an essential part of the research, the list either got added onto the figures-list page, or they weren't listed at all.

Where tables were displayed as a separate page the text was usually organized on a different page plan to either the contents or figures pages; compare the example below with the figures list on page 202. Again, researchers' uncertainty as to the best way to lay the pages out became very apparent. It created a situation where each page in the prelims requires a fresh set of design specifications. And forcing the lines out to fill as much as possible of the text area is a consequence.

One *single line space* between the table details would have been all that was required.

Avoid this configuration

TABLES

Issues of rapid scanning

Although the margins and tab positions are identical to those in the previous contents and figure-list pages the first set of double numerals appear to be closer to the text.

This is a case of the difference between measurable white space – in this instance 36 points from the start of the numerals to the first word in the small example – and optical space. Here the eye gets tricked into thinking that the vertical band of white space used in this example is actually narrower than the one used in previous pages.

This of course is an issue of perception, and the important part that space, and apparent proximity plays when organizing and placing words and images on a page.

See page 222 on the principles of Gestalt perception.

The numbers refer to specific line positions on the grid

1 **Tables**

line drop **7**

36

Enlarge page to **159%**

Acknowledgements The acknowledgements page of dissertations is usually written as continuous text, with a single 'A' heading[4] positioned on line **1**, followed by continuous text, as shown in the example below. This may not be the most helpful way of dealing with the all the content, however. Researchers frequently want to acknowledge the help they have received from individuals, and that results in a list of names, sometimes with the addition of job descriptions, and even the names of the organizations the individuals work for.

If on the other hand these separate pieces of information are run together as a string of words, the individual segments tend to become more difficult to pick out and read. In the example below, some differentiation is achieved by setting the names of the organizations in a sloping roman – known as *italic* – which is also done in the template opposite – but it is still difficult to relate the names to the organization.

4
For more information about hierarchical levels of headings, see pages 211–212

Avoid this configuration

ACKNOWLEDGEMENTS

During this project, I have been fortunate in the support of many individuals and organisations, which, while not diminishing my responsibility, has lightened the load and cheered me on my way.

Without the organisations which consented to be the subject of case studies, indeed, the research would have been impossible, and my first acknowledgments must be to their past and present members who were my main points of contact and principal informants, as well as to their many colleagues who contributed invaluable information. I cannot speak too highly of the care and meticulous attention which they devoted first to helping me understand their organisations' practice in the area of the research, and then to updating the case studies and ensuring factual accuracy. Visits to the organisations, and discussions with colleagues there, were enlivening experiences, which counterbalanced the times of solitary reflection and writing which make up so much of the business of research.

THE CASE-STUDY ORGANISATIONS
Action Aid, Sue Davison, Alison Logsdail, Liz Wintle. *City University*, Wendy Clifton-Sprigg, Kate Guess, Peter Tinson, David Vinograd. *The Co-operative Bank*, Chris Smith, Ann Mannock, Gail Ramouz, Jacqui Williams.

vii

Strings of words or structured lists of words?

An acknowledgements page is a useful way of thanking all those people who have helped in the research work that leads to a dissertation.

This is the first example of one – of a set of threepages – of what is called 'continuous text', interspersed with the names of individuals and organizations whom the researcher personally wishes to acknowledge.

But it has to be questioned whether *setting this information as if it is continuous text, is the best way of displaying individual and company names, considering that these individual items need to be picked out one from another?* If they are structured as if they were sentences, the reader is going to find it far more difficult to read than if they were treated as in the example template opposite.

The numbers refer to specific line positions on the grid

1 **Acknowledgements**

line drop **7**

In postgraduate research, one is on one's own to an exceptional extent; responsibility for the whole enterprise rests solely on the researcher; it is not shared or distributed in the way of most work responsibilities; and while there are real satisfactions in that, it is also a heavy burden.

During this project, I have been fortunate in the support of many individuals and organisations, which, while not diminishing my responsibility, has lightened the load and cheered me on my way.

Without the organisations which consented to be the subject of case studies, indeed, the research would have been impossible, and my first acknowledgments must be to their past and present members who were my main points of contact and principal informants, as well as to their many colleagues who contributed invaluable information. I cannot speak too highly of the care and meticulous attention which they devoted first to helping me understand their organisations' practice in the area of the research, and then to updating the case studies and ensuring factual accuracy. Visits to the organisations, and discussions with colleagues there, were enlivening experiences, which counterbalanced the times of solitary reflection and writing which make up so much of the business of research.

The case-study organisations

Action Aid
Sue Davison, Alison Logsdail, Liz Wintle

City University
Wendy Clifton-Sprigg, Kate Guess, Peter Tinson, David Vinograd

The Co-operative Bank
36 Chris Smith, Ann Mannock, Gail Ramouz, Jacqui Williams

vii

Treatment of paragraphs and headings:
see pages 218–219

Enlarge page to **159%**

Abstract The abstract is usually a requirement in the preliminary section. The abstract gives a brief statement of the research undertaken, the context, the methodology used, and any major findings that have resulted; it is also the page the examiner reads to find a summary of what the research project is about.

The abstract is usually kept short – between 200 and 500 words – and fits on a single page. The fact that the content frequently doesn't make a full page often encourages the researcher to increase the spacing – known as the leading – between the lines of text until it does have the appearance of a full page of text, as the example below shows.

Avoid this configuration

ABSTRACT

The purpose of this dissertation is to examine how the historical background and technological development of typesetting systems has influenced the way that tabular typography has evolved.

The research looks at how difficult designing a table really is, and what role taste, typographical style and fashion have played in shaping the conventions currently in use, particularly in present-day software packages that are designed to make designing tables and spreadsheets easier and less time-consuming.

The research looks at the way the EU and UK drug and food labelling legislation has affected the amount of information that has to be displayed. And what influence this legislation has had on information overload or issues of legibility as they affect an aging population.

vii

Increasing the line space to make a full page of text

Although the proximity of the main **'A'** heading forms a comfortable link with the first paragraph of text, the other two paragraphs appear to be isolated and not visually linked to the overall story.

The start of a new paragraph is conventionally signalled in one of two ways. The most frequently used is by an indent of white space the size of the type size, for example if the typeface has been set to 7.5 pt, then the indent will be 7.5 pt.

Alternatively a new paragraph can be signalled by separating each new paragraph from the one before with a line space or a half line space, as the paragraph space above shows.

Using a line space *with* an indent, as this example setting shows, is unnecessary. Use either an *indent* or a *line space*, but not both.

The numbers refer to specific line positions on the grid

1

Abstract

line drop **7**

This research looks at how organisations manage that area of their activities whose function is to give essential information to their inner and outside worlds, in the form of 'information products' – print on paper or electronic – through which information is presented for use. It sets information products in a context in which they have not commonly been considered: the organisations which create them; and it seeks to illuminate them with relevant research and practice from the disciplines of information science and information design.

The research was conducted by means of case studies over a five-year period in ten organisations – three for whom information products constituted the main 'offering' and seven where they supported other products. In the early stages it appeared that little had changed sincc the 1970s, when the author worked in this field. At that time, few organisations had an overall policy for their whole range of information products, related to their key strategic objectives; few made any serious attempt to assess the costs to themselves and their customers, clients or public of badly presented information products, or sought to assess the value of the products in relation to their objectives; and few employed appropriately trained staff to manage this aspect of their activities.

Over the period of the study, however, the practice of all the organisations in these respects advanced in various ways. The experience of developing web sites and intranets brought about a particularly noticeable change in the approach of some organisations to their information products and their place in a strategy for information.

A pilot extension of one case study into a second stage involved the application of a methodology for assessing the value of intangibles.It provided some useful indications of the value of information products in supporting a main product with which they were associated, and of

36 the value contributed by information and knowledge to the main product.

vi

When text makes more than 36 lines:
see page 192

Enlarge page to **159%**

Chapter opening The first chapter opening in a dissertation signals the beginning of the dissertation proper. Most dissertations are written with a number of different levels of headings, and subheadings, arranged in a hierarchical order usually denoted by letters of the alphabet **A, B, C** etc. **A** is the chapter heading, and the next ones in the sequence mark the different of subheadings (*subheads*) within chapters.

Readers benefit from headings and subheadings because they help to show the structure of the text; in the interests of clarity, however, it is as well not to go down beyond level **D** – too many levels can confuse readers just as effectively as none at all. The main **A** heading is traditionally set in a larger type size, and the subheadings in the same size as the text face, but distinguished by using different weight of type or'blackness', as the example in the template opposite shows. The relationship of the headings to the text structure also needs to be made clear; in the example opposite, this was achieved by placing *one* line space above the headings,and a *half* line below the headings.(In a two-column structure there would have to be *two* units above and *one* below if you wanted the two columns of text to align horizontally.) These units of space act as a visual scale that allows the reader to see clearly which headings are associated with which sections of text. See page 218–219 for more help on headings.

Avoid this configuration

G Brown Page 7 of 51 10 March 2003

2 RIEHL'S FACTUAL REPORTING OF THE NASSAU REVOLUTION

This section of the dissertation is subdivided into seven subdivisions, namely (i) The events of March 1848; (ii) The mood of the people; (iii) Government, parliament and legislation; (iv) The military campaigns; (v) Political expression (vi) The July 1848 troubles in Wiesbaden (vii) The outcome of the revolution in Nassau.

(i) THE EVENTS OF MARCH 1848

In Wiesbaden the population showed great enthusiasm when news of the French Revolution and the people's *Forderungen* in Karlsruhe and Stuttgart arrived, but such was the weakness of the German Reich that for some it was initially more an anti-revolution rather than a revolutionary feeling that prompted them to support the uprising. On 1 March 1848 August Hergenhahn[4] was at the centre of meetings which culminated in the drafting of the "Forderungen der Nassauer", which was in the form of a petition to the Duke[5]. The petition, approved at a huge public meeting the following day, started with the sentence: 'Die neueste franzö-

A chapter opening that at first glance looks like a text page

In this dissertation, lack of extra space separating the page **headers** from the following text, gives the impression that all the lines at the top of the page are linked. As a result the chapter heading looks like a line of normal text set in bold capitals, and fails to signal clearly that this is the start of a new chapter.

In fact throughout this dissertation no *internal space* is used. Each page is filled with text, and every line appears the same. The only relief from the monotony is the very occasional **B** subhead (there are seven of them in the whole dissertation), but because they are so visually weak they can be easily missed.

Horizontal spacing is an important part of making headings and subheadings stand out.

● A4 Chapter opening

The numbers refer to specific line positions on the grid

levels of headings

1 A **Chapter 2**
How the research has been done

line drop 7 B **Finding appropriate research methods**

Decisions about methods for the research were based on a combination of experience-based 'inclinations' related to the character of the research, and support from the literature of organisational research.

C The character of the research

The character of the research is essentially practical. It grew from my experience of working in and with organisations on the process of creating information products (on a number of occasions in conjunction with an information-management role), and it aims at an outcome which will be of practical help to people responsible for decisions about information products at all levels. And what I am looking at is essentially a process, whose nature is closely bound up with organisational objectives, structure and culture.

Therefore the research method needed to be oriented to inquiring, as systematically as possible, into how this process is actually managed in organisations. Experience suggested that I was more likely to find something useful by looking closely at the process through case studies in a small number of organisations than by contemplating it from a distance in a large number, by describing accurately rather than by counting, and by letting people tell the story in their own way (though in response to the same questions) rather than constraining them to select given answers. It was an advantage to have had a good deal of experience of making case studies in the course of writing books – though I had to be careful not to choose that method just because experience in a different context made it look an easier option than an experimental and quantitative approach. Fortunately, contemporary thinking about research relating to organisations lends

36 support to qualitative methodologies.

footer 27

Treatment of A, B and C headings:
see pages 218–199

Enlarge page to **159%**

Left-hand facing page

Modern ideas about organisational research

1

There are three relevant strands of thinking. The earliest is related to action research; the second, more recent, but drawing on many of the same ideas, is the thinking which focuses on organisational behaviour and ways of learning about it; and the third places particular emphasis on qualitative as opposed to quantitative methods (which are also explicitly and implicitly supported by the proponents of action research and organisational behaviour). All the strands involve a search for a model more appropriate to looking at human beings in social systems than the traditional 'scientific' paradigm adopted for many years in social science research.

Action research

The history of action research (Susman & Everet, 1978) began with Kurt Lewin in the United States in 1946, and with parallel but independent developments at the Tavistock Institute in the UK. As a research method, its key feature is the combination of 'generation of theory with change in the social system through the researcher acting on or in the social system ... both changing the system and generating critical knowledge about it.' (op cit p586).

The ideas that inform action research developed as a corrective to what were seen as the deficiencies of positivist science which had led to:

> crisis in the field of organizational science ... as our research methods and techniques have become more sophisticated, they have also become increasingly less useful for solving the practical problems that numbers of organizations face. (op cit, p583)

The crisis has arisen because organisational researchers 'have taken the positivist model of science which has had great heuristic value for the physical and biological sciences and some fields of the social sciences, and have adopted it as the ultimate model of what is best for organizational science. By limiting its methods to what it claims is value-free, logical, and empirical, the positivist model of science when applied to organizations produces a knowledge that may only

36

Chapter 2 How the research has been done 28

The numbers refer to specific line positions on the grid

Facing or 'mirror' pages: see 188 for help in setting up

Enlarge page to 159%

Right-hand facing page

The numbers refer to specific line positions on the grid

1 inadvertently solve and sometimes undermine the values of organizational members' (op cit p583)

In contrast to that traditional model, action[1] research is seen as being future oriented and collaborative, as implying the development of the systems being studied so as to modify their relation to the relevant environment, as generating theory which is grounded in action, and as being 'agnostic' and 'situational', in that the consequences of action[1] cannot be fully known, and what happens depends on how the relevant actors currently define the situation (op cit pp589–590).

The legitimacy of its claim to being regarded as scientific rests on 'locating its foundation in philosophical viewpoints that differ from those used to legitimate positivist science.' Those viewpoints include:

- *Praxis* – the 'art of acting on the conditions one faces in order to change them.'
- *Hermeneutics* – the concept of the hermeneutical circle, based on the idea that 'no knowledge is possible without presuppositions', which, in the social sciences, takes the form of gaining knowledge of social systems dialectically 'by proceeding from the whole to its parts and then back again.'
- *Existentialism* – going back to the writings of Kierkegaard and Neitszche, and based on the idea that human interest lies behind every choice.

Heron's (1971, 1981) model of co-operative inquiry, cited by Reason, argues that orthodox research methods are inadequate for a science of persons, because they undermine the self-determination of their 'subjects'. Orthodox scientific method, with its emphasis on

design of footnotes

[1] The concept of 'grounded theory' was first formulated 30 years ago by Glaser and Strauss (1967). As described by Easterby-Smith et al. (1991), they saw the key task of the researcher as being to develop theory through a 'comparative method', that is, looking at events or processes in different settings; the resultant theory should be 'sufficiently analytic to allow some generalisation to take place, but at the same time it should be possible for people to relate the theory to their
36 own experiences, thus sensitising their own perceptions.' (pp35–36)

Chapter 2 How the research has been done 29

Enlarge page to 159%

Bibliography 'A bibliography is an integral part of a book's system of reference, and should contain all specific sources mentioned – or mentioned more than once – within the book. If a work has only a handful of references it may be possible to do without a bibliography. Authors who cite a number of works frequently but others only or twice may find a list of *Abbrevations and Works Frequently Cited* (in the preliminary matter) sufficient. However, the greater the number and complexity of the references, the greater the need for a bibliography' (Ritter, 2003).

1 References

ABBOTT, R (1997), 'Information transfer and cognitive mismatch: a Popperian model for studies of public understanding', *Journal of Information Science* 23 (2) 129–137
Advisory Council on Science and Technology (1993), *People, Technology and Organisations. The Application of Human Factors and Organisational Design,* Cabinet Office (Office of Public Service and Science) and Advisory Council on Science and Technology, London: HMSO
ARGYRIS, C and SCHON, D (1978), *Organizational Learning: a theory of action perspective,* Addison Wesley

---

2 Baber, C (1993), 'Usability is useless', HCI Newsletter No. 22, 24–25

Barabas, C (1993), 'Uncovering the CYA phenomenon in organizational writing: initial findings', *Technical Communication,* Second Quarter, 344–348

Belkin, N (1990) 'The cognitive viewpoint in information science', *Journal of Information Science,* 16, 11–150

---

3 References

Beabes, M A and Flanders, A (1995), 'Experiences with using contextual inquiry to design information', *Technical Communication,* 42 (3) 409–425

Bist, G, Dixon, K and Chadwick, G (1993) 'Setting up a customer network to review documentation'
Technical Communication, Fourth quarter, 715–719

Blair, R, Roberts, K and McKechnie, P (1985) 'Vertical and network communication in organizations'
In P K Tompkins and R D McPhee (eds) *Organizational Communication: traditional themes and new directions*
Sage Annual Review of Communication Research, Vol 13
Beverly Hills, CA: Sage Publications

Notes on designing references

Bibliographical references are made up of segments of information, with each segment doing a particular job. The typographic challenge is to make the many different kinds of text – author's name, title of book or periodical, dates, different kind of numerals – into a synthesis of all the segments.

In these three examples slightly different approaches are taken:
1 Is the simplest and most economical in the amount of space taken and requires fewer end of line decisions. The use of small capitals helps the author names to stand out, but requires more work to get the spacing of the small capitals correct.
2 Is similar to 1, but easier to typeset; requires work in changing the whole line space into half line spaces that separate each entry.
3 Is the simplest, uses default lining figures, one line space to separate entries. A 2-column layout gives a shorter line length, giving more control in the way that individual lines break.

The numbers refer to specific line positions on the grid

1 **Bibliography**

line drop **7** Abbott, R (1997), 'Information transfer and cognitive mismatch: a Popperian model for studies of public understanding', *Journal of Information Science* 23 (2) 129–137

Advisory Council on Science and Technology (1993), *People, Technology and Organisations. The Application of Human Factors and Organisational Design* Cabinet Office (Office of Public Service and Science) and Advisory Council on Science and Technology. London: HMSO

Argyris, C and Schon, D (1978), *Organizational Learning: a theory of action perspective.* Reading, MA: Addison Wesley

Baber, C (1993), 'Usability is useless', *HCI Newsletter* No. 22, 24–25

Barabas, C (1993), 'Uncovering the CYA phenomenon in organizational writing: initial findings', *Technical Communication,* Second Quarter, 344–348

Bist, G, Dixon, K and Chadwick, G (1993), 'Setting up a customer network to review documentation', *Technical Communication,* Fourth quarter, 715–719

Blair, R, Roberts, K and McKechnie, P (1985), 'Vertical and network communication in organizations'. In P K Tompkins and R D McPhee (eds) *Organizational Communication: traditional themes and new directions.* Sage Annual Review of Communication Research, Vol 13. Beverly Hills, CA: Sage Publications

Boisot, M (1987), *Information and organizations. The manager as anthropologist.* London: HarperCollins (cited in Garratt, 1994)

Bowonder, B and Miyake, T (1992), 'Creating and sustaining competitiveness: information management strategies of Nippon
36 Steel Corporation', *International Journal of Information,* 12, 39–56

27

Bibliography style in a dissertation: see alternative design answers on the opposite page

Enlarge page to **159%**

Tables A table is essentially a systematic arrangement of discrete pieces of information that are scanned horizontally or vertically. They can be principally numeric, as in a timetable, or combine words and numerals. Information presented in rows and columns is so commonplace that it is probably assumed that most people readily understand it. But research commissioned by the Decimal Currency Board in the late 60s and early 70s, to help design conversion tables for the public to use when Britain adopted decimal currency in 1971 – discovered that some types of table were incomprehensible to many of the population (see Wright,1968 and Wright and Fox,1970).

Tabulation is important for displaying certain kinds of research information but most researchers probably find planning the layout of tables and inputting them in Microsoft Word a bit of a chore. It is difficult to find the instructions for setting up tables from the Help menu, and when found they are quite complex. You can create either a simple table by using the *Insert Table* command, or a more complex one by using *Draw Table*. But whichever route you take, you are obliged to capture and place every set of words or numbers in boxes that make a sort of net for imprisoning data.[5] This treatment makes tables not only daunting to look at but also difficult to read (see examples 3 – 5 opposite).

Yet there is another way of doing the job, which demands less of both creator and reader – a design solution that has been available for more than 74 years, since the publication in 1935 of Jan Tschichold's revolutionary work.[6] On tables, he laid down the principles behind the use of the open table, which today are universally accepted as a visually simpler way of organizing data: 'In tabular matter, the usual thick/thin and fine double rules, and indeed all kinds of rule combination, must at last be got rid of.With simple rules,from fine to twelve-point, even the narrowest column spacing can be made clear and better than with the old rule combinations.' (op. cit. page 215). The final British currency-conversion tables resulting from the research described above followed the principles he set out, and did not use vertical or horizontal lines. By the end of the 1970s, boxes had more or less disappeared from general use, their departure speeded by legibility research (see Wright and Fox,1970, Hartley,1978, and Miles 1987). The majority of those in design and the publishing industry adopted simpler and quicker methods, replacing the boxes by the 'open-table' design solution that either dispenses with lines entirely, or uses only the occasional horizontal line.

5
I suspect that the view that all tables should be constructed entirely of interlocking cells has grown out of the design of spreadsheets, which are commonly used to collect raw data for analysis, as a preliminary to converting to tabular form.

6
Typographische Gestaltung (1935) and published in English as *Asymmetric Typography*, in which he made a forceful argument for adopting asymmetric typography (see page 62), using only sans serif typefaces, and simplifying the way that design with type was arranged.

1

2 *Insert Table*

Draw Table

3|4

WARNING: DO NOT EXCEED THE STATED DOSE
Storage Do not store above 25°C Store in the original container.
Ingredients Each modified release capsule contains: **Ibuprofen 200mg.**

DO NOT EXCEED THE STATED DOSE.
Ingredients Each tablet contains **Paracetamol 500mg.** **Caffein 65mg**
Please note Please read the enclosed leaflet which provides more information about this product.

Boxes are far more useful in designing forms, invoices and some pre-printed business stationery – where data has often to be printed in specific data fields – than in designing tablulated matter.

The reason why the Word commands *Insert Table* and *Draw Table* automatically construct boxes is probably that box panels, are such a common design feature on packaging and web pages. In packaging, where legislation requires more and more information to be fitted into small areas, panels do help to separate information zones.

5

Conversion factors	Values are given to three figures except where marked† which signifies an exact figure		
	To convert	*into*	*Multiply by*
Length	inches feet yards miles	millimetres (mm) metres (m) metres (m) kilometres (km)	25.4† 0.3048† 0.91444† 1.61
Area	square inches square feet square yards acres	square millimetres (mm²) square metres (m²) square metres (m²) square metres (m²)	645 0.0929 0.836 4050

6

Conversion factors	Values are given to three figures except where marked† which signifies an exact figure		
	To convert	*into*	*Multiply by*
Length	inches	millimetres (mm)	25.4†
	feet	metres (m)	0.3048†
	yards	metres (m)	0.91444†
	miles	kilometres (km)	1.61
Area	square inches	square millimetres (mm²)	645
	square feet	square metres (m²)	0.0929
	square yards	square metres (m²)	0.836
	acres	square metres (m²)	4050

1 *Insert Table* allows you to construct joined-up boxes to predetermined dimensions.

2 *Draw Table* takes you into the pencil mode, which gives you freedom to draw boxes of varying sizes and rule thickness. Both require preliminary drawn design work.

3|4 Two warning panels on the reverse side of a package giving vital drug information, usually associated with having to read very small type sizes, which increases eye strain. Putting all the text in a separate panel does help to isolate it from the rest of the text.

5 Example of a table where each segment of data is in a box. This kind of table is more difficult to read and takes considerably more time to construct.

6 By comparison the 'open table' is easier to read, and far easier to construct.

(A) Heading
Treatment of headings

(B) or secondary headings sitting on the text
Placing B headings directly over a paragraph can be acceptable if only one level of headings is being used in the dissertation. Placing B headings in this way does, however, mean that all subsequent paragraphs have to be indented by 13.5pts. If you don't indent but separate the paragraphs by one line space, then the heading appears to be visually connected only to the first paragraph and not to the following ones.

(B) or secondary headings with space before and after

A better solution is to separate the headings from the text by using a **half line space** after the heading and **one and a half line** spaces before. To give more visual feedback: with the grid turned on, return to Section 4 change the vertical spacing from **exactly 18 pt** to **exactly 9 pt;** this will allow all the text lines and the headings within the text to be placed on the underlying grid. To automatically vary the vertical spacing to get a half line space, return to Section 5, on page 190, and change your style sheets for B and C headings. Type 18 pt in the **Before** box and 9 pt in the **After** box.

(C) or third level headings in regular OR REGULAR SMALL CAPS

If your dissertation needs a third level heading, you can use the same sans serif typeface changing from bold to the regular weight. Alternatively if you have choosen one of the Microsoft Cleartype fonts you can use small caps, with some letterspacing. See Chapter 9.3, pages 228–229.

Note: When you enlarge the individual templates to **159%** the typefaces get distorted and appear larger than they should. This accurate picture of an A4 page shows how the types should appear in the finished dissertation.

Information on the typefaces used on this A4 page:
(A) headings are set in 15 pt Calibri bold, with 3 pt leading
(B) headings are set in 12 pt Calibri bold, with 6 pt leading
(C) headings are set in 12 pt Calibri regular and small caps, with 6 pt leading
Text is set in 12 pt Cambria regular and bold, with 6 pt leading

All of these typefaces are Microsoft ClearTypes and are suitable for document design

A checklist of things you should have done by this point
Have you:

1 Decided which of the dissertation elements on page 182 you will need, ticked them, photocopied the page and filed for reference? ☐

2 Set up the complete Word typographical design specification following Sections 1 to 7, photocopied and filed for reference? See pages 187 to 191 ☐

3 Photocopied either the A4 or US Letter size grid to 159% and filed pages for future design reference? See pages 194 and 195 ☐

4 Photocopied all the individual templates you have decided to use onto A3 sheets for design guidance and filed for reference? Note: if you are using US Letter size don't forget that you can only fit 34 lines to the page, two less than the A4 size ☐

Now all you have to do is to choose the typefaces you want to use; see Chapter 9.3, pages 228 and 229 for information and advice

✔

tick boxs when completed ☐

References

Websites referred to in this chapter accessed 18 March 2009

BROWN, MICHELLE P (1994)
Understanding Illuminated Manuscripts: A Guide to Technical Terms.
Malibu: J Paul Getty; London: British Library.

FORTE, BRIAN (2002)
A4 vs US Letter.
http://betweenborders.com/wordsmithing/a4-vs-us-letter/

HARTLEY, J (1978)
Designing instructional text.
London: Kogan Page.

MILES, J (1987)
Design for desktop publishing.
London: Gordon Fraser.

RITTER, R M, (2003)
The Oxford Style Manual.
Oxford: Oxford University Press.

TSCHICHOLD, J
Asymmetric typography.
trans. Ruari McLean.
London: Faber & Faber 1967.

WRIGHT, P (1968)
Using tabulated information,
Ergonomics, 11 (4) 331–343.

WRIGHT, P and FOX, K (1970)
Presenting information in tables,
Applied Ergonomics, 1 (4) 234–242.

Further reading

MŰLLER-BROCKMANN, JOSEF (1981)
Grid systems/Raster systeme.
Niederteufen: Arthur Niggli.

PREPPERNAU, J, COX, J and FRYE, C (2008)
Microsoft® Office® Home and Student Step by Step.
Redmond, Washington: Microsoft Press.

HIGGINS, H (2009)
The Grid Book.
Cambridge, MA: MIT Press.

Design is more than cosmetic: seeing is perceiving

Ch 9.3 Contents at a glance

Introduction

This chapter is called 'Seeing is perceiving' because it deals with the design implications of what we put before the eye of readers. Few people are aware that there are design implications and their ignorance causes a lot of trouble – and not just for the readers of dissertations. Since we are writing for researchers, we think we owe it to them to tell them something of the theory that underlies the practical advice in Chapter 9.2.

That theory draws on how the human brain has evolved over the 100,000 years since *homo* became *sapiens*. The first work in understanding what we see is done by our inbuilt visual system. It's a lot older than the technology that presents to us what we see on page or screen, and it doesn't change anywhere near as quickly. It has to be respected, rather than insulted, if its remarkable powers are to work at their best. That means that design decisions have to take into account the interactions of what readers see with how they see and read – and the decisions on all the individual features affect one another.

What do readers see?

When we look at text, our eyes are confronted by: characters grouped into words; words with horizontal spaces between them grouped into lines, which are separated by vertical spaces; lines arranged in blocks; the whole array displayed on a field – page or screen – with a defined outer boundary, and a margin separating text and boundary.

How do they see?[1]

Chapter 9.2 has shown how different ways of arranging what readers see affect how readily they can make sense of it. Research by 'Gestalt'[2] psychologists in the 1920s provided clear evidence of how the human eye responds to the visual structures presented to it. As Dondis (1973) expresses it: 'if several alternative structures are possible, the simplest and most stable will be selected'. The Gestalt principles of 'proximity', and 'similarity' underlie the examples of helpful and unhelpful arrangements of text shown in Chapter 9.2. As defined by Broom (n.d) the first principle is: 'things which are closer together will be seen as belonging together' and the second: 'things which share visual characteristics such as shape, size, colour ... will be seen as belonging together'.

The work of present-day neuroscientists sheds light on how the structure and functioning of the human brain may account for these observations. The British biologist and neuroscientist Steven Rose (2006) explains that

1
For a readable and scholarly account of how we learn to read (and why we sometimes fail to do so), and the role of the human brain in the process, and how it changes as we become expert readers, see Wolf (2008).

2
The word means 'organized whole' (see Broom, n.d.)

information is transformed into perception and becomes meaningful 'in the visual cortex itself; multiple interconnections link the separate modules, integrating their separate analyses; the flow of signals between them is the mechanism of perception'. And the American neuroscientist Antonio Damasio (1994, 2006) writes (in the context of his research on the role of emotion in thinking) of the part played by visual images in the subsequent work of recalling knowledge that is distributed among many brain sites: 'because of the brain's design, the requisite broad-based knowledge depends on numerous systems located in relatively separate brain regions rather than in one region. A large part of such knowledge is recalled in the form of images at many brain sites rather than at a single site.'

How do they read?

The eyes are the front end of the visual system, and research over the past 100 years has revealed what they are up to when we read. It has been known for more than a century that it's an energetic process of jumps forward and back, with pauses between. As Larson, a reading psychologist with Microsoft, describes it (2004), and as shown in Figure 9.3.1 below.

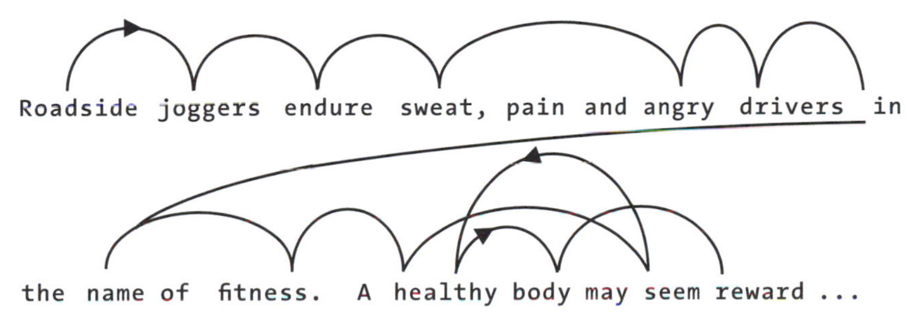

Figure 9.3.2 Saccadic eye movements. Reproduced with permission, from Larson (2004)

'We fixate on a word for a period of time, roughly 200–250ms, then make a ballistic movement to another word. These movements are called saccades and usually take 20–35ms. Most saccades are forward movements from 7 to 9 letters, but 10–15 percent of all saccades are regressive or backwards reading. The location of the fixation is not random. Not all words are fixated; short words and particularly function words are frequently skipped.'

There are various interpretations in the eye-movement literature of what clues are most important in the process of recognizing words – basically word or letter shapes. Larson concludes in the light of the evidence that 'we are using letter information to recognize words, as we are better able to read when more letters are available to us. We combine abstracted letter information across saccades to help facilitate word recognition, so it is letter information that we are gathering in the periphery [of vision]. And finally we are using word space information to program the location of our next saccade'.

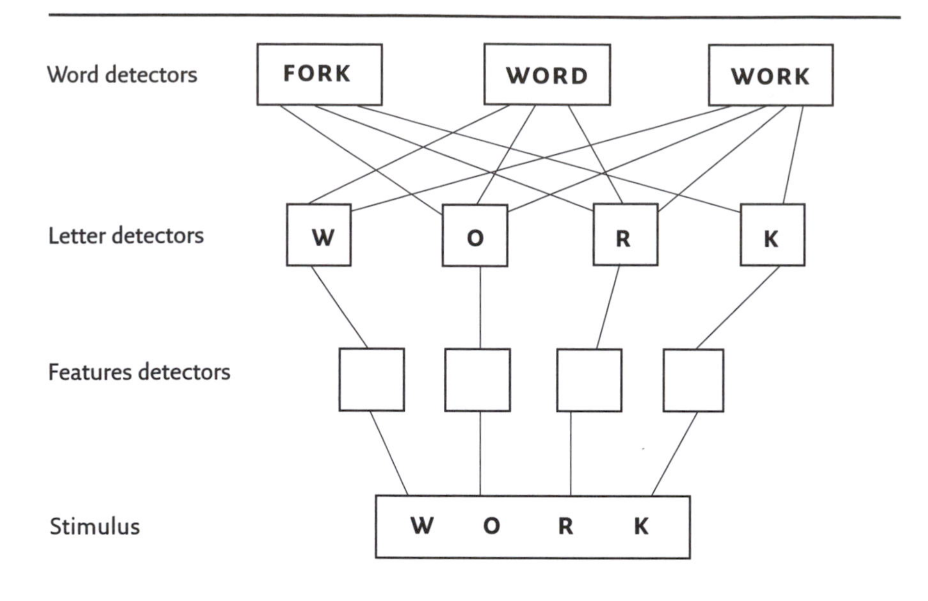

Figure 9.3.2 Parallel letter recognition. Reproduced with permission, from Larson (2004)

Figure 9.3.2 shows the process Larson describes. The lessons from that are:

1. Because the first clue for the eye is the lines that make up letters, and their direction, use typefaces whose letterforms are close to a central norm. Reassuringly, typographers have, from historical studies, also concluded that plain simple unadorned typefaces have survived because their skeleton shapes are identical.
2. Since groups of letters that don't normally occur together in known words slow up the rate of reading, check spelling with care.

These findings about the detail of eye movement complement earlier research on legibility, which can be defined as the ease and accuracy which comprehension of meaningful printed material takes place. Tinker & Paterson (1941), Tinker (1963), and other studies of legibility and eye movement, confirmed that the number of characters, and consequently the number of words, in a line play an important role in ease, accuracy and comprehension of what we read. An average of 60–70 characters and 11 to 14 words gave the best results, but this applies to designing documents or books, not newspapers or magazines.

Overlong lines make for difficulty in reading, because the eye has to make more fixations, and more regressive (backward) movements. There is also the tendency when moving to the beginning of a new line to pick up the start of the line just read. If on the other hand lines are very short, reading is also made more difficult; breaking up the sentences into very small word groups causes the eye to make many backward movements.

Overlong lines make for difficulty in reading, because the eye has to make more fixations, and more regressive (backward) movements. There is also the tendency when moving to the beginning of a new line to pick up the start of the line just read.

If on the other hand lines are very short, reading is also made more difficult; breaking up the sentences into very small word groups causes the eye to make many backward movements

If you count the average number of words per line in the dissertation templates on pages 211–213, you will find they match the research findings. This will be maintained if you get the point size of your style sheets correct (see page 190).

But although the research is well founded and the results have been around for so long, it is still very common to select too long a measure with 16 to 20 words in the average line, especially in documents for an A4 page format – including dissertations.

From the point of view of researchers, there is self-interest in paying heed to these findings, because we human beings have a built-in 'mental-cost calculator' when we meet text; if it looks as though it's going to be hard going, unless there are compelling survival reasons, we avoid reading it.

Now we return to the facts discussed on pages 223–224 about the importance of letter shapes in reading as our first clue in recognizing words, and the help that 'simple unadorned skeleton shapes' give in the task. The next section shows a cross-section of typefaces which you can safely use, and explains how the elements of their anatomy influence the way that readers are able to interact with them, and the implications for choosing appropriate typefaces.

What does history tell us about the shapes of our letters?

Most readers take the shapes of the upright roman typefaces that we read each day entirely for granted, probably not appreciating that our western typography is constructed from what Gerrit Noordzij (2000) calls 'prefabricated letters' which have their origins in an 8th-century national writing style know as Carolingian. It was developed by decree of King Charlemagne of France (742–816) to replace the existing scripts inherited from the Romans, because over time they had become corrupted by scripts imported from Irish and English monasteries and as a result were difficult to read and even illegible.

Figure 9.3.3 on the next page shows a reproduction of 9th-century Carolingian writing. Although this lettering underwent further changes, to evolve by the 12th century into what were known as Gothic characters, as Hans Meyer (1963) comments, 'Both the Gothic and the Carolingian hands had their origins in France, and from there quickly spread to neighbouring countries'.

The Carolingian letterforms became the model for the printed roman alphabet that we use today. The Gothic form developed as a formal book hand known as Gothic Textura, and it was this letterform that was used by Johannes Gutenberg for printing the first books made from movable type. Both these sets of letters evolved from shapes carefully written with a broad

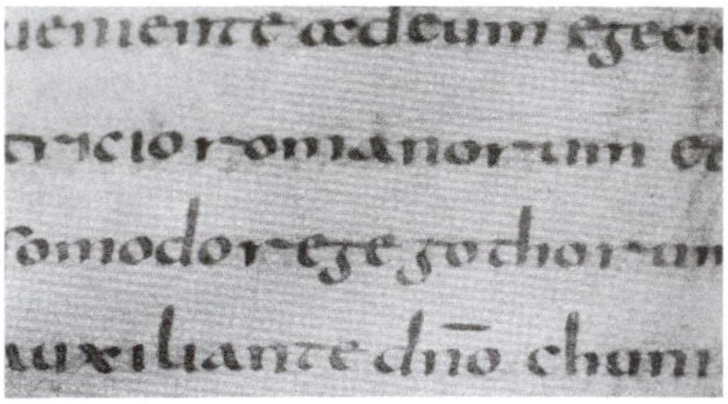

Carolingian minuscules developed over a period from the 9th to the 12th centuries. Over that period of time the letterforms underwent many subtle changes in the way they were written.

As André Gürtler (1965) comments, 'A main feature of Carolingian minuscule script is it high degree of legibility, the letters being well formed'.

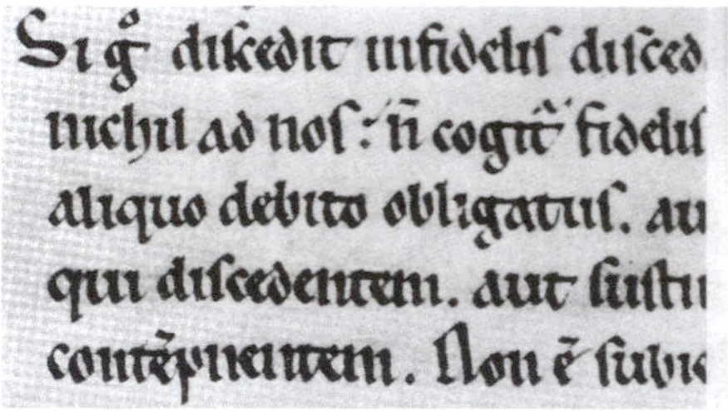

Gürtler comments 'Carolingian minuscule was transformed into an early Gothic, a narrow or condensed script full of broken features'. The arches of the letters were flattened, the letter strokes became heavier, and the interior white shapes become narrower. This letterform was known as Textura.

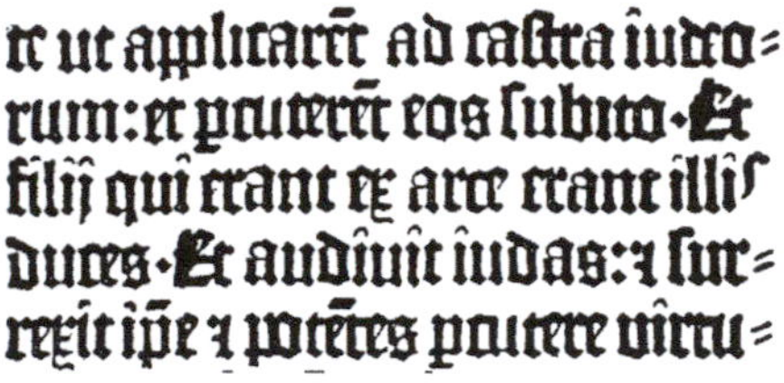

The Gothic Textura was the model used by Johannes Gutenberg when cutting the type for his 42-line Bible which was printed in the period between 1452 and 1454/55. Textura was considered the most beautiful and distinguished script of the Middle Ages.

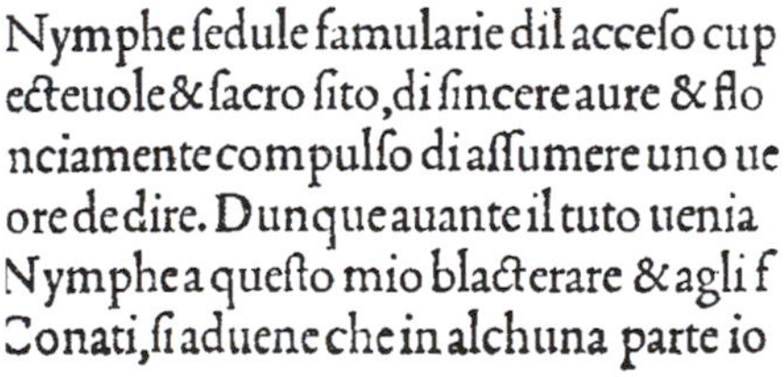

Early Italian roman-style typeface cut by the punchcutter Francesco da Bologna for the printer-publisher Aldus Manutius and used in the book *Hypnerotomachia Poliphili*, which he published in 1499.

The shapes of these early roman typefaces are still used today and form the foundation of our western alphabet.

Figure 9.3.3 This figure shows the link between Carolingian writing and present day roman typefaces

pen; the fact that the letterforms had a heavier stroke, and looked different from the roman model was, according to Noordzij's (2005) analysis, to do with the angle at which letters were written, $\pm 45^{\circ}$ for Textura and a modest $<30^{\circ}$ for the roman. Textura was eventually replaced in the 16th century by Fractur (meaning broken) and this continued to be used in Germany until 1940/41 when it was banned by the Nazi party.

Choosing a typeface

It has been estimated that there are more than 100,000 typefaces available for use on a PC or a Mac,[3] any one of which can be downloaded once you purchase a licence that entitles you to use it. However researchers using word-processing software such as Microsoft Word will find packaged with the software a range of typefaces, from single fonts to entire families, suitable for designing and typesetting a document such as a dissertation.

What is a suitable typeface?

While no guidance is provided on which of these fonts might be suitable for designing documents, common sense – or conditioned association – usually comes into play and leads researchers to choose font designs which are intended for continuous text. Generally these are familiar-looking unadorned fonts which follow a traditional underlying skeleton form.

The letterforms that condition our reading habits have evolved slowly over the last 500 years, but the basic skeleton shape of each letter is more or less fixed in time. The detail of the individual letterforms has been modified over time in ways that are largely the result of how printing and paper-making technology having evolved from hand-based to machine-based production. But many new typefaces are designed to meet new reading situations – for example reading large amounts of text on screen instead of paper, or information that has to be printed in small type sizes; in these and similar cases, type designers produce fonts that meet the very specific requirements of the situation.[4]

To help researchers make decisions on a range of typefaces suitable for setting their dissertations, I have compiled a short list of fonts supplied with Microsoft Word 2004, with Windows OS XP or Word 2006 and Windows Vista. These are shown on the following double-page spread, and are suitable to use in conjunction with the enlarged A4/A3 photocopied templates in 9.2.

3
The OpenType format allows the font to be used on a PC and a Mac, Font in this format are cross-platform and support a greater number of characters and languages.

4
One such typeface was PT, designed in two weights (55 and 56) by Erik Spiekermann for the German Post Office in 1985. The project was cancelled and the typeface was never used, but it was eventually released in 1991 by *FontShop* in Berlin as FF Meta family. Part of the original design brief required that the typeface had to be 'very legible, particularly in small sizes and under the special considerations of finding names and figures rather than reading extensive amounts of copy'. Spiekermann, E (1987)

Serif typefaces suitable for use in a dissertation, or other documents

This page and the next show sample text settings using typefaces available with Microsoft Word: serif below, sans serif opposite (see Figures 9.3 4 & 9.3.5). The samples marked with CT are set in Microsoft Cleartypes (see Berry, 2004).

All text examples are set to the same point size of **11 pts**, but, as you can see, there is little relation between the point size and the appearing size. The examples also use the two forms of arabic numerals: 1234567890 – 'lining' or 'ranging', and 123467890 – 'non-lining' or 'oldface'. Non-lining are more suitable for use within text, and lining are better used in setting tabular matter.

Constantia is available on PCs using *Microsoft Word 2004* with Windows XP or Word 2006 with Windows Vista. Cleartype fonts marked with CT have between 713 & 992 separate glyphs*. CT

Design: John Hudson, as part of the Microsoft Cleartype font collection. **Size 11 pts**

Cambria is available on PCs using *Microsoft Word* 2004 with Windows XP or Word 2006 with Windows Vista. Cleartype fonts marked with CT have between 713 & 992 separate glyphs. CT

Design: Jelle Bosma, with Steve Matterson and Robin Nicholas, as part of the Microsoft Cleartype font collection. **Size 11 pts**

Times New Roman is available on PCs using *Microsoft Word 2004* with Windows XP or Word 2006 with Windows Vista. Cleartype fonts marked with CT have between 713 & 992 separate glyphs.

Original design: Stanley Morrison for the Times newspaper in 1931. **Size 11 pts**

Georgia is available on PCs using *Microsoft Word 2004* with Windows XP or Word 2006 with Windows Vista. Cleartype fonts marked with CT have between 713 & 992 separate glyphs.

Design: Matthew Carter for the Microsoft Corporation. **Size 11 pts**

Glyph: the term used to describe any individual character in a font e.g. ß©™<>=@%1122fiflá•

The technical expressions for parts and forms of serif characters

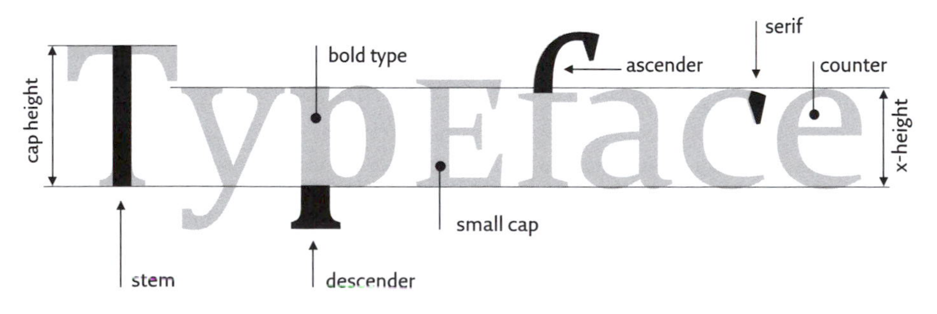

Figure 9.3.4 Serifs are a distinguishing feature of a main group of typefaces. This diagram shows them and the other parts of characters

Sans serif typefaces suitable for text setting dissertations

Although typefaces without serifs might appear to be identical, there are in fact four main groups: 1 Grotesque *sans* 1896 2 Neo-grotesque *sans* 1989
3 Geometric *sans* 1927 4 Humanistic *sans* 1928

Types in groups 1 and 3 are usually not available in Word packages, but groups 2 and 4 are. All the typefaces below are suitable for a dissertation. Their different design characteristics will change its overall appearance, while bold sans is useful for headings when the text is set in a contrasting serif face.

Arial is available on PCs using *Microsoft Word 2004* with Windows XP or Word 2006 with Windows Vista. Cleartype fonts marked with CT have between 713 & 992 separate glyphs.

Design: Monotype Corporation for Microsoft.. **Size 11 pts**

CT **Calibri** is available on PCs using *Microsoft Word 2004* with Windows XP or Word 2006 with Windows Vista. Cleartype fonts marked with CT have between 713 & 992 separate glyphs.

Design: Luc(as) de Groot, as part of the Microsoft Cleartype font collection. **Size 11 pts**

CT **Candara** is available on PCs using *Microsoft Word 2004* with Windows XP or Word 2006 with Windows Vista. Cleartype fonts marked with CT have between 713 & 992 individual separate glyphs.

Design: Gary Munch, as part of the Microsoft Cleartype font collection. **Size 11 pts**

CT **Corbel** is available on PCs using *Microsoft Word 2004* with Windows XP or Word 2006 with Windows Vista. Cleartype fonts marked with CT have between 713 & 992 separate glyphs.

Design: Jeremy Tankard, as part of the Microsoft Cleartype font collection. **Size 11 pts**

Trebuchet MS is available on PCs using *Microsoft Word 2004* with Windows XP or Word 2006 with Windows Vista. Cleartype fonts marked with CT have between 713 & 992 separate glyphs.

Design: Vincent Connare for the Microsoft Corporation in 1996. **Size 11 pts**

There are many design differences between different sans serif typefaces

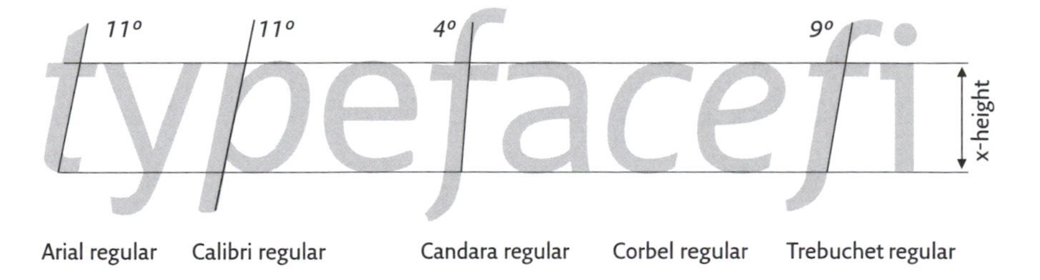

Figure 9.3.5 Sans serif italic types are distinguished by visual differences, not only in their shapes and terminals, but in the angle of slope of the letters

What makes typefaces look different?

The most obvious difference between the two groups of typefaces on page 228 and 229 is that one has serifs and one doesn't. Serif typefaces of every shape and form are more commonly used in the setting of continuous text for books, magazines, newspapers, and research or official documents, although many of the latter are also set in sans type. On balance we read far more texts in serif faces than in sans, which suggests that our reading habits are conditioned towards letters with, rather than without, serifs.

The colour of a typeface

Closer study of the two groups will show differences in what type designers term the 'colour of the type' ('colour' in this context refers the degree of blackness seen in a page of type). Comparison between the passages set in the regular weight of the serif typefaces Cambria and Constantia shows that these two types are not identical in colour values. Similar differences in colour value can be seen in sans serif type as well.

Before you make a final decision on typefaces for your dissertation, set and print out a series of A4 specimen pages in the typefaces on your shortlist, using your master template and outline specification (see pages 187–191). The result will give you invaluable feedback on the appearance and typographical colour of each font.

There are two reasons for differences in type colour: some are related to the 'weight' of the type, and some to design features of different fonts.

Traditionally typefaces were made available in roman and italic forms, and in two weights: regular/normal and bold, and that is the policy still followed with Microsoft Word fonts, with the exception of the sans font Arial which has a more extensive range of weights. Today, many serif and sans serif typefaces are available in larger families; the main font used in this book (Fresco) has five separate weights, but the entire family extends to 21 varients – four of the separate weights are shown on the left in Figure 9.3.6. As you can see, as the weight increases from normal to black the type gets blacker and the internal white spaces smaller. The difference within this single font is achieved by careful changes in the thickness of the underlying shape.

Normal & *italic*	Regular	The degree of blackness
Semi Bold & *italic*	Regular	The degree of blackness
Bold & *italic*	Regular	The degree of blackness
Black	Regular	The degree of blackness

Figure 9.3.6 Left: colour values within a single font family related to a series of weights
Right: a comparison of the colour values of the regular weight of four different fonts

The right-hand column of Figure 9.3.6 gives an idea of how the degree of what typographers call 'colour' is influenced by the design features of the four different fonts. Smal text set in a typeface with a marked contrast between thick and thin strokes and a small x-height is less legible and more of a strain to read, because the individual characters when printed carry less ink; typefaces with less 'contrast' between thick and thin strokes and with larger x-height, carry more ink, appear visually larger and are therefore easier to read.

Measuring the characters: what is the point?

Types are measured in multiples of points – a unique unit of measurement used only in printing and typography. If you look at the sample settings on pages 228 and 229 you will notice they are all set to 11 points (pts), and yet our eyes tell us some types appear larger than others.

The reason for this dates back to the invention in 1450 of movable type consisting of single metal cubes with a character cast on the top surface. For the invention to work, these had to have (see Figure 9.3.7 below): 1 a standard height-to-paper dimension; 2 a standard unit of measurement for the front-to-back dimension (the 'point', which defines the type size); 3 a measurement defining the width of the individual characters (the 'set measurement').

The point unit is unchangeable, but type designs differ, and that is why these two typefaces, set to the identical point size appear and print differently:

a 9 pt type with a small x-height and long ascenders and descenders,

a 9pt type with a large x-height and short ascenders and descenders.

Setting words and setting lines

Historically words haven't always been separated from each other by what we now refer to as the word spaces. As Saenger (1997) points out: 'In the West, the ability to read silently and rapidly is a result of the historical evolution of word separation that, beginning in the seventh century, changed the format of the written page, which had to be read orally and slowly in order to comprehend.'

Metal type

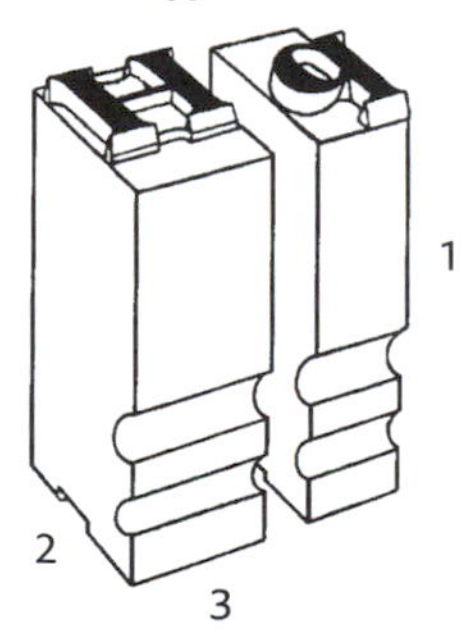

The desktop publishing point

The smallest unit of measurement is one point, there are 72 desktop publishing points to an inch, and twelve of them make a larger unit of measurement known as a pica.

The *body size* is the imaginary design space that fixes the point size of the individual characters. The example characters below are all 19 pts and are fitted into a space of 19 pts, but the typefaces still vary in their appearing size.

Hg IgIg

The body size is invisible to the eye, but its height is made up from multiples of the basic 1 point unit: 0.0139 inch or 0.3528 mm.

Figure 9.3.7 Although the technology has changed from analogue to digital, the system of measuring type sizes has remained more or less the same

Although the word space has not always been a convention, it is now an established law in typography that when setting continuous text, the space between the words should appear visually smaller than the space between the lines. The purpose of this is to link the words, as well as allowing the eye to move across the page without too many impediments, and to separate clearly one line of text from another. In setting a block of text you also have to make decisions about the space between the characters and lines as discussed next.

The character space

In Microsoft Word – as in professional desktop publishing software – the character spacing and the line spacing specification are separated. But in Word, although you have exact control over the distance between lines, the control over the character spacing is far less exact. The character space is fixed at 100% and although you can reduce or increase it by 1 pt increments, doing so also changes the width of the characters. Reducing the width from 100% to 90% condenses the width of typeface as this. Expanding the character space does the opposite. Change to the fundamental proportions of the letterform is to be avoided, and you get the best results by leaving the default setting on 100%.

The line space

If the line space is smaller than the word space it can make the process of reading more difficult; it shunts the lines together, and the visual effect is similar to that of condensing the typeface.

The design characteristics of the typeface will influence the decision about interline space. Typefaces with a large x-height and short ascenders and descenders need more generous space between the lines. If, as here, the text is 'set solid' (i.e. if the interline space is the same point size as the type), the ascenders and descenders can collide, and the lines appear uncomfortably close together. That makes the word spaces (which can't be modified without changing the horizontal scale of the typeface) more prominent, which gives the impression of rivers of white space running vertically through the text. In contrast, typefaces with a small x-height and long ascenders and descenders need less interline space; they can be set solid without appearing crowded, by virtue of their small x-height. The above examples are set solid and the lines are justified without any end-of-line hyphenation.

The Cleartype fonts in the collection available in the full version of Word are of average width, but they do not have identical x-height values, so setting text matter solid could produce the results seen in the first example above. So the best design decision is to avoid setting type solid.

From lines to pages in a dissertation

Most institutions stipulate that dissertations should be A4 (or in Northern America) US Letter. They also mention that the margins either side should be generous, while they give no reason why, or what the internal page structure should look like.

Left: Thread sewn hollow-back book, opens more or less flat.

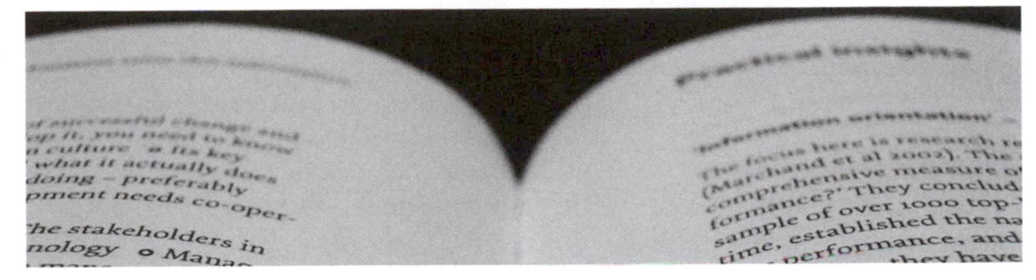

Right: Perfect binding, sheets glued together, book doesn't open flat.

Figure 9.3.8 The process of reading takes place on a curved surface, and the extent of the curve depends on the way the pages of the book are joined together and the grain direction of the paper

Generous margins are needed because there are differences, as well as similarities, between the way the pages of books and dissertations as physical objects are put together, because that has a great effect on the experience of reading, and in particular requires careful decisions about the margins that define the boundaries of the printed page.

Both books and dissertations are 3D physical objects printed on both sides of standard sheets and bound. Books can have many page sizes, dissertations just one – A4 opening to a span of 420 mm, a bulky volume which is not portable like a novel. The great variety of book formats is possible because their pages come from paper of various standard sizes folded into 'sections' of interleaved pages, which are either sewn or glued together and fixed into a binding, with hard or flexible covers. Dissertations, by contrast, are constructed of single, unfolded pages of a standard paper size, and that means there is only one binding option: glueing, or, as it is called, 'perfect' binding (a misnomer).

How binding affects reading

As a hand-bookbinder with 10,000 hours apprenticeship, my first question before I start designing a book is 'how is it going to be bound?' If I am told perfect binding, or adhesive binding, then I know that I need to design the book with wider back margins. Perfect binding joins the pages together by glue, and this physically prevents the pages from opening flat, so if the margins are narrow part of the text area will start to disappear into the spine (as it does on this page), making the reading process far more difficult. If a book is to open flat, the folded printed sheets – known as sections – have to be stitched together. Figure 9.3.8 shows the extent of the curve of the two binding methods.

This book, and the complete set of dissertation templates, are designed to take account of the fact that the printed pages are going to be held together by glue. The book could have been thread sewn (see the original publishers design brief, quoted on page 144), but mechanical thread sewing can't be used on dissertations, simply because the printing is on single A4 pages.

References

Websites referred to in this chapter accessed on 18 March 2009

Berry, J B (2004)
Now Read this: The Microsoft ClearType Font Collection.
Microsoft ClearType and Advanced Reading Technologies Group. Microsoft Corporation.
http://www.microsoft.com/typography/ctfonts

Broom, K (n.d.)
Gestalt Theory of Visual Perception.
http://www.users.totalise.co.uk/~kbroom/Lectures/gestalt.htm

Damasio, A (2006)
Descartes Error.
London: Vintage (Revised edition of 1994 first edition).

Dondis, D A (1973)
Primer of Visual Literacy.
Cambridge, MA, and London, England: The MIT Press.

Gürtler, A (1965)
The development of the Roman Alphabet.
Zurich: Bildungsverband Schweizerischer Buchdrucker and Union éducative des typographes suisses. BS3/UETS.

Larson, K (2004)
The science of word recognition, or how I learned to stop worrying and love the bouma.
Advanced Reading Technologies, Microsoft Corporation.
http://www.microsoft.com/typography/ctfonts/WordRecognition/aspx

Meyer, H (1963)
The Development of Writing.
Zurich: Graphis Press.

Noordzij, G (2000)
Letterletter.
Vancouver: Hartley & Marks.

Noordzij, G (2005)
The stroke theory of writing.
London: Hyphen Press.

Rose, S (2006)
The 21st-century brain.
London: Vintage.

Saenger, P (1997)
Space Between Words. The Origins of Silent Reading.
Stanford, California: Stanford University Press.

Spiekermann, E (1987)
Post Mortem or: How I once designed a typeface for Europe's biggest company,
Baseline. International Typographic Magazine,
Issue Seven.

Tinker, M A (1963)
Legibility of print.
Ames: Iowa State University Press.

Tinker, M A & Paterson, D G (1941)
Eye movement in reading a modern type face and Old English,
American Journal of Psychology
54 (January) 113–114.

Wolf, M (2008)
Proust and the Squid: The Story and Science of the Reading Brain.
Cambridge: Icon Books.

Further reading

Bringhurst, R (2005)
The elements of typographic style. Version 3.1.
Vancouver: Hartley & Marks *Publishers.*

Hochuli, J (2008)
Detail in Typography. Letters, letter-spacing, words, wordspacing, lines, linespacing, columns.
London: Hyphen Press.

Updike, D B (1937)
Printing Types: their history, forms, and use. A study in survivals. Volumes 1&2:
Cambridge, Massachusetts: Harvard University Press.

Zachrisson, B (1965)
Studies in the legibility of printed text.
Stockholm: The Graphic Institute.

Designing your writing

Ch 10 Contents at a glance

'Writing, when properly managed ... is but a different name for conversation'.
Laurence Sterne *The Life and Opinions of Tristram Shandy, Gentleman*

I have as much difficulty as ever in expressing myself clearly and concisely; and this difficulty has caused me a very great loss of time; but it has had the compensating advantage of forcing me to think long and intently about every sentence, and thus I have been often led to see errors in reasoning and in my own observations or those of others.

There seems to be a sort of fatality in my mind leading me to put at first my statement and proposition in a wrong and awkward form. Formerly I used to think about my sentences before writing them down; but for several years I have found that it saves time to scribble in a vile hand whole pages as quickly as I possibly can, contracting half the words; and then correct deliberately. Sentences thus scribbled down are often better ones than I could have written deliberately.

Having said this much about my manner of writing, I will add that with my larger books I spend a good deal of time over the general arrangement of the matter. I first make the rudest outline in two or three pages, and then a larger one in several pages, a few words or one word standing for a whole discussion or series of facts. Each of these headings is again enlarged and often transformed before I begin to write in extenso.

Charles Darwin (Autobiography, edited by Nora Barlow, Collins,1958)

Writing is a design activity

We said at the very beginning of this book (Chapter 1, page 22) that creating the end product of research in the form of a dissertation or thesis should be 'a work of thoughtful information design, in order to do justice to the work that it presents to the outside world'.

The kind of visual thinking about the real physical product described in Chapter 9 is a final step in the progress towards the transformation of invisible knowledge into visible words, through the series of 'design' processes described in earlier chapters – all intended to integrate the business of 'doing research' with that of delivering a worthy end product. It also marks the culminating stage of managing the information we have gathered and transformed into knowledge during our research – the stage when we transform it back into new information that others can see and use.

This chapter will focus on the main tasks involved in 'writing up', and suggest practical experience-based ways of tackling them, and of handling some of the difficulties typical of the job. But before we get into that, it's worth looking at a possible explanation of why most of us find writing so difficult. I've always been intrigued by that question, and finding an explanation helps to alleviate the exasperation and sense of inadequacy I still feel when I'm trying to 'get into' writing a chapter – as I'm doing at this moment.

A difficult and imperfect invention

The feelings so humbly described by Charles Darwin may be accounted for by the facts about the invention of writing set out by Jared Diamond (1997) in a fine and wide-ranging book. As he explains, it was an extraordinary and rare event in human history, which required the inventors to recognize and solve vast problems:

> 'The two indisputably independent inventions of writing were achieved by the Sumerians of Mesopotamia somewhat before 3000 BC and by Mexican Indians before 600 BC. Egyptian writing of 3000 BC and Chinese writing (by 1300 BC) may also have arisen independently. Probably all other peoples who have developed writing since then have borrowed, adapted, or at least been inspired by existing systems. ...
>
> ... Inventing a writing system from scratch must have been incomparably more difficult than borrowing and adapting one. The first scribes had to settle on basic principles that we now take for granted. For example, they had to figure out how to decompose a continuous utterance into speech units, regardless of whether those units were taken as words, syllables, or phonemes. They had to learn to recognize the same sound or speech unit through all our normal variations in speech volume, pitch, speed, emphasis, phrase grouping, and individual idiosyncrasies of pronunciation. They had to decide that a writing system should ignore all of that variation. They then had to devise ways to represent sounds by symbols.'

It is a tribute to the power of the human brain and to human perseverance and vision that they managed to achieve all that. That we still find using the invention so difficult is the result of the encounter between those qualities and the very nature of the human brain at the present stage of its evolution. And that is why writing to make what we know, feel, and think visible to others is one of the hardest things most of us have to do. As Norman (1992) says, '... careful, conscientious writers simplify the task for readers, but at the cost of great time and effort for themselves.' But if we want to be read and understood, the time and effort have to be invested – and when writing is, as we said earlier in this book (see Chapter 5, page 114), 'the only means of creating the visible end product on which [our] efforts will be judged' it's surely in our own interest to do everything in our power to make sure it's read and understood!

Sneaking up on writing

As Levin (2005) says in his helpful book on writing 'excellent dissertations', 'Thinking is an inherently untidy process' in the course of which our minds go in all directions; then out of it '... we have to produce a dissertation that is essentially linear, that takes the reader through a logical progression from Introduction to Conclusion. Quite a challenge!'

To meet the challenge, we suggest – again on the basis of experience – making a gradual approach, rather than a last-minute frontal assault, on writing. In other words giving ourselves all the help we can, and getting every job that could distract from actual writing and the kind of thinking it needs out of the way before we start. Treating your mind kindly in preparing for the most exacting and critical task of research will give you the best chance of finding new thoughts and felicitous expression as you write.

Before we get down to the business of writing, here's a reminder of all the preparatory activities suggested in earlier chapters, and of how they can help when it comes to writing the end product.

Making and updating maps (see Chapter 2, pages 27–44)
Gives you a visible record of the research process from the beginning: how you saw it at the start; what changed during the process; when, how and why it changed.

Managing research information (see Chapter 3, pages 49–86)
Gives you: quick access to your information store to find whatever you need to use in the end product; standard terms for the concepts you deal with; references in the proper format ready to incorporate.

Managing the project and the vital documents about it (see Chapter 4 pages 87–104)
Gives you reminders of: constraints and rules to observe in the writing; what you proposed to do at the start of research; records of communications and key developments; documents prepared for use in the process (some of which

can be taken more or less as they stand into the chapter on method, as example material).

Setting up ways of managing time (see Chapter 5, pages 105–120)
Gives you: a standard way of planning how to fit the things that have to be done into a specified period of time. If you have applied it from the start, by the time you get to writing the dissertation you will have profited from experience and be able to make effective use of whatever way of managing time works best for you, in this final phase.

Forward thinking towards the end product (see Chapter 6, pages 123–140)
Helps you to identify: the people who will read the end product, and their purposes; others whose help you will need in completing it; the most important features of the research which readers must understand; what readers need to understand about you as the researcher. And that makes the basis for the most critical decisions about content and presentation.

Creating a design brief for the end product (see Chapter 7, pages 141–149)
Gives you: a concise record of the decisions you make, and points to the most significant things you have to attend to in designing every aspect of what you submit to the examiners.

Visualizing the end product (see Chapter 8, pages 153–170)
Makes the key features of what you're about to start writing visible to you, and so helps to bring the ideas and knowledge you have gained in research to the point where you are ready to transform them into visible information that others can use for their own purposes.

Designing what readers will see on the page (see Chapter 9.2 pages 181–220)
Gives you: a clear visual framework into which you can write, and a set of standards for all the elements of the dissertation so that your mind is free to concentrate on the content of your writing. Chapter 9.1 to 9.3 explain the role of typography in the design of dissertations, and provide you with example pages of all their main features, and advice on avoiding design pitfalls that researchers often fall into.

How recent researchers did it

We asked the recent researchers who have contributed their experiences to this book how they had planned the end products of their research, and when they started planning. They told us about a variety of approaches, some of them determined by the structure of their course and university requirements, and some the outcome of the individual researcher's temperament and previous experience. None of them, I'm glad to say, belong to the 'sit-up-all-night-and-do-it-at-the-last-moment' persuasion. If you do, please stop and think about whether doing it that way so far has a) been an enjoyable experience and b) brought good results. If not, stay with us and consider whether there are some ideas here that you could try to adopt.

Kerry, on a part-time two-year Master's course, in which the dissertation modules occupied the second year, was compelled by the nature of the course to start serious dissertation planning at the end of the first year.

Kerry the germ of an idea had been planted during the course of my work but actually formulating an idea for a research project began over the summer prior to undertaking the dissertation module. There wasn't really time before this because I was focusing on my other coursework requirements. ...

However, the teaching on Applied Information Research in the first year gave me a real insight into the means by which I should think about undertaking my dissertation research by completing practical tasks devised to introduce us to research concepts ... By undertaking this type of task, I was able to think through the whole process of what I wanted to research, why, how and what I would do with the information gathered.

And so she was well prepared to make a quick start on the dissertation, and to present the required dissertation plan early in the first semester of the second year.

If we hadn't had the opportunity to design research strategies in the Applied Information Research module this would have been much harder to do from a mere understanding of research theory/concepts.

Karen, working on doctoral research over a five-year period, which includes a major qualitative case study, has decided to submit a monograph thesis as the final product (her university allows various options for the form of the end product). She describes how she works through a process of creating 'building blocks' and then assembling them and combining their content in various ways.

Karen I work on several smaller 'building blocks' (files in folders) at a time and usually start by writing a lot on each. Then I put some of them together and try to cut down most of the texts and make them simpler and more readable. I have found that it usually is possible to create new products from combinations of all my texts that are still quite dissimilar. A more affective problem with this approach is that it doesn't feel structured, none of the chapters of my final monograph is 'really' ready yet, although most of them are 'quite' ready. ...

For the seminar texts ... in one way, I started planning some three months before; in another I had kept them in mind during the whole process of writing smaller files. But when I really started creating the texts, I started by writing a schema of what I wanted to represent, with headings and sub-headings, I transferred all my 'small files' to

> their place under the appropriate titles, and incidentally found out which topics I didn't have enough material on. Then I would start summarizing the smaller files, turning them around and making them fit into the whole.

I find this an interesting insight, with which I have a fellow-feeling. It makes the point that we should try never to waste what we have written, but look for opportunities to 'recycle' it. When I'm asked to write articles or give lectures, I usually go back and look at other things I've written on related subjects, to remind myself of approaches, diagrams, or ways of expressing ideas that may be useful for this product for a new audience. That makes a good starter for developing new ideas, and a new structure that incorporates the recycled material. It's pleasing to think that it's comparable with the practice of such composers as Handel, who never wasted a good tune!

As Karen points out, this approach leaves you with the final task of editing to achieve a fully integrated structure so that the thesis is a proper building. You can't just leave it as a set of loosely constructed sheds! And you have to do that job yourself if possible – few people will be able, let alone willing, to do it. (see pages 255–256 and 263–264 for more on editing).

Karen and Kerry, and most of the other researchers quoted in this book, have been required to do a good deal of writing in the course of their education and in their work. The case is different for many 'practice-based' researchers, whose whole education, sometimes from their early teens, may well have been focused on developing other capacities and skills than handling words. This can make for some unhappy experiences when they undertake research that requires some form of written submission as well as artefacts of various kinds. On the other hand, they *can* put their special kinds of skill and knowledge – particularly in visualizing structures – to good use in the ways we have been suggesting throughout this book.[1]

[1] When I first started working with graphic- and industrial-design students who were undertaking their first postgraduate research, I quickly found that many of them felt, as one expressed it,'Like an adult when I'm designing, but like a school-kid when I try to write', and consequently felt less than enthusiastic about the dissertation they had to present as part of their MA.
To help them feel more confident, I devised what I thought was probably a cheering fiction. I told them that as designers they had something that those of us who can only put things down in words hadn't got–the ability to create expressive visual structures where all the elements and their relations are simultaneously present in the same plane–and I suggested they could try applying it to their writing, making images in whichever way they found worked for them as a starter for writing, rather than trying to capture ideas that won't stay still by putting them down one at a time in long strings of words. They thought that was worth a try, and to my surprise it worked; the fiction seemed to have some basis in reality.

Industrial design MA student Ismaril describes how he overcame the difficulty of starting to put words on paper:

Ismaril Putting pen to blank paper was difficult so I started the thesis by simply combining on the page the strongest elements of my research findings in the form of quotes and images, I then wrote text around this basic structure and built it up with more quotes and images in a process of refining both structure and content.

Many years ago my typographer co-author developed a way of applying his design skills to interpreting the writing of others, which he describes below. Today, when he himself is an author, he uses the knowledge gained from it to create a visual framework for his own writing.

Graham When I started to take a deep interest in the idea that typography was a process of interpreting visual language rather than an entirely formalist aesthetic activity – although aesthetics are an extremely important part of design – I developed working practices which allowed me to bring together writing and designing into a single integrated process the final result of which simulated the finished printed page. This work needed good eyesight, high levels of concentration, and the skill to work in a small scale.

I carried out the process of writing, designing and interpreting on tracing paper, because it allowed me to copy accurately the type fonts available on my printer, as well as to scrape away any mistakes I made. I used specialist drawing pens and permanent black ink, and the finished sheets looked like a printed page – and frequently better than the finished job produced by the printer. The process was lengthy and exacting, but it helped me to explore the problem at first hand, as well as to lay down in my memory bank visual solutions which could be drawn on later; and it developed the essential skills of hand and eye coordination.

Today my visual acuity is not up to working in such an exacting way, even with the best industrial magnifying lights, but fortunately Mac technology and advanced screen definition allow me to work in a comparable manner and in real time. I still draw on my memory bank of visual design models, but the working process is more fluid. I still do numerous concept drawings by hand, which essentially explore the communication problem and spatial relationships. These start off as rough thumb-nail sketches, which by definition are drawn small; then they are developed at full size in greater detail.

The results fascinated me. Though I lacked the knowledge and skill to emulate them, I felt there was something underlying that could be adapted to help me as a writer. I began drawing layouts of pages before writing a chapter (for an example, see Figure 10.4 on page 247), and found they made my ideas for its structure visible to me; that in turn helped me to keep my thoughts in focus as I started to get them down in words. Having a visible framework seems to relieve the stress of trying to run two different mental activities at once: keeping a sense of the structure and where you are in it, and turning thoughts into words and sentences.

After that look at the strategies of some recent researchers, the next section is an illustrated account of the stages by which I prepare to start writing. It is based on what I've been doing over the past few days in setting about this chapter, but it reflects the practice developed over many years, which I followed in writing my own thesis. Please note that I am not putting it forward as the One Best Way of writing a dissertation; writing is a very individual matter and I know that what one person finds helpful can look like an appalling idea to another. But I also know that students facing this particular writing task for the first time find it useful to have practical accounts of how those who have done it before set about the job, from which they can select ideas that look congenial, try them out, and build up their own approach.

Getting down to it

As explained in Chapter 8 (page 156), from the point when the synopsis of this book was agreed with the publishers, I've been building up a 'holdall' folder for each chapter, into which I dropped, in no sort of order, useful quotes, ideas, relevant answers from our recent-researcher contributors to the questions we asked them, references to books, articles, and websites for quotation or mention as further reading. This looks rather like what Justin describes:

> Justin — I created a 'Thesis' folder on my computer. Under it, I created subfolders, each corresponding to the research questions that I had proposed as chapters for the thesis.

The other file I have had on hand when starting to write each chapter is the original synopsis for it set out in the proposal for the book, which contains ideas for main headings for the topics to be covered.

As this particular chapter is the final one, and there have been many mentions in earlier chapters of matters relevant to writing, its holdall also contains a collection of them, so that I can remind readers of them in the appropriate place. They found their place on pages 238–239, as a straightforward list.

But deciding how to explain the steps by which I progressively sorted the miscellany in the holdall into an ordered sequence to make a framework that I could write into gave me some difficulty. The solution came from talking my designer co-author through a series of images starting from tipping out the holdall; the outcome was Figures 10.1–10.4, which describe the essentials of the process that I now realize I follow, supported by minimal words.

The first thing to do was tip out the contents of the holdall folder, to see what was in it. Figure 10.1 shows what was in the holdall for this chapter.

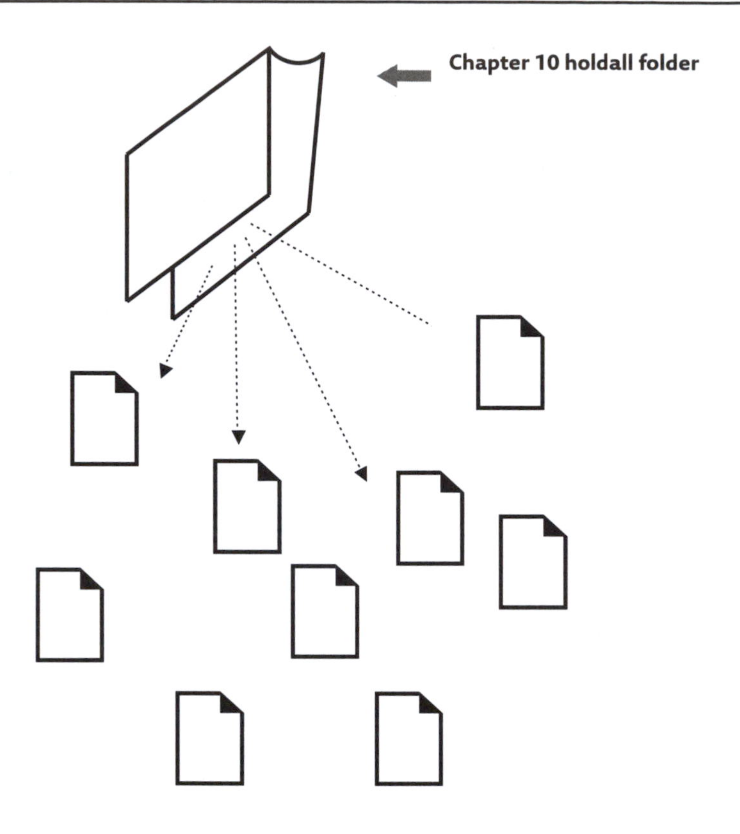

The files in the folder

Original chapter synopsis

How supervisors can help writing

Cross-references to pick up from earlier chapters

Quotes about writing from researchers

Email exchange with co-author about how I write

Where software can help, and where it's useless

Quotes about why writing is difficult

References to articles and websites

Ideas for illustrations

Now the information in the files needs to be sorted into an organized structure

Figure 10.1 Getting down to writing a chapter. Stage 1: tipping out the holdall

Next came a re-sort of the material to bring like together with like, under an appropriate heading, and try to arrange them in a logical sequence that would tell the story that the chapter was intended to present. Figure 10.2 shows the results for this chapter – I was able to use some of the headings from the original synopsis, but experience of writing the earlier chapters suggested some changes to make links between them and this one.

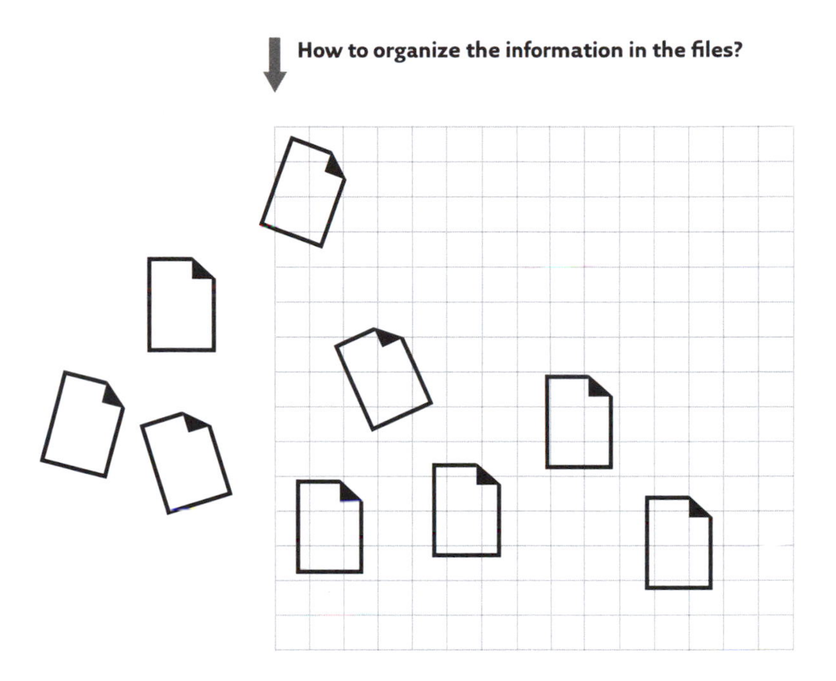

The files from the holdall folder
Now the information in them needs to be sorted to make a structure for the chapter

The results of thinking

Key themes:

Writing as a design process

A difficult and imperfect invention

Stages in the process

Sequence of writing

Creating a structure, making connections

Tips, timesavers, overcoming troubles

Meeting the institution's requirements

Finding the appropriate style

Help: from supervisors, friends, technology

Being your own editor

Ideas for figures:
A series showing progressive sorting, based on metaphor of a holdall for each chapter

Figure 10.2 Getting down to writing a chapter. *Stage 2*: Sorting the information in the files

Then I was able to make a sort of 'Table of contents' for the chapter, with main <**B**> headings, as shown in Figure 10.3.

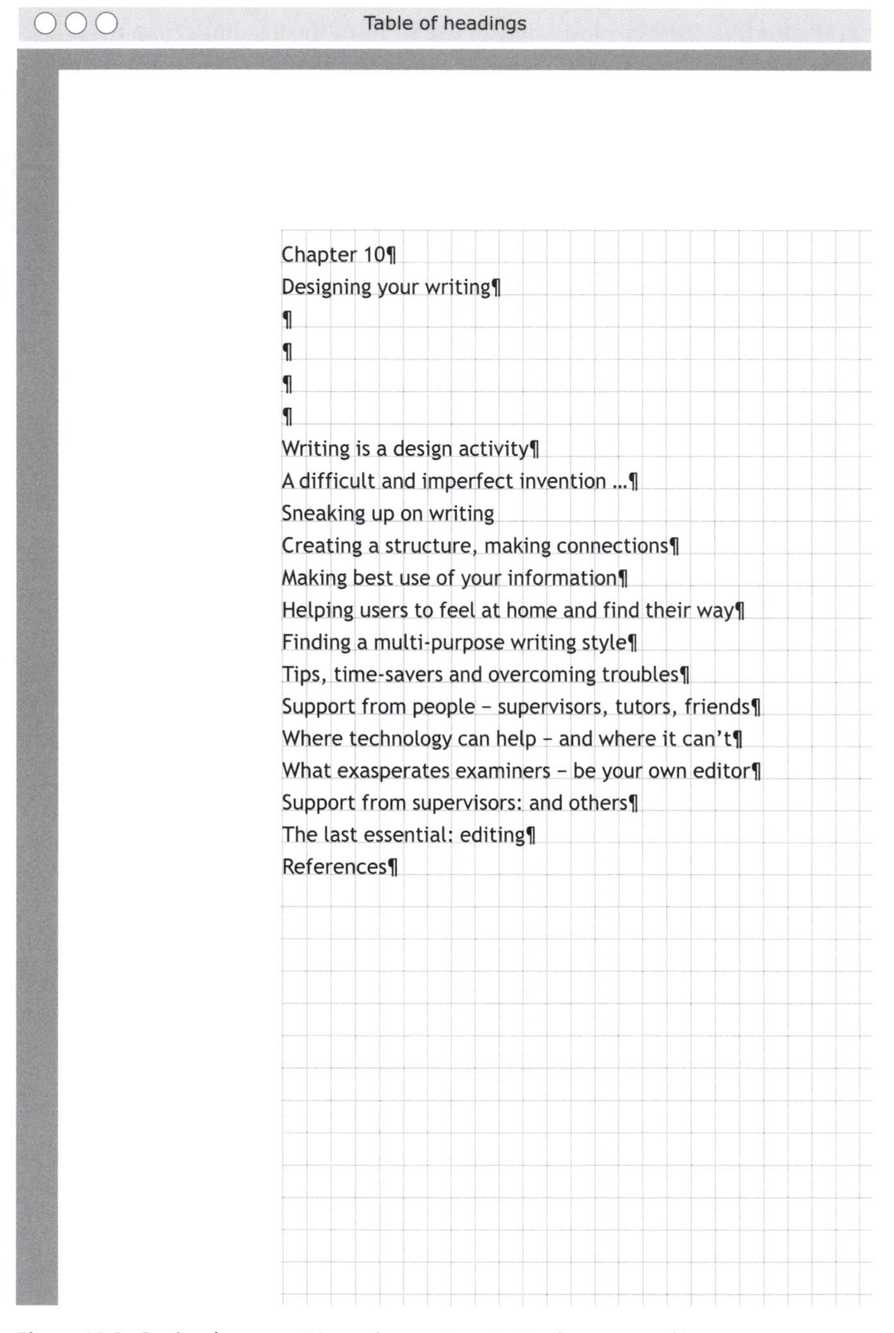

Figure 10.3 Getting down to writing a chapter. *Stage 3*: Key themes sorted into sequence

Next, I produced rough layouts for the pages of the chapter, using the headings to show myself the space available on the pages of the chapter and how it might be divided up between text and diagrams; and then annotated the layouts to remind myself where I wanted to quote or refer to particular materials, as shown in Figure 10.4.

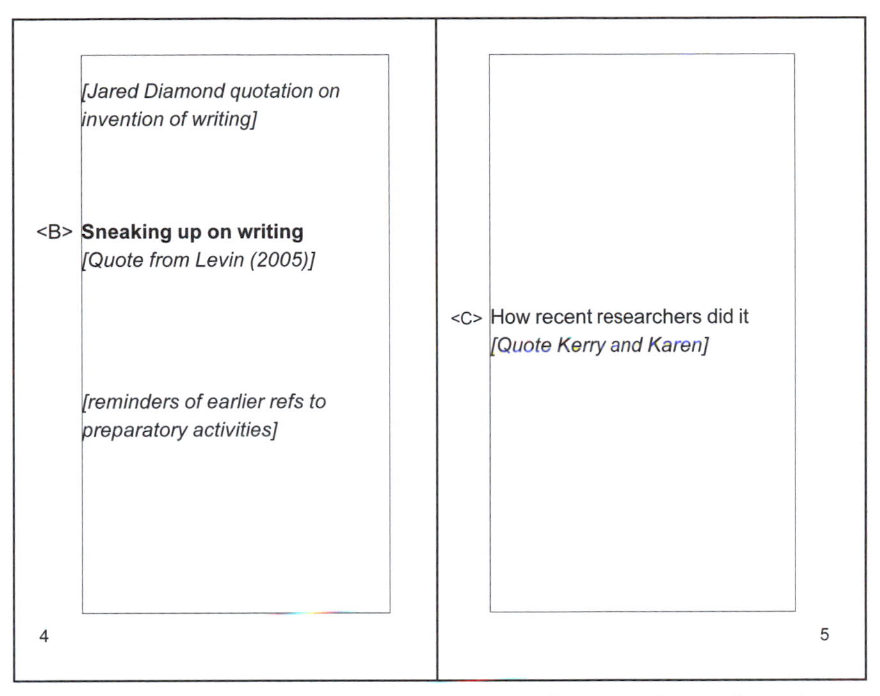

Figure 10.4 Getting down to writing a chapter. *Stage 4*: Headings entered on rough page layouts

Writing in layers

At that point I felt ready to set up a Chapter 10 draft file, into which I input the main headings, and to start writing – and not before time, you may think; but it's only after this kind of preparation that I am ready to write; otherwise I waste time going round in circles because I literally don't yet know my own mind. (You may notice that I have made some changes to the headings in the course of writing – this always happens, because it's not possible to envisage everything that emerges in the course of actually writing. See below for an account of how it came about in this chapter!)

If you have followed the advice in Chapter 9.2 (pages 187–195) and set up a style for margins and all the elements such as headings that you will need in your dissertation, you will have that ready to use as your framework for drafting online, as well as print-on-paper rough layouts to help you for reference – and that will take a large weight off your mind and allow you to concentrate on the writing!

When I actually start writing, I write 'in layers': first inputting text in pretty rough draft form, mostly not bothering about making complete sentences, and concentrating on catching the thoughts before they slide out of view, using the rough layouts as a guide, and bringing in material from the holdall folder as needed. At the end of each main section, I print out what I've written, read it, and annotate for things that need changing, additional material to take in, etc. I find it helps to refine it a section at a time; when I've got down the essence of what I want to say, it becomes much easier to turn it into complete sentences. I seem to have a mental store of sentence structures, comparable to Graham's memory bank of visual solutions (page 242), but I can't use it properly at the same time as thinking about the content I'm trying to get down (it's cheering to think that Charles Darwin had similar difficulties!).

That brings us to the point of talking about the down-to-earth details of writing, and it is also the point in this chapter where I found I needed to change the original headings shown in Figure 10.3. When I looked at the material I had marked for using under them, I realized that it really consisted of the experiences of a number of researchers, including the present authors, in dealing with the usual difficulties of the process. The problem was finding a way of presenting them that would be most helpful to readers. I finally decided that the best solution was to put them all under the heading 'Tips, time-savers and trouble-shooting', to make a kind of 'Dissertation Writer's Inquire Within'.

And that is what I have done. Now read on!

Tips, time-savers and trouble-shooting

This section is arranged as a sort of directory. Under the three topics of its heading, you will find:

- Brief experience-based advice on the questions and problems that writing a dissertation presents
- Reminders of relevant points from earlier chapters
- Pointers to fuller treatments of some topics.

Tips and reminders

Clear the decks

Isolate the one thing you need to write at any one time; removing physical clutter tidies up thoughts too.

Kerry Having a clear desktop apart from a pen, blank paper for notes and the text book/article/questionnaire I was reviewing was a good visual indicator of what I should be focusing on (even if everything else was shoved under the desk in piles!)

My own desk isn't exactly a good example of that at the moment! I clear the decks by taking the material for a particular bit of writing (sometimes with the laptop, sometimes just with pen and paper to sort out ideas) away from the desk, to somewhere where I feel comfortable – to a different part of the house, to a favourite café or pub, into the garden in good weather, or even to stay a few days somewhere away from the distractions and everyday demands of home.

Sequence for writing

You don't have to wait until you have done everything else before starting to write. Paula found she could make a start on some elements of her dissertation while the research was still in progress.

Paula *Write from the beginning*
Literature Review
Methodology
Title page, contents page – quite small tasks that can be started and added to – saves time at the end.
These can be started early and revised later but gets a good chunk of work out of the way to free up time for other things.

Leave until last
Discussion
Conclusion
Review Introduction
Abstract

First impressions are critical

The title and contents page, and the other elements that make up what publishers call the prelims (the bits of text that identify the product, show its origins and author and when and where it was issued, and give the reader a quick overview of what's inside it) are the first things that meet the eye of any-one who picks up a dissertation, and consequently the most often accessed. Potential readers use them to judge whether they want to read further or whether it's not of sufficient interest for their purposes; readers who *have* to read them (i.e. examiners) get their first impressions of the writer from them; and librarians use them to compile catalogue entries. The first pages of the introductory chapter are of equal importance in giving first impressions of the product.

So here is some help towards getting the best out of them.

What goes into the 'Prelims'

* = obligatory element   [ ] = optional

* Abstract
standard description of objectives of dissertation
how it was conducted
any important changes in course of research
significant findings
(see De Guire, 2006 for useful tips on writing abstracts)

* Contents List
Contents of prelims

[ ] Part titles
Chapter titles with page numbers (make sure you get page numbers correct!)
Bibliography with page number

[ ] Index with page number

* List of Tables
* List of Figures

[ ] Author's preface
[ ] Acknowledgements:
To organizations and individuals who have given help of various kinds (make sure you get their names, job titles, etc. right; in case of doubt, check what form of acknowledgement is preferred)
Remember to thank supervisors/tutors.

Things that need to be said clearly in the introductory chapter:

- What the research was about; innovative features (standard statement)
- Questions it sought to answer (and what it did *not* aim to do)
- Definitions of key terms used in the dissertation
- Why the study was undertaken
- The researcher's background relevant to the research (see Chapter 6 pages 136 and 138).
- The content and how it is arranged.

Helping readers helps the writer

And the readers whom dissertation writers have the greatest interest in helping are *the examiners.*

Reminders of where you will find helpful information and ideas in earlier chapters of this book:

In Chapter 6

- Identifying the users and their purposes (pages 128–131)
- The most important points they need to understand about the research (pages 132–136)
- What they need to understand about you as the researcher (pages 136 and 138)
- Examiners: what they want to be able to do, and what will enable them to do it (Table 6.1, page 129)

In Chapter 7

- Example of a design brief for a dissertation (pages 146–149)

The design brief described on pages 146–149 covers the basic questions researchers need to ask and answer before they start their dissertation. From their answers a clearer picture will emerge of the key visual features their dissertation will need to incorporate to make its sense and structure clear. These characteristics then have to be mapped onto the relevant features found in Word, which are identified in Chapters 9.1 to 9.3.

In Chapter 8

- Think of yourself as a reader: what most turns readers off when they are trying to find useful information in text? (page 155)
- Information elements that dissertation writers need (page 159)
- More about helping users (pages 159–162)

In Chapter 9.2

- Standards for the information elements you need (pages 194–217)

Making the connections

What researchers have to tell readers is seldom a linear story; more often they need to make them aware of complex interactions, but without losing the main story line in a maze of digressions. Chapters 9.1–9.3 are a good example of the problem and of ways of meeting it.

1 Identify all the topics involved, and how they are related. Then sort them into main themes, and try out ideas for a structure to accommodate them. Originally there was to be a single Chapter 9, covering: findings on what researchers actually do in the way of dissertation design; practical help in the task for non-designers; and an explanation of the theory underlying the advice. It soon became clear that its structure would be so complex as to baffle readers. So it became three linked chapters. The first made a straightforward story (9.1); the second resolved itself into a toolkit for dissertation design with instructions for setting up a design specification, and templates for the standard dissertation elements (9.2). That left for 9.3 the complex explanation of why some design choices will give readers a hard time and others smooth their path, which had to bring together insights from the psychology of reading, neuroscience, the history of European letterforms and of printing, and typography.

2 Show readers where you are about to take them. All three chapters start with 'Contents at a glance' and 9.2 follows it up with a visual overview of the basic toolkit.

3 Give meaningful headings and sub-headings all the way through to show readers what they're coming to next. Help them make the connections by cross references to relevant material already given or to come; and use footnotes to give supplementary information. Chapters 9.2 and 9.3 are rich in these features, because the more complex the route the greater the need for signposts.

4 Remember that diagrams can make plain interactions and their effects that are difficult to convey in words – as do the figures in Chapters 9.2 and 9.3.

Keeping within length

Institutions usually specify maximum (and sometimes minimum) numbers of words or pages for the end products of research. They have to be observed, and doing so demands self-discipline from writers.

Paula	Never enough words! – 15,000 words seems a lot but it isn't.
Kerry	A 12–15,000 word limit means you have to be really tight with your writing.

The most painless way of keeping within the maximum is to allocate appropriate target lengths for each chapter at the point when you have decided how many chapters you need and what they will deal with. Then, when you have done everything in the checklist on page 220 and decided on typeface and type size (see Chapter 9.2 pages 196–219) you can work out the average number of words to a page. If you then follow the suggestion of giving yourself rough layout (see pages 242–249) you will see from them how many words you should aim to write under each heading. As you write each main section, use Word Count in the Word Tools menu, so that you can see how the total is going so far, and if necessary note possible cuts. It's easier to adjust for length as you go than to remove a given number of words when you've written the whole thing (a lesson I learned from having to do that to the first book I wrote!)

Hand-writing or typing? Paper or on-screen?

Find the mix that suits you best! Both have advantages for particular tasks; neither is to be despised. Some find pen and paper is essential for working out first ideas, and then go to the computer keyboard for developing the themes; many people find it easier to compare different parts of a piece of writing if they have it printed out on paper. As Paula found:

Paula Make use of the PC – I used to write drafts on paper and rewrite. It saves a lot of time if you can get used to writing on a PC. You can print out drafts for editing where it is easier to see to see the 'whole' and then cut and paste etc.

See also: Time-savers (see page 257).

Style – what's 'appropriate'?

The current version of the Research Studies Handbook of the university where I did my PhD says:

> '... there are several matters on which discretion may be used in choosing the most appropriate style.
>
> Theses should be as far as possible be written in the manner of a formal research report. ... It is in your own interest that your thesis should be written in a style that is clear, pleasing to read, and has a minimum of jargon.'
>
> *(City University, London, Research Studies Handbook 2006/2007)*

The general sense, of those guidelines at least, is that the style of a dissertation should match the nature of the content, and the needs of the people who will use it, and that so far as possible it should observe the relevant conventions, but without going overboard.

So you don't have to stop being yourself when you write a dissertation; you don't have to write as if you're an automaton programmed to deliver 'academic' jargon and complicated statements of simple things. As two of our contributors express it:

Karen [One of the most important decisions was] ... to change my individual style from a fairly hedging and 'flowery' language to a more direct, no-nonsense language ...

Kerry	It's too easy to throw flashy jargon in when plain English would do so much better!'

First person or third?

A dissertation or thesis is the outcome of work undertaken on the decision of the individual researcher, who has sole responsibility for carrying it through. So if there was ever a situation that required the author to use 'I' from time to time (rather than 'it was decided' or 'the present author decided') this is it.

Legitimate uses of the first person: when you are describing your own decisions, reasons for them, actions taken to implement them. Obviously there is no reason to use it when talking about what other people have written, the theories they have advanced, etc, because they, not the researcher, are the subject. The tricky decisions are the ones that have to be made when it comes to developing arguments, interpreting findings, and drawing conclusions. Here, it's self-evident that the researcher originates the arguments, etc, but it's wise to go easy on phrases such as 'I think/believe', and to avoid 'I feel' (a polite fiction is maintained in academia that researchers don't have feelings!). The emphasis here is on the evidence to support arguments, and the logic and validity of the steps by which conclusions are reached, and while you hope the readers will respect you for their quality, it is better to step modestly aside, and use such phrases as 'It can reasonably be concluded from ... that ... ', 'The evidence suggests ... '. See also: If writing terrifies you (page 258).

Set it aside to clear

When you finish a piece of writing, or when your mind can go no further with it for the present: stop, note the point where you finished, put that work aside, give yourself a reminder of when to come back to it, and do something else. The mind needs time out, as Paula explains:

Paula	Go away and come back – to identify errors. ... Regular breaks – re-read. After a while you can't see your mistakes because you know the chapter so well. It was useful to move to a different section for a while and come back and spot mistakes.

The necessity for these pauses is another good reason for not leaving writing to the last moment.

Regular review

Setting writing aside and then going back to it is part of the process of regular reviewing mentioned in Chapter 4 (see page 101), which should go from a section of a chapter at a time, to the whole chapter, to the chapter in the context of the earlier chapters, and then all the chapters taken as a whole. If you follow this process, you will be able to pick up and rectify inconsistencies of treatment and contradictions between what you say in different places, and so save work on the final *essential* editing of the whole dissertation. See also: Editing, below and pages 263–264.

A second pair of eyes

A number of our researcher contributors have mentioned how helpful it is to invite selected readers to comment on work in progress; they are likely to spot things that we have missed through familiarity with the subject matter, and sometimes to ask awkward questions that alert us to features which, if left as they stand, might lead to even more awkward ones from examiners! As Paula and Kerry express it:

Paula	Be brave and allow others to comment on drafts.

Kerry	Enlisting a couple of friends to proof read for me, and asking a non-LIS (library- and information-studies) professional to read it through and honestly tell me if the report has not only a beginning, middle and satisfactory end, but also whether it was comprehensible! ... Having a non-LIS proof reader also meant that they could be far more objective on the report as a piece of writing.

Editing

All end products of research should be put through this separate final process, but too often they are not.

What does it consist of? Editing is the application of a series of rigorous checks to different aspects of the work, for purposes of 'quality assurance', to ensure that it's fit to go out into the world.
The checks cover:

- Features of structure; content; arguments; evidence; internal consistency etc, (see Table 6.1 on page 129). This kind of editing, which looks at the text as a whole, and requires qualitative judgement and knowledge of the subject matter, is usually called 'content editing'.

The following checks come under the heading of 'copy editing' or 'proof reading'. That used to mean checking text set by a compositor against the author's original MS or typescript for errors in the course of setting, but now that typesetting is normally based on the author's own keystrokes, it covers this range:

- Presentation standards – e.g. for references – and consistency in observing them
- Heading hierarchies and consistency in observing them
- Use of language to check that acceptable standards of spelling, punctuation, grammar and sentence structure are maintained.

In book publishing, editing is a professional job which used to be done in-house (I worked for some years in a publishing house as a technical-book editor), but is now usually free-lance. It is not normally left to the authors of books, with good reason; they tend to see what they *meant* to write, not what they did.

So how should researchers, with limited opportunities for input from other people, deal with the task?

- Allow time in the schedule *(at least a week).*
- Use the Editing Checklist on pages 263–264.
- Benefit from whatever help supervisor/tutors and friends can give, which will vary according to their experience and the time they are prepared to give (see pages 261–262 of this chapter for suggestions to supervisors on this question).
- If all else fails, and if your supervisor/tutor recommends it, pay a professional to edit it (a step sometimes advised for researchers who are writing in a second language, to deal with any linguistic obstacles to clarity).

Citing and quoting

Check that every quote is truly relevant to the context in which you are putting it, accurately reproduced, and correctly cited in standard form, both in text and in reference lists and/or bibliography.

Reminder: see Chapter 3, page 68 on plagiarism, and pages 68–69 on taking notes.

Kerry [from a list of the most important decisions she took]
Being absolutely scrupulous when checking and re-checking my final report for spelling/formatting errors.
Rechecking every citation and cross-reference.

Check *all citations of websites* in a final complete pass through to make sure they're still accurate, and give an overall date for the final check in a note to the bibliography; the web is a fluid medium, referring to it has been described as being like trying to pin jelly to a wall, and this is the best one can do!

Illustrating it

The whole of this book is based on the well-founded belief that words are not the only way of expressing and communicating ideas. It has argued, with evidence from experience, that if researchers visualize what they have in mind and make various kinds of pictures, it can help them at every stage of research to clarify their thoughts, see connections, and take decisions on action.

So when it comes to writing the dissertation, take good advantage of the maps and pictures you have created to help your own thinking, and use them to help readers to grasp your ideas.

Reminders: see Chapter 8, pages 164–167 (Beverley's account of visualizing to interpret data).

Indexing it?

If the end product of your research is a PhD thesis and/or makes over 100,000 or more words (200 or more pages), you should think seriously of making an index for it. You will know from writing it how discussions of key topics are dispersed throughout the chapters, to the extent that even the author can't be too sure of locating them all. So think of how much more difficult it will be for examiners, who are very likely to want to do just that. They really appreciate thoughtful researchers who provide an index! There is no room to provide even a quick DIY guide here; instead, consult Mulvany (2005) for authoritative instruction.

Incentives and rewards

Give yourself tangible incentives, as well as targets, in writing. When I read the contributions of recent researchers, I was cheered to find that I am not alone in promising myself small treats as a reward for progress when writing. Kerry's answer to the question 'What were the most important decisions you took about research?' included 'Booking a fortnight's holiday in Mallorca as a reward for finishing!' It was an act of faith that paid off.

Time-savers

Start early on writing and add value as you go

As we've seen, researchers can come to regret not making an earlier start on writing when they find how much time it takes, and those who do start early are glad that they did so.

Whenever you pick up a piece of writing on which you've already done some work, make sure that the next stage of your work on it adds something useful. Reminders: If you're working from hand-written notes, never just copy type them (see Chapter 5, page 120); when you've input rough notes, print them out and mark things for changing, then amend the file of notes on-screen (see Paula's advice on page 253 of this chapter).

Where was I? Picking up the threads

Whenever you finish writing – even if you will be coming back to it within the hour – put a note at the point where you stopped, to remind yourself what to do next, so that you see it as soon as you return to the job. It helps to save the time that otherwise goes on wondering 'What on earth was I doing? Did I really write that? What did I mean to say next?'

Cross off items as done, e.g. if you are taking material from the holdall folder for a chapter into the master file, either delete each piece of it from the holdall as you transfer it, or (safer) leave it there, but mark it as 'transferred'.

As you finish writing a chapter, go through it for cross-references to later chapters (e.g. topics you have undertaken to deal with in a later chapter), and copy them into the holdall folders for the relevant chapters, so that when you get to them you are reminded to do what you promised readers.

References – deal with them as you go
Reminder: see Chapter 3, page 76 (good advice from Paula and Kerry).

Set modest targets
In planning writing tasks, break targets down to a realistic and manageable size; that will save the discouragement, loss of confidence and wasted time that comes from unmet targets.
Reminder: see Chapter 5, page 116 (advice from recent researchers).

Never do nothing
If prevented for reasons beyond your control from doing what you have planned for a particular time, bring in something else from the 'anytime' or 'less-urgent' jobs – a lesson Hamid learned during his research:

Hamid now if I want to do something and I realise that I am not doing it or I don't feel like doing it right now or I am stuck and can't move for the time being, I switch quickly to another task and make use of my time and restart the unfinished task another time with a fresh mind.

Reminder: see Chapter 5, page 115 (advice from recent researchers).

Run jobs in parallel, alternate writing with other tasks
Reminder: See Chapter 5, page 113 Figure 5.1: Breakdown of key activities into tasks: sequential and parallel working.

Trouble-shooting

It is impossible to get through such a major job as writing a dissertation without hitting obstacles and getting into tight corners. Here are some suggestions for dealing with common occasions of that kind.

If writing terrifies you
If any or all of these points apply to your experience:

- You've never been any good at it
- Have always hated it
- Were never taught systematically about grammar or syntax
- Your school essays always came back covered with red ink.

You've been living with a situation likely to rob all but the hardiest of confidence, and to make them approach writing a dissertation with the reverse of joyful anticipation.

If that is how you feel: remember that if you're good enough at whatever you are studying in your higher education to be able to undertake a research project, you're bright enough to beat the blight.

Experience of working with designers who lack confidence in writing (see page 241 in this chapter) suggests how to find a way round: use your strengths in the things you're accustomed to doing, and do competently.

Deal with *structure, sequence, and connections* first, and don't even think about writing until you're clear about them! Try thinking of it as planning an exhibition in which the exhibits are the story of your research. First decide what the rooms for the exhibition should contain (the chapters, and the most important content that readers need to understand – see Chapter 6, pages 133–138). Then work out the best path for readers to follow through it (the sequence of chapters, and of the content within each chapter). And then think about the connections and links you need to give them to help them understand the relations between different elements.

When you've done that, you can work out the best ways of presenting the various kinds of information you have to give; choose the ones that minimize the number of words you need to write and maximize the use of diagrams, tables, etc.

Follow the advice earlier in this chapter on making a rough layout, with just the headings in place, and seeing how much space you have to fill with words, etc. under each.

Only then move on to actual writing, and take that in stages too, write in notes first; give it a rest, then come back to putting them into sentences. Try explaining the notes to a friend to help make it clear to yourself – if you can talk someone through it, you can write it.

If the underlying problem is in fact dyslexia, this kind of approach should help; it has features in common with methods that are used to help dyslexic students in colleges of art and design. If you haven't already done so, find out what help your institution offers, and take advantage of it, with the support of your supervisor.

A final illuminating reflection from the thesis of a student on an MA in graphic design, who found the 'mutual interference' between the analytic and the intuitive modes of thinking a serious obstacle to both visual creation and writing in her research:

Ann — [The] mutual interference between different functions became apparent early on. Attention to ordering received ideas in language (inspiring, confusing, verbose, banal), listening to lectures, reading and then writing – blocked any visually creative flow. The muse of visual exploration did not want to play. And I was finally compelled to shut up the mind's several voices and pay heed to my intuition which spoke to me in the quiet pre-language voice of its authority. To follow where it led, side-stepping the voices of anxiety, intellectual scepticism and analytic enquiry. ... intuition walked me, in darkness, in silence, sensing my way.' Chasseaud, 1993

Once she had recognized the two modes, she was able to allow each its due time, and the final result was a truly mature piece of work that benefited from both.

Keeping out of the language traps

The last edition included some pages of advice, under the heading 'Watch your language', about avoiding some of the traps of grammar, syntax and punctuation that lie in wait for writers. It wasn't a very satisfactory way of dealing with the subject; it couldn't be comprehensive enough to be really useful, and, while as an editor I know how revise text to rescue writers from linguistic traps they have fallen into, I am not a specialist in language. So this time round we give details of some really useful – and brief – texts by experts; you will find them under Further Reading, on page 265.[2]

See also: Support from supervisors, pages 261–262.

When the going gets sticky

Make your mind work hard, but give it time to itself!

After all these years of writing, there are still days when I find it's 'sticky' and ideas don't flow. That's usually a sign that there's something I haven't thought through fully and that I have started writing about it before I'm really ready. The solution: think as hard as you can about it for a while; then give your mind a chance to be on its own while you do something else. It will go on at its own pace, and hand you the answer. My typographer co-author relates similar experiences in book design, also after a working life in the job. Paula too has wise words from her experience of research (some of them have been quoted earlier – in Chapter 6, page 138 – but it is worth having the full passage here):

Paula — The perfect piece of work – This was a piece of work at the end of several years of study. It was a very precious piece of work and I wanted it to be perfect. There has to be a level of acceptance towards the end that it will never be quite perfect! My reflection diary has a number of entries – asking: Why am I so slow? I think this was to do with trying to get everything right – I learned that at times you just have to write a rough idea and come back later. I seem to problem solve while doing other activities e.g. running at the gym.

2

Having said that, there is one group of punctuation marks that has given us some problems in this book, because they are similar in appearance, though the function of each in conveying meaning is very different. Many writers of dissertations aren't aware of the distinction, and in consequence use them in ways that undermine the sense they are trying to convey. We are talking about

- the hyphen
– the en dash
— and the em dash

For a brief clear explanation of their proper use, see Ritter (2003).

The difficulty in using them is compounded by the fact that some typefaces make the difference between them difficult to see, particularly in sizes below 9 pt.

Take the problem out of the frame of whatever you're trying to write, make notes for yourself in no particular order of what's troubling you about it, what are main things you want to say, want readers to understand. As Paula puts it, 'Try "free writing" to express ideas, collect notes and overcome writer's block.'

Visualize the things you are trying to write about – processes, interpretations of findings, relations between ideas, etc.

Reminders: see Chapter 2 pages 29–30, 36–41 (on research maps); Chapter 8, pages 162–167 (on visualizing knowledge).

Support from supervisors

Though writing gets only this final chapter to itself, the message throughout the book has been that supervisors and tutors can help researchers prepare for the last, critical stage of their research if they require them to present relevant written work from the start, identify any problems that they have with it as early as possible, and give or obtain specialist remedial help where necessary (see pages 42–43, 101–102, 108, 117, 138–139, 168).

As researchers enter on the phase of work with which this chapter deals, editorial support is likely to be the main need for most of them – and providing it can be a problem for their supervisors. While it is no part of the job to be a copy-editor or proof-reader for their students, they are the right people to exercise the role of 'content editor', and they should carry it out from the start of projects.

Their subject expertise means that they are able to ask searching questions about structure, sequence, evidence, and strength of arguments whenever written work is presented to them, and to require revision where necessary. Their help here is irreplaceable, and we have seen from some of our researcher contributors how much it is appreciated and how it helps them in constructing a sound dissertation.

When it comes to writing the end product, supervisors can lighten the load for themselves as well as their students if they insist on seeing a chapter at a time, starting early and spreading the writing over an extended period, with time targets for delivery (which can be built into any Learning Contract that the institution uses).

There remains the vexed question of what to do about the cavalier treatment of language (nearly always by people writing in their first language!) in the matter of grammar, sentence structure and punctuation, which can do researchers so much damage in the eyes of examiners. This will show itself as soon as they present any writing, and needs to be dealt with as soon as it does.

Idiosyncratic grammar and syntax, confusions between spellings of homophones (there/their; its/it's; were/where, etc), erratic punctuation (especially apostrophes, use of semi-colons and colons, etc) may arise either from lack of knowledge, or from insufficient care because the writers believe it's not important. Whatever the cause, supervisors should make sure as soon as it manifests itself that researchers understand how much they will harm their chances with examiners if they do not improve their use of language; that they attend whatever remedial teaching is available; and that they help themselves by reading some good straightforward texts (see pages 265–266 for some recommendations).

Though supervisors can't be expected to act as copy-editors/proof-readers, they should do their best to show clearly what is wrong, suggest how to put it right – and insist on seeing a revision.

Appropriate methods (based on personal experience and that of colleagues):

- Mark up and annotate a page or so of text, and talk it through together, explaining why it doesn't work properly and how to correct it. If researchers' school education was in a period when formal teaching of grammar was not on the syllabus, it is necessary to find non-technical equivalents for the technical terms they lack – and that is quite a challenge in itself (some of the texts on pages 265–266 are flagged as useful for the purpose).
- Compare a piece of their text with an extract from a text on the same subject which they themselves have read and found useful, and highlight the differences in the use of language which make a difference to the readability of the two.

It is hardly necessary to remind readers that in dealing with problems of this kind they need to be aware that difficulties in writing can be a sensitive area with students whose earlier experiences are likely to have undermined their confidence (see pages 258–260 of this chapter.)

Where technology can help

Caution! Don't leave learning the essential features of the software that you will need in writing your dissertation until the point when you start 'writing up'! This is no time to learn an unfamiliar software tool.

The main software most researchers will need is Word. Get to know the Word environment thoroughly, especially these features of it: clicking on the *Microsoft Office Button* opens the window relating to the commands for managing documents. In that window clicking on *New* opens a new document window, where you will find the *Taskbar*, the *Quick Access Toolbar,* the *Title bar,* and below that the *Ribbon* which makes all the Word features available in a single area. Explore all these individual features, then try a dummy run using the step by step Word instructions on pages 186–191 of Chapter 9.2.

Apart from that, use any other software you have been using during your research for mapping, managing information, etc. in order to: assemble information you want for particular chapters, and on specific subjects; create diagrams for use in the dissertation; demonstrate methods followed for collecting data; present findings from questionnaire responses.

And finally, if you learn to type with all your fingers and without looking at the keyboard you will save both time and energy.

When it comes to the driving force for writing, however, though the technology tools can be slick assistants, the real work has to be done by the human mind. If you have learned to respect its powers, and to treat it well, trust it now, and it will see you through!

Summary

Writing is a great invention, but it's not easy to use for most of us, so we need to give ourselves all the help we can by clearing other tasks that would distract us from writing out of the way first, and making a gradual approach to it. In particular:

- Make all the decisions about page layout, style for information elements, etc (see Chapter 9.2) before starting to write.
- Before starting to write each chapter, give yourself a visible framework to act as a guide to where you are, what to treat next, how to treat it, and at what length.
- Start early and spread the job of writing over time.
- Write in layers – get the ideas down first, and refine the expression as a separate job.
- Use the directory of Tips, Time-savers and Trouble-shooting (pages 249–261) to find possible solutions to *your* problems from the experience of others who have travelled the same road.
- Allow plenty of time for final editing and tidying – doing it properly takes longer than you would imagine!
- If the going gets rough, use all the help that's available, and do it quickly; don't struggle alone.
- Get to know the software you will need for the dissertation as thoroughly and as early as possible!

Appendix: Editing checklist

The checklist given here is based on the one I use when editing other people's work for publication. When I apply it to my own writing, as I did with my thesis, and as I have done with this book, I make two lots of checks: one as I write, and the other when the text is complete in draft.

It will help you a lot in editing if you learn the basic standard proofreading marks – you can download a useful set based on the British Standard from http://www.journalismcareers.com/articles/downloads/proofreadingsymbols.pdf

As you write

As you complete a chapter (or section), print it out and make these checks:

1 *Content editing*

Read through for *content* asking these basic questions, and make notes for yourself on things you need to amend.

Will this help readers to get the point?

Does it tell them all they need to know? Too much? Anything essential missing?
Does it tell the story in the right order?
Does it show readers the links and connections they need to understand?
Are statements backed by evidence?
Any internal contradictions/inconsistencies?
Is there enough help for readers to see where they are and to find their way through?

2 *Copy editing*
A friend's critical eye can be particularly helpful here; not being as close to the text as the author, it is likely to pick up things you may miss!
Go through again, this time to pick up anything that gets in the way of a smooth read. Mark corrections as you go.
Sentences correctly constructed? Any that fall apart in the middle? Literally mean something different from what you meant to say?
Is the punctuation right?
Any incorrect spellings?

3 *Standards editing*
Another check through, this time concentrating on the typographic standards you have set for information elements (see Chapter 9.2 page 227 and Chapter 9.3 page 229.)
Have the standards been followed correctly?

4 *Take in the corrections*
Work from the marked-up printout straight to the file on screen, and when the checks are completed, make a note on the file 'Edited on [date]' and save this latest version.

Final editing

When the whole dissertation is ready in draft, including all the initial material such as contents list, etc (see page 250), and is paginated throughout, make these checks on a printout of the edited chapters, and mark up for final corrections:

1 Re-read making the content checks, paying special attention to internal consistency as between chapters (it's better that you rather than the examiner should spot any contradictions between what you've said in different places). Keep in mind the marking scheme that will be applied (see Biggam, 2008).
2 Check all the cross-references between chapters, and make sure the links mentioned are there, and the page numbers are correct.
3 Another complete pass through the whole text to pick up anything missed in copy editing in the first stage, in particular any inconsistencies in spelling and punctuation.

4 A series of passes through the whole text to check:
Consistency in applying typographical standards.
Consistency between chapter headings and page numbers in contents list and as they appear in the text; between table titles/figure titles and page numbers as given in prelims and in text.
Accuracy of pagination.

References

Websites referred to in this chapter accessed on 18 March 2009

Biggam, J (2008)
Succeeding with your Master's Dissertation: A step-by-step handbook.
Maidenhead: Open University Press.

Chasseaud, A (1993)
Transformations and the Hate Object.
Unpublished MA dissertation. London: Central St Martins College of Art and Design.

De Guire, E (2006)
Publish or perish: afterlife of a published article.
http://www.csa.com/discoveryguides/publish/review.php

Diamond, Jared (1997)
Guns, germs and steel: a short history of everybody for the last 13,000 years.
London: Chatto & Windus.

Levin, P (2005)
Excellent dissertations.
Maidenhead: Open University Press.

Mulvany, N C (2005)
Indexing Books, Ed 2.
Chicago: University of Chicago Press.

Norman, D (1992)
Turn signals are the facial expression of automobiles.
Cambridge, MA: Perseus Publishing.
Chapter available on the author's website:
http://www.jnd.org/dn.mss/chapter_11_turn_sig.html

Ritter, R M (Ed) (2003)
Oxford Style Manual.
Oxford: Oxford University Press.
The OUP's own style guide; combines the successor to the 19th century Hart's *Rules for compositors and readers at the University Press, Oxford*, and the *Oxford Dictionary for Writers and Editors.* A great reference book; lives on my desk!

Further reading on use of language

There are many books on this subject! This selection is from my own collection. Some of the items were recommended by students who had come across them for themselves and found them useful.

Beardshaw, D (1982)
The Old Fashioned Rules of Punctuation Book.
London: Ward Lock Educational.
Issued 1982, and still in print. A lot of what you need to know, in just 10 pages, and with a rhymed couplet for each punctuation mark!

Glanville Price, B (2008)
MHRA Style Guide. A handbook for authors, editors, and writers of theses. Ed.2.
London: Modern Humanities Research Association.
Highly recommended by Mantex (http://mantex.co.uk/reviews/mrha.htm) and modestly priced.

Joshi, Y (2003)
Communicating in Style.
New Delhi: teri (The Energy and Resources Institute).
Elegantly written guide by an author who is also a designer; covers many of the topics discussed in this book. John le Carré rightly recommends as 'Courteous, unfrightening and essential'.

The next three titles are straightforward, well-written and accessible guides by experts. Supervisors should keep them on hand to recommend to researchers who have problems in this direction!

SEELEY, J (2004)
Oxford A-Z of Grammar and Punctuation.
Oxford: Oxford University Press.

TRASK, R L (1997)
The Penguin Guide to Punctuation.
London: Penguin.

TRASK, R L (2002)
Mind the Gaffe. The Penguin Guide to common errors in English.
London: Penguin.

TRUSS, L (2003)
Eats, Shoots & Leaves. The zero tolerance approach to punctuation.
London: Profile Books.
So well known it hardly needs a recommendation. An easy read, with great stories to reinforce the rules.

WATERHOUSE, K (1991)
English our English (and how to sing it).
London: Viking.
Written from inside knowledge and experience by a witty author with a keen eye.
Good on how to avoid the 'tin ear' that leads to plodding text.

WHALE, J (1984)
Put it in Writing.
London: J M Dent.
(Most recent edition 1999). Also by a journalist author, who approaches written English through how it sounds.

Websites

A RESEARCH GUIDE FOR STUDENTS
'The goal of this site is to provide all the necessary tools for students to conduct research and to present their findings.'
Gives access to a range of North American guides for researchers, and guidelines on writing research papers, quoting, avoiding plagiarism, references and bibliographies + a 'Virtual library of Useful URLs'.
http://www.aresearchguide.com/styleguides.html

MANTEX PUNCTUATION GUIDANCE NOTES
Free downloadable guidance notes on punctuation. Covers, besides commas, semicolons, colons, full stops, sentences and paragraphs (subsitute name of each for 'commas' in website address to access).
http://www.mantex.co.uk/samples/commas.htm

ROYAL LITERARY FUND, REPORT ON STUDENT WRITING IN HIGHER EDUCATION (2006)
Writing Matters.
Recommends all higher education institutions should have a 'Writing Development Policy', help students to develop writing skills, give explicit feedback on written assignments, etc.
Lists RLF partner institutions in UK.
http://www.rlf.org.uk/fellowshipscheme/research.cfm/

Index

S

T

U

V

W